THE COMPLETE IDIOT'S GUIDE TO

Microsoft® FrontPage 97

by Aaron Weiss

A Division of Macmillan Computer Publishing
201 W.103rd Street, Indianapolis, IN 46290 USA

Library of Congress Catalog Card Number: 96-72205

International Standard Book Number: 0-7897-1135-4

99 98 97   8 7 6 5 4 3 2

Interpretation of the printing code: the rightmost double-digit number is the year of the book's first printing; the rightmost single-digit number is the number of the book's printing. For example, a printing code of 97-1 shows that this copy of the book was printed during the first printing of the book in 1997.

Printed in the United States of America

Publisher
Roland Elgey

Publishing Director
Lynn E. Zingraf

Editorial Services Director
Elizabeth Keaffaber

Managing Editor
Michael Cunningham

Director of Marketing
Lynn E. Zingraf

Acquisitions Editor
Martha O'Sullivan

Technical Specialist
Nadeem Muhammed

Product Development Specialist
John Gosney

Technical Editor
Kyle Bryant

Production Editor
Tom Lamoureux

Editors
Kate Girens, Nick Zafran, Elizabeth A. Barrett

Book Designer
Glenn Larsen

Cover Designer
Dan Armstrong

Production Team
*Lori Cliburn, Maureen Hanrahan, Linda Knose,
Daniela Raderstorf, Scott Tullis*

Indexer
Eric Brinkman, C. J. East

We'd Like to Hear from You!

As part of our continuing effort to produce books of the highest possible quality, Que would like to hear your comments. To stay competitive, we *really* want you, as a computer book reader and user, to let us know what you like or dislike most about this book or other Que products.

You can mail comments, ideas, or suggestions for improving future editions to the address below, or send us a fax at (317) 581-4663. For the online inclined, Macmillan Computer Publishing has a forum on CompuServe (type **GO QUEBOOKS** at any prompt) through which our staff and authors are available for questions and comments. The address of our Internet site is **http://www.mcp.com/que** (World Wide Web).

In addition to exploring our forum, please feel free to contact me personally to discuss your opinions of this book: I'm **104436,2300** on CompuServe, and I'm **jgosney@que.mcp.com** on the Internet.

Thanks in advance—your comments will help us to continue publishing the best books available on computer topics in today's market.

John Gosney
Product Development Specialist
Que Corporation
201 W. 103rd Street
Indianapolis, Indiana 46290
USA

Although we cannot provide general technical support, we're happy to help you resolve problems you encounter related to our books, disks, or other products. If you need such assistance, please contact our Technical Support department at 800-545-5914 ext. 3833.

To order other Que or Macmillan Computer Publishing books or products, please call our Customer Service department at 800-835-3202 ext. 666.

Contents at a Glance

Contents

Introduction

Unlike the vastly underrated hoola hoops, Web pages aren't merely a trend. True, they *are* a trend, but they will likely outlive that pupal stage. The advantages of Web sites are becoming well-known: They're low-cost, they're interactive, and they can reach global audiences. But, there's always a bit of jelly in the peanut butter (or vice versa, depending on your preference), and as Web pages grow increasingly complex and capable, they've also become more difficult to create and design.

Not anymore! (You knew that was coming). Now, anyone who's seen a Web page and used a word processor can spend a few intimate evenings with FrontPage 97 and churn out Web masterpieces. All right, perhaps *masterpiece* is a tad strong. *Modestpiece* at the least. The fact remains, with FrontPage 97 we can create, design, manage, and serve Web sites with relative ease, while retaining much of the power commonly billed for by Web consultants with expensive cars.

Bien Venue à FrontPage 97

With this book, attractively styled and bound, we'll work through FrontPage 97 from end to end, top to bottom, through and through, so forth and so on. Plus, it's fun! Sort of. Honestly.

We'll learn how to manage and administer an entire Web site, and how to run a Web server, with which we can deliver our Web content within an Intranet or to the entire Internet. We'll spend lots of quality time designing Web pages, adding attractively fashioned text, graphic images, sounds, and hyperlinks. Wading into the deep end, we'll even spend some time looking at more advanced Web page design techniques, such as using ActiveX and Java technology, and creating scripts to program the behavior of a Web page.

That's a lot of material. Clearly, despite its punny title, this book is not intended for "Idiots." Rather, we assume you have a moderate amount of computing experience, and—given the particular subject of this book—have spent some time using the Internet and visiting Web sites. Some of our other assumptions:

➤ You have at least used a typical word processor, and have a passing familiarity with the likes of Microsoft Word or Corel Wordperfect (or any of the myriad similar products).

➤ You haven't necessarily created any Web pages before, but you have visited at least a few.

➤ You have a moderate familiarity with general computer use, and Windows 95 (or Windows NT) in particular.

➤ You've seen some kittens or puppies recently. In fact, this is not required for reading this book, but it's highly recommended; they're very cute!

Our goal is to present FrontPage 97 in a clear, concise, comprehensible fashion, with a conversational style that most official software manuals lack.

If, perhaps, you feel that you may not be quite up-to-speed on some of the experience this book assumes, feel free to pick up extra background knowledge, from such books as *The Complete Idiot's Guide to the Internet, Third Edition* by Peter Kent or *The Complete Idiot's Guide to Netscape Navigator 3.0* and *The Complete Idiot's Guide to Internet Explorer 3.0,* both by Joe Kraynak.

How to Read this Book

Since it's in English, a working knowledge of said language is a real help. Furthermore, it probably helps to read these chapters in order. While most books in this series try not to require "cover-to-cover" reading, we build on important concepts from chapter to chapter in this book. Novices should probably stick to a linear read, while more advanced users are in a better position to pick-and-choose chapters of interest. Readers who have no desire to run their own Web server can skip Part 5 "Broadcasting from Bed: the FrontPage 97 Web Server" entirely.

To clarify our discussions, we've used some style conventions that differentiate certain types of information.

When referring to buttons to click or text that you are required to enter, we use **bold type**. For instance, we may say "click the **OK** button", in which case, you'd click the button which is labelled "OK".

Onscreen text appears as monospace font like this:

> **This text appears on your computer screen.**

We often make reference to items contained in pull-down menus at the top of the program window. In this case, we use a convention such as "Select the menu item **File, Open.**" This means you should pull down the menu named "File" and select the item named "Open." Also, field names, and window and menu titles appear with the first letter uppercased, as in the "Create" dialog box.

Trademarks

We don't enjoy lawsuits, and as such, are inclined to make statements such as the following:

All terms mentioned in this book that are known to be trademarks have been appropriately capitalized. Que Corporation cannot attest to the accuracy of this information. Use of a term in this book should not be regarded as affecting the validity of any trademark or service mark.

Right on!

Part 1
Grasping at the Web

FrontPage 97 is all about the Web: Web sites, Web pages, Web servers. It's a full meal, so we begin with some appetizers. Some background information on the World Wide Web, and how it works, will bring us up to speed. We will then understand the terminology used with FrontPage 97. Additionally, we look at how FrontPage 97 can help us with every aspect of Web site design and management.

1996 WORST WEB SITES volume 2

Chapter 1

Why We Web (and How!)

In This Chapter

➤ Clients and servers

➤ Protocol play

➤ Where the Web pages are (Earl has them)

➤ Incentives to Web

➤ The browsers and the bees

When I was in grade school, I had a teacher—or what seemed like a series of teachers—who thought it clever to forewarn us against the dangers of assumptions by using a word game. They simply scrawled and scratched the word "ASSUME" on the chalkboard, and then proceeded to illustrate what would happen to us were we to engage in such behavior. This lesson did not go unheard, and so here we cannot assume what some readers do and others do not already understand about the World Wide Web. Skip ahead if you're a pro, but you'll miss some good jokes.

Brief history lesson: The war began with the assassination of Archduke Francis Ferdinand...oops, wrong lesson, darn these stacks of notes...ah, yes...

Before the Web

Even before the introduction of the World Wide Web as we know it, most applications on the Internet functioned on a client/server model. The client/server model is a fundamental concept behind much of the Internet, and, fortunately, it's also a fairly straightforward concept (no snoring!).

The client/server model has two components, surprisingly known as the *client* and the *server*. These two components have a special relationship—the client makes requests, and the server fulfills them. Consider a restaurant, as it is an almost perfect analogy. In a restaurant, the patron wants something (food or a cool drink). To get that something, the patron must request it from the waiter ("I'd like the house salad, please"). The waiter's role is to bring the patron what she wants, and ask any questions necessary to help specify what is to be served ("Would you like Italian or Russian dressing?").

Similarly, on the Internet, a client is a computer program which makes requests for data, and the server fulfills those requests, or asks further questions to help specify what data to retrieve. Specific protocols insure that the communication between client and server is smooth.

"Straight Back, Soldier" and Other Matters of Protocol

A "protocol" is a set of rules by which two computers exchange data. Each protocol is tailored to a specific need, depending on the type of data to be delivered. That's why we have several protocols in use on the Internet, such as the FTP protocol for transmitting files, the POP protocol for retrieving e-mail messages, and so forth.

Modern Times—The Reign of HTTP!

The World Wide Web, therefore, also works on the client/server principle: The Web client requests data from the Web server. In the case of the Web, unlike other Internet protocols, the data requested and delivered can be text, graphics, sound, or a computer program. In short, the Web server can deliver any type of data necessary.

The ubiquitous protocol HTTP (short for HyperText Transfer Protocol) is the workhorse that drives data delivery on the World Wide Web. Hypertext enables selected "hot spots" of text to link to other pages and sources of data—to jump from point A in one page to point B in another. HTTP is the raison d'etre ("raisin of the etre") of the Web, as it were.

A Web Client by Any Other Name...

In typical speech, Web clients are more commonly called "browsers." This term became popular early in the Web's beginnings, as the Web client was thought to allow users to "browse" information. Information specialists and other literalists sometimes object to this term, since one may do more than "browse" data with a Web client, but nonetheless, the term sticks.

The Web browser is a smart client, and can request data from several different types of servers (rather like a patron who can order food in several languages, depending on the restaurant). Typically, the Web browser requests data from a Web server. When doing so, it uses HTTP protocol; hence the proliferation of Web sites whose addresses look like **http://www.ourgreatsite.com**. However, the browser can also request data from servers using different types of protocols (for example, FTP, gopher, and others). We'll explore this issue of protocols in more detail later in the book, when we learn to create Web pages.

Fun with URLs

We use the term "URL" (pronounced either "earl" or "u-r-l") to refer to a whole Web address, as in **http://some.computer.com**. Note that some URL's are much longer than that, and may include subdirectories and filenames, as in:

> **http://some.computer.com/in/here/mypage.html**.

In any case, the URL specifies *exactly* where on the Internet the Web server, and the Web page, are located. The natural follow-up question, then, is, "How much *should* a pound of bananas cost?" Oh, I meant the *logical* follow-up question, which actually is, "Just what is a Web page?"

Earl

Just as every house has an exact address (number, street, city, postal code, country), so does every Web page. The URL—or, "Uniform Resource Locator"—is the way we specify a Web page's address on the Internet. As is oft the case among humans, people disagree (that is, yell at each other with vast amounts of scorn) about how to pronounce the acronym... some prefer it to sound like the distinguished, gentlemanly name "Earl," while others simply spell it out. Word has it that future editions of the Cosmo Quiz will rely on this crucial personality difference in pronouncing couples fit or unfit.

Because this book is about using FrontPage 97, which is a Web site design application, Web pages will become intimately familiar to us. Creating Web pages, after all, is the meat of creating a Web site. So, if it doesn't seem like much more is said about this topic right now, that's because much of the remainder of this book will be concerned with the very issue of creating Web pages.

A Web of Your Own

The World Wide Web has become a major, bona fide communications medium in the past few years. These days, there are sites covering as wide an array of topics as exists in our world. There are loud, flashy Web sites which advertise corporate wares, such as music and movies and Coca Cola and wrinkle creams. There are informative sites offering knowledge and contact between consumers and producers. There are sites for shopping, sites for learning, and sites where people simply write about what's on their minds.

Line of Site

It almost seems as if the terms "Web site" and "Web page" are interchangeable. In certain respects, they are, but there is a distinction. A Web *page* is generally a file or set of files which consist of the information (text, video, sound) to appear in the Web browser's window. A Web *site* may refer to a collection of Web pages that are all somehow interrelated. For example, information about the history of combs might appear on the "History of Combs" page, which is itself part of the "Hair Care" site, also containing other pages, such as the "History of Hairdryers" and the "Do's and Don'ts of Curling Irons."

There is no definitive reason to sponsor one's own Web site, but there are plenty of smaller, valid reasons. The Web is a medium driven by self-publishing, and this has many benefits:

➤ **It's cheap**—For the personal user who wants to share his/her knowledge or thoughts with the world, it shouldn't cost more than a few dollars a month to own your own Web site. Users who already have Internet access may be able to have their own Web pages for free. For businesses and corporations who want to advertise, sell, or maintain close contact with their customers, Web sites are far cheaper than any of the traditional alternatives (TV or print advertising, printed catalogs, or banks of phone operators).

➤ **It's easy**—While a company with the resources to hire talent may produce Web sites of superb quality (or simply glitz), even individuals can produce Web sites of respectable-to-excellent quality, with only a moderate amount of labor or technical knowledge.

➤ **It's fast**—Depending on the scope and complexity of your ambitions, you can create a Web site in a day, or in minutes. However you cut it, you can create Web sites quicker than any alternative media. Secondly, you can modify your Web site at any time, and instantly. If you have information which rapidly changes, such as retail prices or news items, a few minutes spent updating the site will automatically be reflected when a user comes to visit.

➤ **It's everywhere**—Look, behind you! Seriously, the *World Wide Web* is named that for a reason. People can visit your Web site from Egypt, or the U.S., or South Africa, or anywhere on the Earth where there's Internet access (almost everywhere). In most cases, and depending on the complexity of your site, folks from half-way around the world can access what you have to offer just as readily and as quickly as friends 15 blocks away. That's a potential audience of millions.

How the Users Won the West

Now that we're in a jubilant frenzy after the previous love-the-Web-fest, there are differences between Web sites and other media that you must keep in mind. The Web is a *user-directed* medium—this means that the person visiting the Web site is in control. People will only visit your Web site if they want to, or if they feel there will be something worthwhile there. They have a fair amount of control over how your site will appear on *their* screens; they might turn off graphics (thus disabling any advertising images you may have), or alter the color scheme, the font, and so forth.

In the old days, on television and in print, the deliverer of content had total say. The listener or viewer either took in the content as delivered, or changed the station (or turned the page). On the Web, readers have less patience. They don't need it. Every site is a few mouse-clicks away, and if your site isn't giving them what they came for, they'll find another one. This might sound cold, but it's quite reasonable. Let's say that I'm shopping for a sweater and I find a likely site. I visit this site, but instead of a catalog of sweaters, I'm greeted with a large ad, touting how wonderful their sweaters are. I click on a link and I am led to another page, where I encounter a huge graphic that downloads very slowly. I am still waiting for an indication that there is a catalog here. In frustration, and a couple mouse-clicks later, I'm visiting the site of a competitor who anticipates my needs.

Some of the issues above are matters of the new medium: "We're not a captive audience, and won't be treated like one." Others are issues of site design (such as having large graphics without alternative navigation tools), and we'll address some of those as we learn how to create Web pages with FrontPage 97 throughout this book.

What You Need

While it may seem obvious (OK, it *is* obvious), if we're going to be creating Web sites and Web pages in this book (which we are), you'll need to be able to browse the Web. This is the best way to view other sites, and to test your own.

The ability to browse the Web requires, minimally, a computer. Assuming you've got that, you need an Internet connection and a Web browser. Since FrontPage 97 is a product for Windows 95 and Windows NT, we can assume for the purposes of this book that you have Windows 95 or Windows NT. Having established that...

So Many Browsers!

There are lots of browsers out there. However, the feature set of the Web is often changing, and only a small number of browsers keep up with the latest and greatest technologies that Web pages can offer. For most users, the battle comes down to Netscape Navigator and Microsoft Internet Explorer. In many respects, the browser you use is a matter of preference. FrontPage 97, as a Web design application, can create pages which can be viewed with any browser, or very few browsers, depending on the features you choose to implement on your page.

Of course, Microsoft would prefer that you use Internet Explorer, and it is true (as of this writing) that some Web page features available in FrontPage 97 can only be viewed when using Internet Explorer (version 3.0 or later).

The feature-support issue between Web browsers is a constant arms race. Both Netscape and Microsoft release versions of their browsers which try to match or top the features offered by the other brand. It's very difficult to keep track of every advanced feature, which browser will support it, and which will not.

Having said all that, Netscape Navigator (version 3.0 and later) is a very capable browser (**http://www.netscape.com**), and will view Web pages with most of the features that FrontPage 97 provides. However, because Microsoft Internet Explorer supports *all* FrontPage 97 capabilities, and is freely available (if not on your CD-ROM, then from **http://www.microsoft.com/ie**), in this book we will be using Internet Explorer 3.0 as our browser.

Switch Hitting

It's perfectly possible to install both Netscape Navigator and Microsoft Internet Explorer on your computer. You can then run whichever you like at a particular moment, or both simultaneously if you have enough RAM (at least 16 megabytes). By doing this, you have the "best of both worlds," and can view pages that take advantage of special features of each. This also helps in testing your own Web pages to see how they will appear to users of each browser.

Well-equipped with computer, Internet connection, and the Web browser(s) of our choice, we have everything necessary to browse the Web. Certain Web pages require specific programs to view portions of their content, but those can always be picked up along the way. The Web browsers discussed above are sufficient to view Web pages, especially those we create ourselves using FrontPage 97.

The Least You Need to Know

➤ The World Wide Web works on a client/server model—the client requests data and the server delivers it.

➤ Web clients, or *browsers*, are capable of making requests of several types of servers, using HTTP and other protocols.

➤ A URL is the specific Internet address of a Web page, and often looks like **http:// www.somecomputer.com**

➤ Web sites are a cheap, fast, easy, and expansive way to deliver information or services to people around the world.

➤ Browsing the Web, and testing one's own pages, is best done with a leading browser, such as Netscape Navigator or Internet Explorer. Only Internet Explorer supports *all* features of FrontPage 97, but Netscape and other browsers support most features.

Chapter 2

FrontPage 97: A New Era in Web Design

In This Chapter

➤ How the Web got its knows

➤ An extremely abridged look at HTML

➤ Editors of the past

➤ The FrontPage 97 way

One of FrontPage 97's significant contributions to the state of Web design is that it completely redefines how an entire Web site can be created. Before we get nitty and gritty about FrontPage 97 itself, let's take some time to discuss how Web sites and pages have been designed up until now, and how FrontPage 97's approach changes all that. This will be a cheery chapter—read it with a nice cup of tea.

"In My Day"...Web Design in "Olden Times"

Commentaries often note (and, well, comment) on the rapid pace of change in our modern techno world. It's all true. Nowhere is it more so than in the world of the Internet, at such a pace that "Olden Times" was sometime circa 1990.

Way back then, one of the questions at hand was how to deliver data across a computer network in a convenient, easy-to-read, and easy-to-navigate fashion. What developed was a system of marking data with special codes. These codes defined how a particular piece of data should be represented to the reader. For example, imagine that we want to be able to distinguish a headline (that is, text which is large and bold) from regular type. We have the following data which we want to deliver to whomever requested it:

Monkeys Break Free From Metro Zoo

Earlier today, a pack of 15 monkeys broke free from the Metro Zoo by cutting a deal with their guards and cheating in 3-card monty. Reports indicate that the monkeys headed straight for Bill's Banana Discount House.

There needs to be some way to specify how different portions of the above will appear. Several late nights and angry spouses later, we hit upon a solution! We can use a "tag" to mark which sections of data should appear a certain way. Then, the computer program which displays the data to the reader will watch for these tags, and display the data accordingly. We'll enclose our tags in brackets, and develop a system something like this:

<H1>Monkeys Break Free From Metro Zoo</H1><HR>

Earlier today, a pack of 15 monkeys broke free from the Metro Zoo by cutting a deal with their guards and cheating in 3-card monty. Reports indicate that the monkeys headed straight for *<I>Bill's Banana Discount House</I>*.

In the above example, we've used three tags: <H1>, which we'll imagine has been defined as "very large bold text"; <HR>, which we can think of as meaning "hit return"; and <I>, which means italic text. For most tags, we also have an "off" version, which we precede with a backslash, as in </H1> ("stop using very large bold text").

Our intrepid reader, using the appropriate software (a "browser"), requests today's top news story and receives the above data. But the tags are not shown—those are taken as instructions by the browser as to how to display the data. Rather, the reader sees:

Monkeys Break Free From Metro Zoo

Earlier today, a pack of 15 monkeys broke free from the Metro Zoo by cutting a deal with their guards and cheating in 3-card monty. Reports indicate that the monkeys headed straight for *Bill's Banana Discount House.*

Magic Markings

The above is exactly the solution computer scientists came up with several years ago (albeit, they were more excited than I let on). The way they figured it, using the above technique, they could "mark up" a page of data with all sorts of "tags" to define how it should appear. Thus, they christened this new technique HTML—the Hypertext Markup Language.

Soon after this invention, they began work on devising many tags to serve a variety of purposes. There were tags for the size of characters on-screen, tags for bold, italic, and right-alignments and left-alignments. There were tags which defined data as a link; that is, if selected (such as by a mouse-click)—the linked data would automatically retrieve another page of data. There were tags which allowed for a graphic image to be put in place, and so forth.

Once word got out about HTML, computer users ("nerds", not that that's a bad thing) everywhere began preparing data in this format. This allowed the data to be shared by anyone connecting to their server; and thus the birth of the World Wide Web.

Over time, an increasing number of tags were created, making it quite difficult to remember them all. Furthermore, their functions grew more complex, allowing for more advanced capabilities beyond mere appearance. Some tags allowed for reader input from the keyboard, for instance, or selecting an option on the screen. Understanding how each tag worked became a specialized area, and those who kept in-the-know about these matters quickly became valued Web designers.

These days, keeping up with every new tag is a time-consuming job. Every time a new version of a Web browser is released, such as the latest by Netscape or Microsoft, new tags are introduced. Clever folks devised two strategies to help people design Web pages in this complex environment:

Strategy 1: The HTML Editor

The original Web designers created their HTML "documents" in a simple text editor. They merely typed everything directly in, as in <H1>This is my headline</H1> and so forth. This works just fine, but it can become quite a tax on one's mental skills considering how many tags there are to remember.

Enterprising netizens wrote programs called HTML editors, which offered menus of tags for a Web designer to choose from. The Web designer would typically enter his data into the HTML editor, and then select the appropriate tag from a menu or button. For instance, I might type This is my headline, then highlight that text with my mouse, and select **Headline 1** from the HTML editor menu. The HTML editor would then pop the correct tags into place in the document.

As you can imagine, HTML editors can be convenient, especially if you need help remembering tags. You still have to know which tag to ask for, though. HTML editors have become more advanced, and can often help users with the more complex tags. This is well and good if you have some knowledge of HTML, and simply need a tool to make your Web design quicker.

Editing a Web page with an HTML editor. Whether or not you remember every tag, you'd still need to understand what they do, to make sense of this picture.

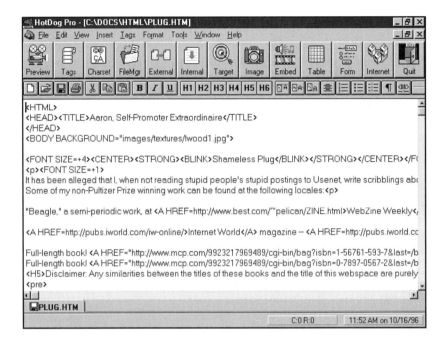

Editors À La Carte

In case you feel like looking at an HTML editor, HotDog Pro, WebEdit Professional, HomeSite, and HTML Assistant Pro are a few currently popular titles. You can find these programs either by running a Web search, or checking the HTML editors page at Yahoo! (**http://www.yahoo.com**). Keep in mind, however, that these editors require at least some knowledge of HTML, and are not equal competitors with FrontPage 97, as will be explained in the next section.

However, what if you don't know HTML, you don't have the time or interest in learning it, but you still want to design Web pages? Please allow me to introduce to you Strategy #2.

Strategy 2: The WYSIWYG Frontier—Goodbye Tags, Hello FrontPage 97!

For many years, the adorable acronym "WYSIWYG" has been applied to word processors and stands for "What You See is What You Get"—the notion not being that of caveat emptor, but rather, what you design on-screen is exactly the appearance that you want for the final product.

In the realm of word processors, this meant that the documents looked the same on-screen as they did printed onto paper. Bold words were bold, indented paragraphs were indented, and so forth. Logically, this approach as been brought to Web design.

FrontPage 97 is just such an application (*quel surprise!*). Rather than needing to understand HTML tags, with FrontPage 97 you design on-screen just as the page will appear in a reader's browser window. A variety of menus and tools provide the necessary functions to this end, quite like a modern-day word processor. All it takes is a mouse and a dream, as they say.

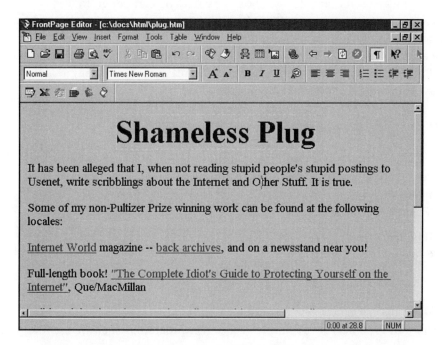

Using the WYSIWYG editor of FrontPage 97. Goodbye tags, hello mouse. The page as we design it looks quite close to how a reader will see it when visiting it on the Web.

HTML Options

For the technically interested, keep in mind that FrontPage 97 does not eliminate the existence of HTML. Rather, it generates HTML documents based on the page you've designed. If you do know HTML, you can always edit these documents at a later time in their HTML form. However, if you never want to look at HTML, that's fine, too. Like a leftover piece of cake, it's there if you want it. You needn't know a single HTML tag to design a Web site with FrontPage 97.

Why All This HTML Yammerin' Then?

It's a fair rebuff—if we don't need to know any HTML, why spend the past few pages introducing it? It's my belief that awareness of the HTML concept, even if you never write a single tag of it, will still aid in Web page design. While I may never use a wrench on my own car (for everyone's good, really), having some idea of how the car functions (gas makes the car go) can be helpful if problems arise down the road. ("The car isn't moving, maybe I have no gas").

Similarly, you should understand that the limitations of what you can design in FrontPage 97 are subject to the limitations of HTML. HTML is not yet a free-for-all design language. That is, one cannot place any data simply anywhere on a page. There are constraints, which are limitations of HTML tags. Those constraints must be duplicated, by necessity, in FrontPage 97 because underneath the hood, FrontPage 97 is creating HTML documents. This is a matter we'll encounter later in the book.

FrontPage 97: Web from Start to Finish

I've been intentionally unclear about something up until now, and it's time to clear the air. Hopefully this won't endanger our here-to-fore warm relationship. FrontPage 97 is, in fact, a collection of programs known as a "suite." In fact, to be ever more specific, two suites: FrontPage 97 and the Bonus Pack.

The FrontPage 97 suite includes:

➤ **FrontPage Explorer** Used to view and manage a Web site, which is a collection of interlinked Web pages.

➤ **FrontPage Editor** The heart of the suite, with which we actually design the Web page.

➤ **FrontPage Personal Web Server** A simple Web server program, which we eschew in this book, in preference for another (also included, see below).

The Bonus Pack suite includes:

➤ **Microsoft Image Composer** An image processing program, with which one can create or modify graphic images with advanced tools. Not covered in this book, because of its complexity, and its tangential relationship to FrontPage 97.

➤ **Web Publishing Wizard** Allows one to transfer one's Web sites to an Internet Service Provider's Web server.

➤ **Microsoft Personal Web Server** A capable Web server program, which we prefer to use in this book.

➤ **Microsoft Internet Explorer** The famous Web browser.

The main point here is that FrontPage 97 has everything covered from Web design to delivery. However, keep in mind that you aren't limited to the applications included in the FrontPage 97 suite. If, for instance, you like the FrontPage Editor, but prefer a different Web server (such as that from another manufacturer), that's fine, too. The Web is based on "open standards"—a Web page designed with the FrontPage Editor can be viewed or even edited with a different editor.

For the remainder of this book, we're going to narrow our focus to the FrontPage 97 suite itself. Up until now, we've explored the background behind the World Wide Web, the construction of Web pages, and the evolution of Web design editors. Belts a-tightened, now it's time to start creating a Web site with FrontPage 97.

The Least You Need to Know

In truth, you *truly* only need to know the last two points listed. But as a whole, this chapter did mention:

➤ Web pages exist as documents with special markings. These markings, known as HTML tags, delineate how to represent portions of data.

➤ To simplify the design of Web pages, programmer's developed HTML editors. These programs make it simpler to insert the proper HTML tags into a document.

➤ A different approach to Web page design is offered by WYSIWYG editors such as FrontPage 97. With it, Web pages can be created graphically, just as they will appear on the Web. No knowledge of HTML tags is needed.

➤ FrontPage 97 is, in fact, a suite of software, which offers the facilities to create, design, manage, and deliver Web content. Web sites created with FrontPage can be edited, managed, or delivered by competing products.

Part 2
Conceiving the Web

The calories start here. FrontPage 97 provides us with several tools for developing our Web sites, and we begin learning about two of them: the FrontPage Explorer and the FrontPage Editor. With this talented duo at our side, we'll begin creating a Web site, and adding content.

The truth about the World Wide Web...

A Brand New Web

A Web site, like a folder on your hard drive, is an umbrella under which a number of files live. These files make up each of the individual Web pages, including text, images, sounds, and so forth. FrontPage Explorer saves your Web site exactly this way—as a folder. The name of your Web is stored as the name of a folder, and within that folder are all the files that make up your Web. In this chapter, you'll learn how to create the structure of this folder; for example, a Web site using Explorer's templates and Wizards.

The Web Wizard—Creating Webs from Templates

To begin designing your Web, you first need to launch FrontPage Explorer. In Windows 95, open **Start**, **Programs** from the taskbar, and select **Microsoft FrontPage** from the menu that pops up. The FrontPage Exolorer will load, and present you with the screen shown in the next figure.

FrontPage Explorer's startup window. It needs to know where to load a Web site from.

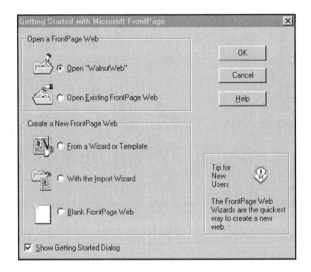

Explorer's startup window is divided into two sections: Open a FrontPage Web and Create a New FrontPage Web. For the time being, let's assume that you want to create a new Web, having never done this before.

One of the easiest ways to get started quickly is to use the Web Wizard to create a new Web site, so let's click on the option **From a Wizard or Template**. This will allow us to use a pre-designed structure for our Web site, not unlike using templates in a word processor (such as for an invoice, résumé, resignation, etc.) Click **OK** to finalize the decision, and a list of possible templates will appear.

A menu of prefab Web sites. Using these templates, we can get our Web up and working quickly, albeit with less creative control.

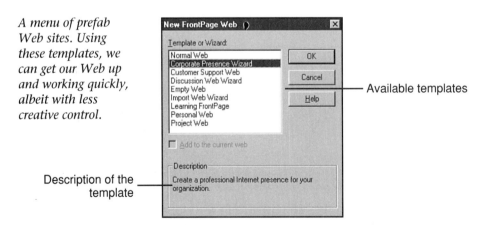

Available templates

Description of the template

What's a Wizard?

Notice that some of the templates are called Wizards, such as the Discussion Web Wizard. A Wizard is a Web site template which will ask a series of questions to help customize the site to our needs. They are helpful little muses and will get our site ready quickly. However, because they have pre-designed the site, some creative control is taken out of our hands. Wizards are a great way to start, to gain a feel for creating Web sites. Those templates which do not say "Wizard" are still pre-fabricated sites, but they are not complex enough that we need to answer further questions.

Making Room for a Web

As we merrily scroll through the list of templates, a small description appears at the bottom of the window. We'll try the **Corporate Presence Wizard**, in an attempt to bring our company WalNut-Mart ("Products made entirely out of walnuts — we pass the savings on to you") on-line. After selecting the Corporate Presence Wizard, we click **OK**, and the ride begins.

We must choose a residence and a name for our new corporate presence Web site.

Where to create the new Web site

The name of the new Web site

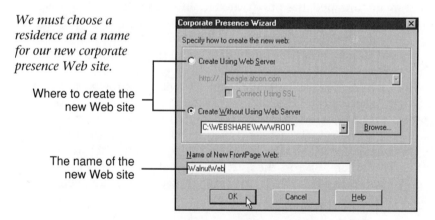

The decision of where to create the new Web site requires some explanation. For those who may not need the full explanation, here's the shortened version: Enter either a local path, such as **C:\docs\mywebs** (from which we can publish the site to a server later), or a server address, such as **server.machine.com**).

A more verbose explanation of where to create the Web site: Ultimately, the Web site must reside on a server to be accessible over the network, be it an intranet or the Internet.

To create the Web site on a server, we'd need to fulfill either of the following two criteria:

➤ We are running a Web server on our own computer. See Chapter 19, "Bringing the Server to Life" for information on doing just that.

➤ We have access to a Web server provided by a service provider.

In either of the above cases, we create our Web sites on the server by using the server's network address, such as *server.machine.com*.

Alternatively, we may choose to create our Web sites on the local hard drive. These will not be accessible to anyone else until they are published to a server (see Chapter 12, "If I Only Had a Crane—Hauling Your Web to a Server"). However, if we are not running a Web server on our own computer, then creating them on the local hard drive will allow us to develop the site internally before publishing it to a Web server. To create the Web site on the local hard drive, simply enter a local path name where the site folder should be created; for example, **c:\docs\mywebs**.

What About Intranets?

The notion of an "intranet" has proliferated recently, as software developers have caught onto the buzzword in defining a new market. However, an intranet is only marginally different from the Internet. The Internet, to be brief, consists of a dynamic set of computers around the globe, that can communicate. This is a type of network—a network with a very wide area (the Earth). An intranet, by contrast, is also a network, but one with a narrow area, usually within a single organization. Thus, you may belong to a business which has a "local area network" (or LAN), which connects the computers within the organization. This is an intranet. As far as Web pages and Web servers go, the distinction is minimal—the Web server delivers Web pages to Web clients, whether they are all located within a single intranet, or across the Internet. Typically, intranets, because they belong to and are controlled by a single organization, require higher levels of security. Read Chapter 20, "Tinker Tinker Little Server."

Now that we've straightened out the question of where to create the Web site, let's work through the process and do so. Recalling the previous image, follow these steps:

1. First, if creating this site on a Web server, enter the name of your server in the box provided (if the server name hasn't already been filled in by FrontPage 97). If creating the Web site on the local hard drive, enter a local path.

2. Next, if we enable the option **Connect Using SSL**, then the Secure Sockets Layer will be used in communicating with the Web server. This is a form of encryption that will prevent anyone from spying on our data as it's being transmitted to the

Web server. This option is important when security matters, less important otherwise. Note that this option only applies if we are creating our Web site on a Web server which supports SSL (such as the Microsoft Personal Web Server included in the FrontPage 97 Bonus Pack).

3. Finally, we must name the Web site, at the bottom of the window where it's labelled **Name of New FrontPage Web**. Choose something memorable so that in the future, you'll know this site is by its name. For example, WalnutWeb would be a good name for the WalNut-Mart Web site, which we'll create shortly. Each Web server has its own restrictions on how long and what characters a Web site name may contain. If you're not sure of the naming restrictions on your server, stick with a "safe" name—one that is less than 16 characters long and doesn't contains spaces or other non-alphanumeric characters.

4. When you've finished entering the information, click **OK**. The FrontPage Explorer will now take us to the Corporate Presence Wizard, where we begin designing the site itself. Whew!

Guide Us, Oh Wizard

The Corporate Presence Web Wizard will launch, and present its opening descriptive screen.

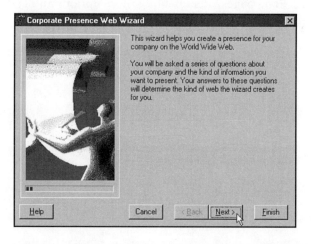

Introducing a Web Wizard. It will be our step-by-step guide to creating a new Web site.

The Wizard is relatively straightforward. It will ask for information, and we'll answer it. Using the Back and Next buttons at the bottom of the Wizard window, we can move to previous questions and change our information, or move ahead to the next question. Each Wizard has different questions to ask, depending on what it will generate. In this case, we're using the Corporate Presence Web Wizard, because we want to bring our company, WalNut-Mart, online. So let's take the Wizard's tour. Clicking **Next** on the introductory screen takes us to our first set of options.

Hmmm...selecting which main pages to include in our Corporate Presence Web site.

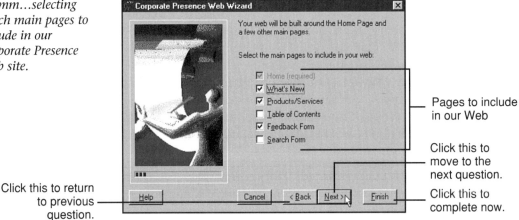

Pages to include in our Web

Click this to move to the next question.

Click this to return to previous question.

Click this to complete now.

Not unlike a fast food menu, we're asked to tick off the items we want. In this case the question is which pages to include in our Web site. As the Wizard explains, we're required to have a Home Page; meaning, an initial page which readers will see when connecting to our site. In this case, let's also choose to have a What's New page, a Products/Services page, and a Feedback Form page. After enabling those options and clicking **Next**, the Wizard asks us some more questions about our Home Page.

What sections to include on our WalNut-Mart Home Page.

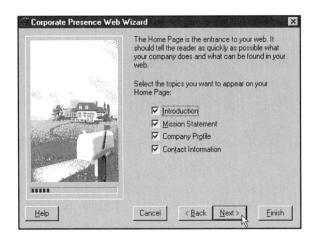

Home Sweet Home Page

Like an astro turf Welcome mat lying at the front door, a home page is often the first meeting place between your Web site and a visitor. Home pages, then, are often designed as "Entryways," describing what content lies within the Web site, and offering navigational tools to reach that content.

Smart home pages are often attractively designed, and have a good introduction to the site. They may use well chosen graphics, so as not to take too many seconds to download, and include intuitive navigation tools to other pages within the site.

The Wizard, ever an inquisitive sort, now asks which sections to include on our home page. Being an "in-touch" kind of company, we'd like to include all sections – an Introduction, a Mission Statement, a Company Profile, and Contact Information. Note that these are not separate pages, but will all appear on our home page, which visitors will see first.

After enabling those options and clicking **Next**, we're asked to determine what should appear on our What's New page. We'll choose **Web Changes** and **Press Releases**, and click **Next** again.

Earlier, we chose to include a page about our products and services. Now, the Wizard would like to create a separate page for each product or service we want to highlight. It asks how many pages to create for products, and how many to create for services. To keep our life, and example, simple, let's imagine we'll highlight two products (the WalNut Alarm Clock and the WalNut Electric Carving Knife), and one service (the WalNut Car Wash).

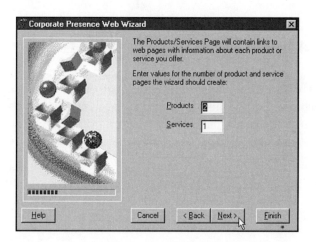

Telling the Wizard to create 2 product pages and 1 service page. The Wizard listens.

27

The Corporate Presence Web Wizard happens to ask a lot of questions, so we'll speed things up using the magic of time-lapse publishing. We've continued using the **Next >** button to move through additional questions, including what information to provide about our products and services, what to include on the Feedback Form, headers and footers for each page, what graphic motifs to use, and so forth. Don't feel terribly left out—the above selections are a matter of personal choice, and our future examples don't rely on them. Therefore, we haven't bored you with images of option after option. With a bag of chips and a soft drink, we've completed the Wizard, and reached the final page, where we click **Finish** to comlete the wizardry.

Last stage of the Wizard. It will now create the structure of our Web site.

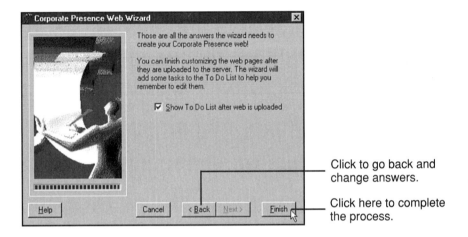

Click to go back and change answers.

Click here to complete the process.

While the Wizard creates the Corporate Presence Web site and each of the pages we've told it to, the hard drive whirs for a bit and pages are created. Once it is finished, the FrontPage Explorer will show our new Web site. We'll pick up from here in the next chapter.

"Web"ula Rasa, or Starting from Scratch

Templates and Wizards are great for helping new Web designers along, but they do have their limitations. For one, there may not be a template or wizard appropriate for the mission of our Web site. Even if there is a template or wizard, we might prefer to design the site ourselves from the ground up. When cooking from scratch, there's nothing better than an empty sink and a clean slate.

From its startup screen, the FrontPage Explorer allows us to choose **Blank FrontPage Web**, instead of using a template. In choosing to create a blank Web site, we're asked where to create and what to name this new, empty, blank site. We should already be familiar with these options from working with the Wizard earlier, but if not, read the earlier section "Making Room for a Web" in this chapter.

After choosing where to create the blank Web site, and deciding upon a name, FrontPage Explorer will whir a bit, and present a blank Web. Despite its name, a "blank Web" is not *completely* blank. Rather, it is a Web site consisting of one Web page. However, that Web page *is* blank, as it has no data in it yet. Learning to use the FrontPage Editor will allow us to add information to our blank Web site. We'll touch on the FrontPage Editor in the following chapter, and begin adding to our page in earnest beginning with Chapter 6, "The Joy of Text."

For the record, and apparently for the sake of redundancy, note that choosing the **Normal Web** template creates the same blank Web as does choosing **Blank FrontPage Web**.

Webs of Old

So far in this chapter, we've looked at two methods for bringing new Web sites to life: Using a template or Web Wizard, and creating a blank Web. But what about Web sites or pages that already exist? You came to the right section!

In fact, there are two ways to load existing Web sites or pages. The first is quite logical: loading Web sites which we've already created with FrontPage.

Opening an Existing Web

In Explorer terminology, "an existing Web" refers to a Web site you've previously created with the FrontPage Explorer. From the Explorer's opening screen, select **Open Existing FrontPage Web**.

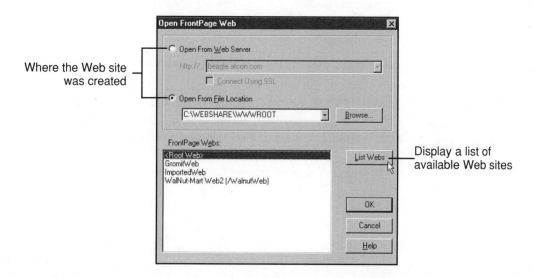

Where the Web site was created

Display a list of available Web sites

If a list of available Web sites does not appear for the selected server or local path, click the **List Webs** button. Simply select which Web site to open and click **OK**. That's it. Really. I mean it.

Importing an Existing Web

In some cases, we may have existing Web sites which were created without FrontPage 97, or they were created onto a different Web server than our current one. To use these sites in the FrontPage Explorer, we need to "import" them into a new Web site, compatible with FrontPage 97 and our Web server. However, note that we can only import Web sites from our local hard drive—we cannot import a Web site from a Web server.

To import an existing Web, we can select the **With the Import Wizard** option from the Explorer's opening screen. Alternatively, we can select the Import Wizard from the list of available templates—it's the same Wizard.

Selecting the Import Wizard, with which we can re-cast old Web sites into a new FrontPage 97 Web.

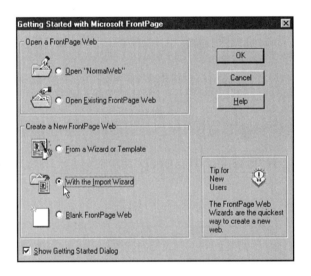

Next, the FrontPage Explorer asks us the now-familiar questions for creating a new FrontPage 97 Web. The Import Wizard, whom we're about to meet, is going to move the Web site from its old location into this new Web, so we should select the appropriate location (server or local path) and name for the new incarnation of this Web site.

Creating a new Web site, into which the Import Wizard will place our old site.

After this is done, the Import Wizard appears, asking us to select the source location of our old Web site. The Wizard, being less-than-omnipotent, can only import Web sites from our local hard drive.

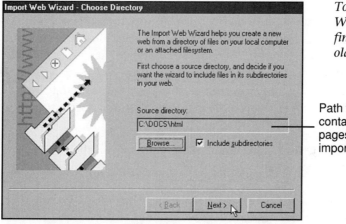

To please the Import Wizard, we must find the path to our old Web site.

Path to directory containing Web pages to be imported

Clicking the **Browse** button allows us to find the correct directory where our old Web pages lay. If the Include Subdirectories option is check marked, then all files within subdirectories (folders) of the chosen directory will also be marked for import. Next, the Import Wizard poses us with a list of files found within the selected directory.

*The counterintuitive file import list. Here we select which files **not** to import.*

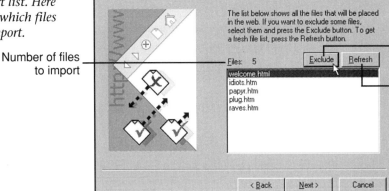

Number of files to import

Eliminates file from import list

Redisplays entire file list

The Import Wizard is an eccentric sort. As shown in the previous figure, a list of files is presented. By default, all of these files *will* be imported. If you *don't* want one or more files to be imported, you must select them with the mouse and click the **Exclude** button (excluding doesn't delete the file from the hard drive, it simply takes it off the list of files to-be-imported). If you've changed your mind after excluding a file, click the **Refresh** button to see the original file list again. This may seem a strange interface design (selecting which files *to import* seems more intuitive), but one does not question the Wizard.

Once we've settled on the list of files to import, clicking **Next >** will bring about the final congratulations of the Wizard. The **Finish >** button will then generate the new Web site, containing the files chosen.

Check This Out...

Web Pages and Files, Oh My

When choosing which files to import, remember that some Web pages require multiple files. For instance, we might have a Web page which consists of one .html file, and two .gif files (which serve as images on the page). Remember to import all the files which make up the Web page. If you're not sure, it's always better to import too many files than too few. Imported files which aren't part of any page cause no harm, although they do take up extra storage space.

A Simple Copy

If you've chosen not to create the imported Web on a server, then you've selected a local hard drive path for the new Web. The Import Wizard adds special FrontPage 97 folders and files to the new Web location, followed by a file copy from the old location to the new. This means you'll have two copies of the imported files on your machine: the originals, and the copies stored in the new FrontPage 97 Web folder. This may be worth noting in terms of storage space. Once you've imported the Web pages to a new Web site, you could delete them from their original location to save space.

The Least You Need to Know

The FrontPage Explorer has to be told which Web site it should open. In this chapter, we looked at the options for creating new, or using old, Web sites.

➤ A Web site is an umbrella under which one or more Web pages reside.

➤ Web pages are made up of files, containing the text and any images, sounds, and so forth, that are included on the page.

➤ FrontPage Explorer stores Web sites as a directory, inside which are all the files which make up the site's Web pages.

➤ Using Web Wizards or templates is a quick way to get a Web site up and running, based on prefabricated styles.

➤ Creating a blank Web allows you to begin desiging a site from scratch.

➤ If you have old Web pages on your machine which you want to use in FrontPage Explorer, import them into a new Web site using the Import Wizard.

➤ Opening an existing Web allows you to load existing FrontPage 97 Web sites into the FrontPage Explorer.

Discovering the Explorer

One could say that a Web site has a skeleton. Besides sounding spooky, the skeleton analogy is befitting for the FrontPage Explorer. Consider that a Web site usually consists of several Web pages, some of which are connected to other pages. Within each Web page, there are even smaller connections, such as to an image file.

The FrontPage Explorer is, as you'll recall, our main control center for designing a Web site. In this chapter, we'll consider the Explorer's ability to project an X-Ray of our Web's skeleton. Such a perspective allows us to see the interconnections in our Web, and configure them in a variety of ways. It's fun.

Web Anatomy: The Ankle Bone's Connected to the...

After a thorough reading of the previous chapter, we've decided to create or open a Web site. For our first trick—er—our first example, we're using the WalNut-Mart Web site, created previously with the Corporate Presence Wizard. The FrontPage Explorer offers us the following perspective, known as the Hyperlink View.

FrontPage Explorer's x-ray view of our Web site.

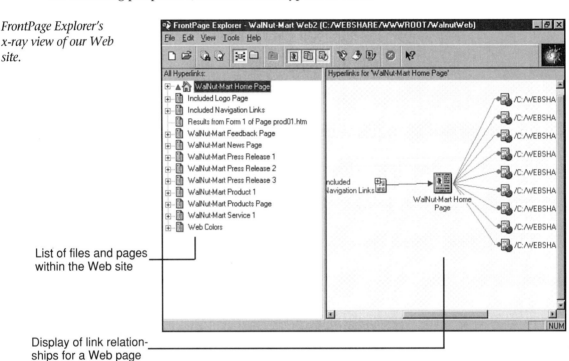

List of files and pages within the Web site

Display of link relationships for a Web page

The Hyperlinks View consists of two main windows:

All Hyperlinks (left-hand window)   Here, we see a list of all files and pages within this Web site. If a page contains any links to other files, a plus sign (+) precedes its name in the list. Clicking on the plus sign will "expand" the list, showing which files are linked. This transforms the plus sign into a minus sign (-), and clicking the minus sign will "collapse" the list, hiding the links.

Click to collapse this list

List has been expanded

Click to expand this list

*Accordion fun—
expanding and collaps-
ing the hyperlink list.*

Hyperlinks for 'WalNut-Mart Home Page' (right-hand window)   Two main qualities differentiate this window from the left-hand one. The first quality is immediately notice-able—links are displayed graphically. In the center of the page, we see the WalNut-Mart Home Page, out of whose right side sprouts a series of links to other pages.

The second quality of note in this graphical window is that it focuses on the page selected in the left-hand window. For instance, in the case of the above picture, we clicked on the page named WalNut-Mart Home Page in the left-hand window, and the above graphic appeared.

Looking back at the left-hand window, we'll now click on the page named **Included Navigation Links** (which is shown because we've expanded the Home Page list). The image in the right-hand window transforms, as in the next figure.

*Visualizing the
WalNut-Mart Home
Page in graphical form.
See the branches.*

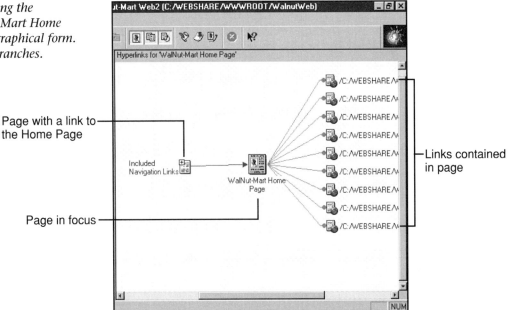

*Changing the focus to
another page. A new set
of branches.*

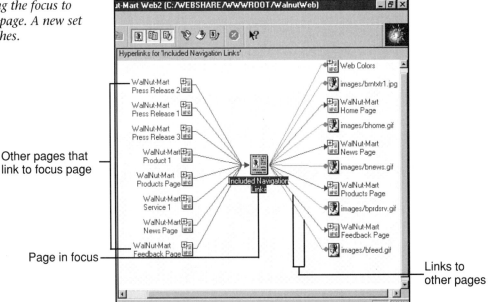

As a Web site grows with complexity (the site we're using here is of medium complexity), the number of links, and hence, the number of branches, will increase. This fact can appear confusing at first glance, but take the time to look and follow each individual branch. Soon, the Web site will make sense, and Hyperlinks View should become a convenient way to see the structure of our Web site.

Home Bones

Some attention has been given to what the FrontPage Explorer calls our Home Page, and if you'll recall it appears at the top of the All Hyperlinks list. (A cozy cottage icon reminds us which page is the Home Page). Let's understand the purpose of this page, and why it gets top billing.

If you've checked recently, you'll notice that human beings have a spine, the central backbone of our skeleton (check now, nobody will notice). Similarly, a Web site has a central Home Page that serves three functions:

➤ **Presentational**   The Home Page is the first page that a visitor to our Web site sees.

➤ **Informational**   It provides some information as to what the visitor can expect to find throughout the Web site.

➤ **Navigational**   Visitors can reach any other major page in the Web site via a hyperlink provided somewhere on the Home Page. Conversely, most pages within the site offer hyperlinks back to the Home Page.

Playing the Links

In the right-hand window of the Hyperlinks View, the right mouse button has a small handful of uses. Right-clicking on the page in center focus pops up a little menu as shown in the next figure.

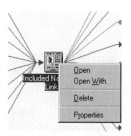

Right-clicking the page in center focus.

From this menu, we can open the page in the FrontPage Editor (**Open**), or another application (**Open With**), or delete it from the Web entirely (**Delete**). Note that if you delete a Web page from the Web, links *to* that page from other pages will *not* be deleted. The result will be "broken links," which we'll look at in Chapter 11. Similarly, deleting images in this manner would also result in broken links on the pages which connect to those images.

In Focus Right-clicking a page which is on a branch pops up the same menu, with an added item: **Move to center**. This selection will reposition the chosen page as the center focus, and show all relevant branches thereof.

Another form of link-play involves hiding or showing certain types of links (branches). There are three types of links we can hide or display, in any combination, offered in the View menu as: Hyperlinks to Images, Repeated Hyperlinks, and Hyperlinks Inside Page. You can also access them by clicking on the appropriate icon on the toolbar.

Hyperlinks to Images Enabling this will display branches which lead to images. Disabling it will cause these branches not to be shown. If your page has tons of images, disabling this option may help reduce clutter.

Repeated Hyperlinks Sometimes, a specific link may appear multiple times within one page. For instance, perhaps we have a link to our Home Page at both the top and bottom of our Products page. Enabling this option will show each of the links described above, even though they both lead to the same page. Disabling this option will only show one branch for the hyperlink, even if we have multiple instances of the same hyperlink on one page.

Hyperlinks Inside Page As we'll see in Chapter 6, "The Joy of Text," when discussing bookmarks, sometimes we create hyperlinks which point to places on the same page (as the hyperlink). Enabling this option will show those links, while disabling it will keep them hidden. For instance, we might be primarily concerned with viewing the links which point to other pages—thus, we'd disable this option to reduce visual clutter.

New Perspectives—the Folder View

Computers and humans rarely see matters the same way. It is often a case of bad feelings, where a heartfelt talk would smooth everything over. So it is with Web sites—the views described above, featuring links and graphical representation of page connections, pleases the human mind. It conforms to how we think and organize data in our brains.

On the other hand, the computer is not so evolved as we are (he says, smugly). As far as the computer is concerned, our Web site is a list of folders and files. Each folder or file has a name. The computer delivers whatever file we ask for, and it's satisfied. No higher aspirations, no struggle for meaning in existence. FrontPage Explorer offers us the option to see our Web site this way. The option is called the Folder View, and we can switch to its perspective either from the menu **View**, **Folder View**, or by clicking the Folder icon on the toolbar.

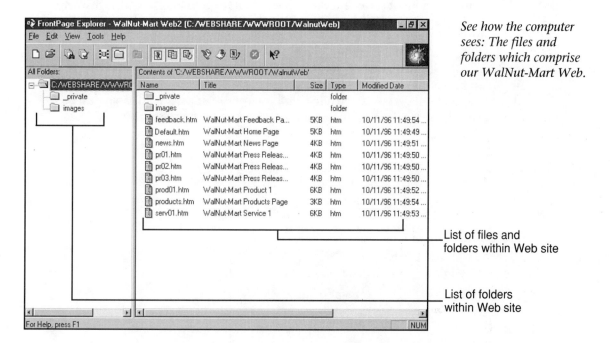

See how the computer sees: The files and folders which comprise our WalNut-Mart Web.

List of files and folders within Web site

List of folders within Web site

In the left-hand window, at the top, we see the folder in which our Web site resides. Expanding this list (clicking the plus sign) reveals any subfolders within. As represented above, we've already clicked the plus sign to expand the list, hence a minus sign now precedes the folder name. The WalNut-Mart site contains two subfolders: private, where we keep pages that visitors cannot view, and images, where any graphic images used in this site are stored. These two folders are created by default when FrontPage Explorer generates a Web site. The use of folders is largely up to the individual, and you need not use any. However, they can help to keep files organized within the site, especially a complex site with many images, sounds, and so forth. Again, we don't *have* to put our images in the images folder. The Corporate Presence Web Wizard did place its images in the image folder of our WalNut-Mart Web site, however.

Notice a file named Default.htm. This is what FrontPage Explorer has named the Home Page. To the right of the filenames appears the human-friendly title of the page: WalNut-Mart Home Page. Right-clicking a filename brings up a list of options, from where we might rename the file name of the page, or delete the page from our Web altogether.

The Home Page Filename

When we create a new Web with the FrontPage Explorer, it automatically creates at least one page—the Home Page. It saves that page with a particular filename. However, *which* filename depends on where we create the Web site. Imagine that we're creating the new site on a Web server. Each Web server has its own preferred filename for a home page. On the FrontPage Personal Web Server, the preferred home page filename is *index.htm*. On the Microsoft Personal Web Server, the preferred filename is *Default.htm*. In this book, as detailed in Chapter 19, "Bringing the Server to Life," we use the Microsoft Personal Web Server, and therefore our home pages are created with the filename *Default.htm*. Also, if we create the Web site on a local path rather than on a Web server, the FrontPage Explorer will assign the filename *index.htm* to the home page.

Right-clicking a file name offers a few handy options.

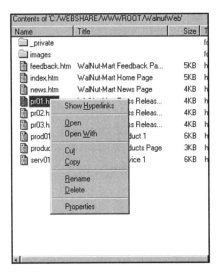

Because hyperlinks are at the very essence of a useful Web site, the Hyperlink View offers a skeletal perspective on our site which provides the "big picture." The Folder View is far more limited in scope, but allows us to tinker with the underpinnings of the site (such as the filenames of particular Web pages, or image files).

Setting the, well, Settings

Reviving our skeleton analogy, a human is *more* than a skeleton, of course (that's what my mom used to say to cheer me up. Give it a try!). Each person has a set of personal characteristics, such as name, languages spoken, favorite ice cream, favorite *type* of chocolate ice cream, and so on. Our Web site also has a set of personality traits and other characteristics, which we can configure via the menu **Tools, Web Settings**.

First page of Web Settings. Here we modify or add any substitution variables used in our Web pages.

The Parameters Tab

The first tab of Web settings is labelled Parameters. Pictured are a list of variable names followed by their values. As we'll see in a later chapter, the FrontPage Editor provides a feature called the Substitution WebBot, which we can use when creating the pages on a FrontPage-compatible Web server. This particular WebBot allows for placement of variables within a Web page, whose actual values (which are what appear in the reader's browser) can be modified quickly via the Web Settings.

Very Variable

In programming parlance, a "variable" is a word which refers to a value. For instance, let's choose the word *number*. Used as a variable, we can designate that *number* refers to the value 5. We then use this word *number* as a placeholder in our program, whenever we need to use the value it refers to. The reason for doing this is that the value can be changed in one instance (suppose we now decide that *number* refers to the value *10*), and every instance where we used *number* is automatically updated.

Within a Web page, we might want to list the winner of the weekly lottery, for example. If we were not using a variable, we'd have to re-edit the Web page each week and replace the old name with the new. Using a variable to substitute for the winner's actual name, we can edit the current winner's name in the Web Settings dialog and the page will then reflect that change. Please see the discussion of the Substitution WebBot, in Chapter 18, "Pump Up Your Page: Plug-Ins and WebBots," for a full discussion and example of this.

The Configuration Tab

Moving to the second page of Web Settings, we see a few characteristics of the Web site itself.

The second page of Web Settings—brief and to the point.

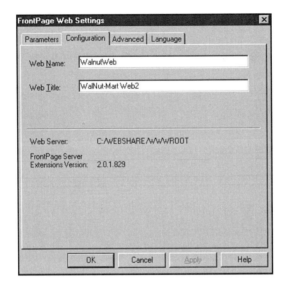

This lonely settings page only has two modifiable properties:

Web Name   This is the name by which the Web is saved on the Web server or local machine. Therefore, when the FrontPage Explorer creates a directory on the Web server or local machine, it names that directory whatever is entered for Web Name.

Web Title   This is the "title" of the Web which Web surfers will see in the Web browser window title. For example, we might have chosen the Web Name "walnutweb" for our current site, but chosen "WalNut-Mart Web" for the Web Title. In most cases, it's least confusing to simply choose the same name for both the Web Name and Web Title (unless the human-friendly Web Title would violate filename rules).

In the bottom portion of this window is a report on what Web server this site is on (or what local directory, if not using a server), and what version of "FrontPage Extensions" are in use. FrontPage Extensions are discussed in more detail in Part 5, "Broadcasting from Bed: The Microsoft FrontPage Web Server," but suffice it to say, they provide special functionality for a Web server, allowing special FrontPage features, such as WebBots, to be used.

The Advanced Settings Tab

The third tab of the Web Settings contain the Advanced settings for our Web site.

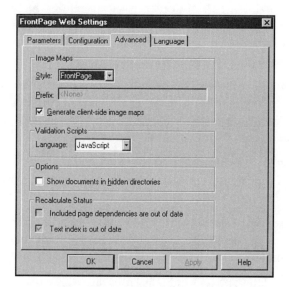

Careful in these parts, these are the Advanced characteristics of our Web page—only occasionally do these need to be altered.

In most cases, the settings on this page do not need to be modified. However, there are certain instances where tweaks are called for. Let's run through each of the items.

Image Maps   On some Web pages, you'll see a large graphic image. Mouse-clicking different areas of the image brings about different results, such as leading us to different Web pages. This ability for one image to be sensitive to mouse-clicks within certain regions is called an *Image Map.*

Furthermore, when you click on a part of the image, there is the question of who analyzes where the click took place. In one scenario, the browser sends the click information to the Web server, and the Web server then determines what action to take. This is known as *server-side image mapping*, because the server is making the final call. In the second scenario, the browser can decide what to do all by itself; this is known as *client-side image mapping*. Client-side image mapping is almost always preferable, because it is much quicker (less information needs to be sent to the server), and easier to configure.

Notice that there is a check box in this window labelled Generate Client-Side Image Maps. In almost all cases, we should have this box enabled. FrontPage is the preferred option for the Image Maps: Style selection.

Validation Scripts   As we'll discover in Chapter 7, "Friendly Forms," we may create form fields (user input areas) which require input constraints. To enforce these input constraints, FrontPage 97 will generate scripts in the Web page (more on scripts in Chapter 16, "The Art of the Script"). This option allows us to select which scripting language to use: VBScript or JavaScript. Using JavaScript allows the page to be compatible with more Web browsers, but beyond that, we should stay consistent with whichever scripting language we choose to use in Chapter 16.

Options and Recalculate Status   Show documents in hidden directories: Enabling this allows the FrontPage Explorer to display files which reside in hidden folders. Hidden folders are named with a preceding underscore, such as "_private." By default, the FrontPage Explorer does not show files within these folders.

Recalculate Status   At the bottom of the Settings window are two status reports. We can't alter these, as they're not options. Rather, they are reports from FrontPage 97 on the current status of two site-related functions:

Included page dependencies are out of date: If this is check marked, this means that any Include WebBots in our pages have lost validity. For further explanation of Include WebBots, see Chapter 18, "Pump Up Your Page: Plug-Ins and WebBots."

Text index is out of date: The text index is FrontPage 97's current database of words on every page of our Web site. This is used by FrontPage 97 in combination with the Search WebBot (again, more information on this in Chapter 18). If selected, this means that the text index for our site is not current. Selecting the FrontPage Explorer menu item **Tools**, **Recalculate Hyperlinks** will create a new, current text index.

The Language Tab

The final tab of FrontPage Web Settings allows us to configure any language properties of our Web site. Most Web sites are in English, and so most users won't need to change this setting. However, if your site is in another language, or uses a different alphabet, these settings matter.

Non-English users of the Web can configure their Web browsers to display pages in their language, using the correct alphabet font, and so forth. If you are designing a Web site intended for use in a non-English environment, select the correct language and alphabet (known here as "HTML encoding").

A Small Bevy of Options

The settings we've tickled thus far affect the specific Web site loaded. Another set of options, found in the menu under **Tools, Options**, configure the behavior of the FrontPage Explorer application itself. These options do not change our Web site—just how the Explorer behaves.

The General Options Tab

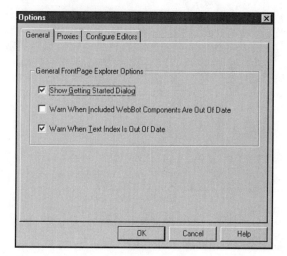

The General Options page, telling the Explorer how to behave itself.

The General Options page only contains three options.

➤ **Show Getting Started Dialog**   When we launch the FrontPage Explorer, it presents us with a dialog box from which we can open an existing Web, create a new one, or import an old one. We saw this dialog box several times in Chapter 3, "A Brand New Web." Disabling this option will skip that dialog, and open directly into the FrontPage Explorer. From there we'd use the items under the File menu to create or open Web sites.

➤ **Warn When Included WebBot Components are Out of Date**   If an Include WebBot has lost validity, enabling this will show a warning to that effect upon opening this site into the FrontPage Explorer.

➤ **Warn When Text Index is Out of Date**   If the text index for this site, used with the Search WebBot, has become stale, enabling this will warn us upon opening this site into the FrontPage Explorer. We'll then be offered the option to Recalculate Hyperlinks.

The Proxies Tab

On the second tab of the Options window, we can configure any necessary proxy server. If you're using a proxy server, enter its name in the box. Enter the names and ports of any Web servers which you don't want to be proxied in the box labelled List of Hosts Without Proxy.

Foxy Proxy Moxy

When you send out a connection request to a Web server, it normally travels from your PC along the Internet, to the server machine. A Proxy is a machine supplied by your service provider which intercepts these requests. The Proxy evaluates your requests, and might choose to deny it (if your service provider bans you from accessing certain Web sites), or might deliver the data from its local cache, if someone else has visited that same site recently (the local cache process is much faster than receiving the data from the real server).

The best way to be certain about whether you need to use a proxy server or not is to ask your service provider, be it the network manager at a workplace, or a private service provider whom you pay.

The Configure Editors Tab

The final tab of the Options window allows us to choose which editors to use for certain types of files. Again, for most users, the defaults will all be sufficient.

Pairing files types with editors. Matchmaker, matchmaker...

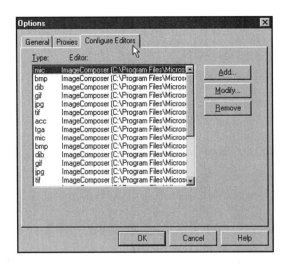

For example, if we look for the file types listed as htm and html, we see that they are matched with the FrontPage Editor. Assuming you want to use the FrontPage Editor, that should be fine. Many of the image file types (gif, jpg, bmp) are matched to the Microsoft Image Composer. Feel free to change these pairings by clicking the **Modify** button, should you prefer a different image editor.

Important note: These pairings *only* apply to functions within the FrontPage Explorer. They do not affect the general Windows 95 file associations in any way.

The Least You Need to Know

The FrontPage Explorer allows us an overview perspective of our Web site. It provides a variety of means to navigate this view or alter its contents.

➤ The default Hyperlinks View provides a tree-structure of our Web, the pages within, and their interconnections.

➤ Right-clicking the icons of pages in the Hyperlinks View allows us to edit, delete, or shift focus.

➤ The Folder View displays the official directories and filenames of our Web pages as stored on the server, or the local hard drive.

➤ Expand or contract the listings in either view by clicking the plus (+) and minus (-) signs that precede branch names.

➤ Web Settings modify characteristics of the loaded Web site, including its name, folder name, and how to generate image maps.

➤ The Options dialog box of the FrontPage Explorer configures its own general behavior, including whether to use a proxy server, and the up-to-dateness warnings.

Chapter 5

Mission Statement: Editor at Large

In This Chapter

➤ The Editor as canvas, sort of

➤ Elements of a page

➤ Limitations: A degree of freedom

➤ Limitations: Tech kept a rollin

➤ Starting anew (page)

The canvas is often used as a metaphor for the stage on which people create. In that vein, then, one *might* say that the FrontPage Editor is the Web designer's canvas. But we won't say that. The canvas is not a perfect metaphor for the FrontPage Editor. Having not said that, the canvas concept *is* in the general ballpark. In this chapter, we'll consider the role of the FrontPage Editor, and how it does, and doesn't, fit the metaphor. In doing so, we're laying the groundwork for using the FrontPage editor, which is the subject of the chapters in Part 3, "Our Evolving Web."

Pros: What the Editor Can Do

In an earlier, more innocent, time (Chapter 2, "FrontPage 97: A New Era in Web Design"), we discussed the significance of the What-You-See-is-What-You-Get (WYSIWYG) approach to Web design that the FrontPage Editor provides. In this respect, the FrontPage Editor is similar to a painting canvas—what the artist creates on the workspace is the final result.

Web pages, however, are not merely "a look." Unlike a canvas, where paint is the single medium through which an image is conveyed, a Web page may be made up of a combination of five elements:

➤ **Passive Data**   Any information which appears on a Web page, but has no interactive function, can be classified as passive data. For instance, the body of a news article about the difficulty of finding licorice tea, may be entirely passive data. It appears on the screen for the reader to read, but no interaction is possible. Superficially, passive data may have any look —italic, bold, large, small—but it retains its inert property.

➤ **Hyperlinked Data**   This is onscreen information that may possess any of the visual characteristics of passive data, but, if "followed" or "clicked," brings about some action: leading to a new page, playing a sound file, and so on. Often in Web pages, passive data is punctuated with bits of hyperlinked data. For instance, our news article about licorice tea might be largely passive data, but the phrase "licorice tea" is hyperlinked data, which could lead the reader to another Web site about tea.

➤ **External Objects**   External objects appear in a page, but are provided by a file other than the page's HTML document. The most common example of an external object is an image file. Many Web pages contain images, such as backgrounds, divider lines, puppies, and so forth. These images exist in separate image files, and are linked into the Web page. However, external objects can also be more advanced than still images. Animated videos, sounds, Java applets, and Netscape Plug-Ins are all examples of external objects (See Part 4, "It's Alive! Advanced Web Tactics," for more information on these external objects).

➤ **Interactive Forms**   For any number of reasons (42), we might want the reader to provide us with interaction, perhaps supplying their name, or to select a favorite variety of apple. "Forms" are any type of interactive questionnaire: Text boxes where a user can type, menus from which a user can select options, or buttons a user can click. Some forms can also be external objects, such as Java applets and ActiveX controls.

➤ **Conditional/Result Data**   The actions of a user, be it clicking certain options, or typing in certain data (such as ordering items for a catalog), might be used to generate new data (passive or hyperlinked) on a page. For instance, suppose a user clicked on the apple seedling varieties she wanted to purchase from our company. Following that, she entered a name and shipping address. We might then want to generate and display a new Web page, summarizing her order, costs, and address (an invoice).

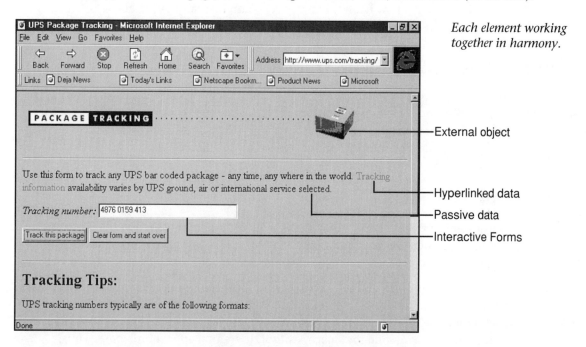

Each element working together in harmony.

————External object

————Hyperlinked data

————Passive data

————Interactive Forms

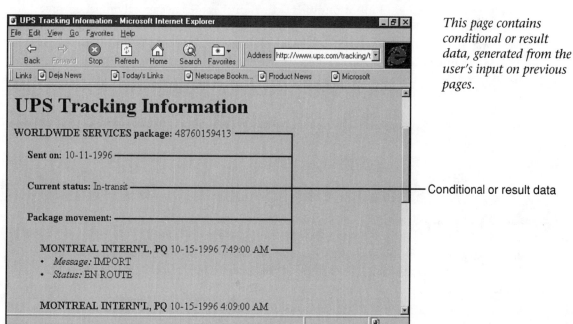

This page contains conditional or result data, generated from the user's input on previous pages.

————Conditional or result data

Of the Web page elements, some are easier to represent in a WYSIWYG format than others. The FrontPage Editor cannot show all elements with equal visual accuracy, and this is an issue we'll discuss in detail in the next section of this chapter. What the FrontPage Editor *does* allow us to do, however, is combine any of the above in creating our Web pages.

Cons: What the Editor Doesn't Do

Learning a new tool is as much about understanding what it can't do as what it can. The FrontPage Editor does have its limitations, and they're important to note. Some of these limitations are unavoidable, and are part of the territory of using a WYSIWYG Web page editor. Others could be improved in updates to the FrontPage Editor, but whether this will or won't occur is unknown.

Degrees of Freedom

On the degrees-of-freedom spectrum, WYSYWIG Web designers such as the FrontPage Editor fall somewhere below word processors. We cannot place any image and any block of text anywhere on a page.

Why not? "Blame it on the HTML," to misquote a certain non-singing duo (hint: rhymes with Silli Banilli). Recall from Chapter 2 that Web pages are built out of the HTML page description language. This language defines what can appear on a page. Conversely, what the language does *not* define for a page, cannot, therefore, appear on a page. Thus, whatever the placement limitations of HTML, FrontPage 97 necessarily must enforce those restrictions. For instance, HTML (in its current incarnation) offers no straightforward way to align one phrase of text to the left edge of a page, and another to the right, along the same horizontal. Thus, when we use the FrontPage Editor, there's no easy way to do this. Web designers may find this frustrating, especially if they are used to word processors or page layout applications with more degrees of freedom. In some cases, there are "tricks" or "workarounds" which can achieve similar effects to those we want (as there are with the above text-wrapping example, which we'll explain when discussing tables in Chapter 9).

As HTML advances, and the Web continues to evolve, we can expect freedoms to expand. Which carries us neatly to the FrontPage Editor's second notable limitation.

External Objects

In some cases, the FrontPage Editor does not or cannot know what an external object looks like. Or, perhaps that object is an animation clip or a sound. In these cases, the Editor cannot easily display these elements in the WYSIWYG environment. For instance, imagine that we want to add a Java applet of a scrolling LED sign to our page. The FrontPage Editor allows us to insert a Java applet, but it doesn't know that the applet is an LED sign. Rather than accurately display the applet in the Editor, it must show a place-holder, such as a coffee mug (a "java" joke), letting us know that the applet will appear in this place.

Similarly, an animated movie cannot be shown on the page, because to keep the anima-tion running within the editor would require too much computing power. Again, a placeholder is used so that we know an object belongs there. While this approach is generally satisfactory, it does separate the Editor from a true "WYSIWYG" interface, in which every element on the final page would be accurately represented in the editor.

The March of Progress

When the first version of the Netscape Navigator Web browser was released, it quickly became popular. The most capable, and fastest, browser on the market, Netscape grabbed a huge market share. In doing so, the makers of Netscape were dissatisfied with some of the early limitations of HTML. They wanted new tags that could make pages flashier, so they unilaterally decided to invent new tags.

Competing browsers had to decide whether to stick to the "official" HTML, as described by the standards body, or copy Netscape's new tags. Browser wars grew ever fiercer as the Web exploded in popularity, and browsers had to compete on any front they could. As a consequence, caution was thrown to the wind, and the invention of new tags, and the copying of competitor's tags, became commonplace. The HTML standards body was left in the dust, although in recent times it has decided to catch-up, and amend HTML to include the newly invented tags. To this day, the major browsers such as Netscape and Microsoft Internet Explorer invent new tags and other features (ActiveX, JavaScript, and so on) with each new release. The major advantage of this is an ever-expanding war chest of authoring tools. Web pages can be more advanced than ever.

The major disadvantage of the HTML arms race is simply keeping up. An application such as the FrontPage Editor or any HTML editor, for that matter, can only, *at most*, offer the HTML features that exist at the time it was created.

Hopefully, the above paragraphs did not come across as complete downers. The point is not that the FrontPage Editor is a bastion of obstacles and limitations. Rather, it tries very hard to do what it claims to do, and in most cases, succeeds. However, due to limitations in the technology the editor is based on, as well as the pace of that technology's change, the FrontPage Editor will always be a slight step behind. For most users, this shouldn't prove a major problem, and is one of the tradeoffs for the ease of WYSIWYG design.

Prepare for Takeoff

Concepts firmly grounded, it's now time to begin working with the FrontPage Editor itself. There are a few ways to launch the editor:

1. While exploring a Web site in the FrontPage Explorer Hyperlinks View, locate the page to edit in the right-hand window. Either double-clicking or right-clicking and choosing **Open** from the pop-up menu will open the FrontPage Editor with the page in question.

Double-clicking or right-clicking the Web page will launch the FrontPage Editor. Whee.

Double-click or right-click

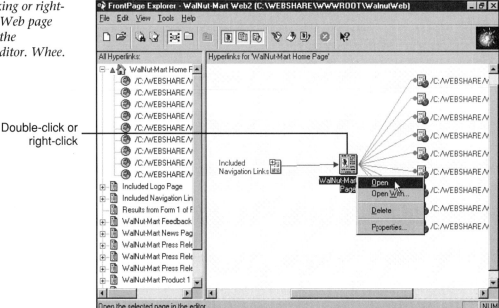

2. When FrontPage is installed on a machine, a new icon is added to the Internet Explorer Web browser. Labelled **Edit**, clicking this button will open the FrontPage Editor, with which we can edit a copy of the Web page currently in view.

3. Create a shortcut on the desktop which directly opens the FrontPage Editor. To do so, first locate the FrontPage Editor (by default, it lives at **Program Files\Microsoft FrontPage\bin\fpeditor.exe**. Here's the easy way:

➤ In the Windows 95 desktop, click **Start**, **Find**, **Files** or **Folders**.

➤ The File Find utility will pop up. Be sure the box labelled **Look** in is set to the drive on which FrontPage was installed (*usually pathname*).

➤ In the box labelled **Named**, enter **fpeditor** then click **Find Now**.

➤ Your drive will be searched, and matches will be listed (this may take several minutes). It should have found at least one file named fpeditor.exe, somewhere between 1,500KB to 2,000KB in size.

➤ Right-click the fpeditor icon that was found, and drag it anywhere on the desktop. Let go of the right mouse button, and a menu will pop up. Select **Create shortcut here**. A new icon will appear on the desktop. Anytime you double-click this icon, the FrontPage Editor will be launched.

A Shiny New Page—Templates and Wizards

Suppose that after launching the FrontPage Editor, we want to begin work on a new page. At some point down the road, we may link this page into our current Web site. To begin creating a new page, choose the menu **File**, **New**. Déjà vu! A choice list of templates and wizards appears, not dissimilar to the list we saw when creating a new Web site.

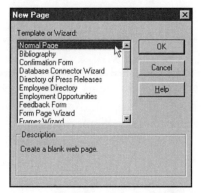

Beginning to create a new Web page—prefab or original design.

There are a few templates and wizards to choose from. Highlighting any one in the list will initiate a brief description of its purpose. Of course, using a template or wizard is largely a personal choice. We can create a page from scratch (Normal Page) if we like. There are a couple of wizards which even seasoned page designers will appreciate: the Frames Wizard, for instance, is one we'll be looking at later.

Most templates, if selected, include comments to direct us to complete the page. For instance, suppose that we chose the "Hot List" template. A page appears in the FrontPage Editor which looks remarkably similar to the next figure.

Using the Hot List template, we have a basic page with helpful commentary. Readers will not see the commentary; only the designer does.

Instructional comments

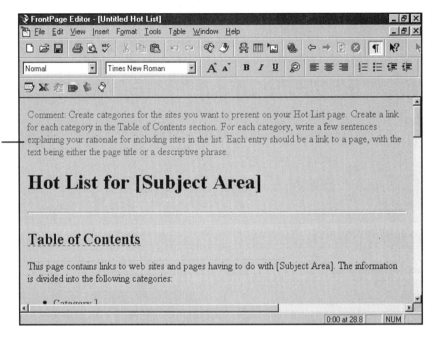

At the top of the page, we can see a few lines prefaced with Comment. This is an instruction provided to us, the page designers, by the template we chose. It *will not* appear on the Web page when a reader views it. (Adding comments to a page is simple, as we'll see in Chapter 18, where we discuss WebBots.) Were we to have selected to create a new page from the ground up ("Normal Page"), a completely blank page would appear. From there, we would begin designing.

The Least You Need to Know

The FrontPage Editor is a quasi-canvas on which we visually design Web pages. But it's not an exact canvas:

➤ Several different elements can be combined on a Web page, including passive data, hyperlinked data, external objects, interactive forms, and result data.

➤ The FrontPage Editor does not have infinite degrees of freedom; there are restrictions on where elements can be placed on a page.

➤ The FrontPage Editor cannot represent all page elements in WYSIWYG format, notably some external objects such as Java applets.

➤ We launch the FrontPage Editor from the FrontPage Explorer or the Internet Explorer or from the Start button cascading menu.

➤ Creating a new Web page is as simple as selecting **File**, **New** in the FrontPage Editor, and selecting an appropriate template or wizard. Use **Normal Page** to start a page from scratch.

Part 3
Our Evolving Web

If you read no other section of this book, or if you want to jump right into the fray, this is the section. We touch all the bases here, from adding text to Web pages, to creating hyperlinks and tables, forms and frames. Our Web sites have really shaped up by the end of this section, so we close out by publishing our Web site to a Web server—where all the world can see it!

The "Peggy Tyler is a lying tramp" web page closes up shop.

Chapter 6

The Joy of Text

In This Chapter

➤ Putting Text to page

➤ Fashionable words—Style and Color

➤ A little to the left, no...right, no...left

➤ Hyperlink Power

Every good page has text. Web pages which only contain graphics are generally considered poor uses of the Web medium, because not every user has the time or capability to receive graphics. In addition, text is (still) the major means by which we communicate. This chapter will look at how we place and design the text that appears on our Web page. Although the Web is touted for its multimedia stylings, we'll re-assert that the backbone of a good Web page is its text; despite claims about the decreasing level of literacy among, um, er...the, all the people who live together inside a big...society, yes, society.

Inserting and Importing

For the sake of Zen clarity, let's assume that we start this chapter with a completely blank Web page. The FrontPage Editor has been launched, we've selected **File, New** from the menu, and chosen "Normal Page." Blank as a beaver. Not that that makes any sense.

Fresh as a new spring day, starting with a blank Web page. Smell the bleach.

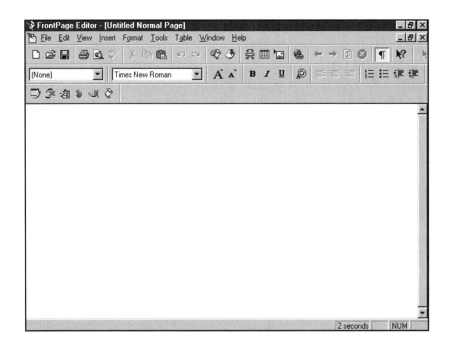

Premixed Pages: Selecting a Template

Rather than starting with a blank Web page ("Normal Web"), we could jump-start our design effort with a prefabricated template. When a user selects the menu **File, New**, a number of additional page templates are offered, such as:

Bibliography: Used to create a Web page with citations to other works.

Feedback Form: A Web page with which readers can submit feedback to you or your organization.

Form Page Wizard: If you're not entirely comfortable with creating forms from scratch (see Chapter 7, "Friendly Forms"), try this Wizard.

Frames Wizard: The main subject of Chapter 8 "But Your Honor...I Was Framed!" this Wizard walks us through the process of creating a page with multiple frames.

Personal Home Page Wizard: A step-by-step walk-through for creating your own individualized personal Web presence.

When we place text onto a Web page, the process is as follows:

1. Put text onto page

2. Fashion text in desired manner

In the case of the first (which is what this section is about) we're concerned with putting text onto the page. Not its color, or font, or size, or alignment. Those are aspects of fashioning the text, which we'll discuss a bit later in this chapter.

Our text may come from two sources: That which is typed directly onto the page, or that which is imported into the page from a text file. In many cases, when designing Web pages, we'll be typing text directly onto the page. However, there may be times where we want to use text from an existing file.

Type Type Tap

When typing text directly onto the Web page, the FrontPage Editor behaves similar to a word processor. A blinking straight-line cursor can be seen, and it represents where typed text will appear. Entering text is the default mode of the FrontPage Editor, and so the cursor should be blinking right now, after we have created our blank Normal Web page.

Simply, then, we begin typing. In this case, **All About Me**. That will be the main header of the page, but we won't format it just yet. We keep typing in our text, pressing enter to move to the next line. After all the information has been entered, we have the beginnings of a Web page. Do keep in mind that when building a Web page, we needn't place the text first, but in this case it seems most logical.

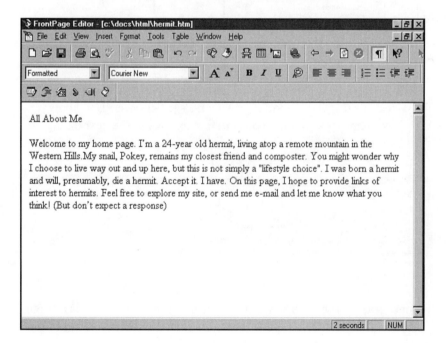

Typing our text directly onto the Web page. We'll fashion it afterwards.

Bring It in, Boys

Our hero, the hermit, has a poem he wrote some years ago. Wanting also to place it onto his Web page, we look at importing text from a file. The poem, we'll imagine, lives in a file called "poem1.doc" on the hermit's hard drive. The FrontPage Editor can import files from a variety of sources: Plain text files , HTML files (other Web pages), and files created in Microsoft Word, Microsoft Excel, or WordPerfect.

When importing a word processor file, the FrontPage Editor will retain any formatting that the Web page supports (bold, italic, and so on), but any advanced formatting will likely be ignored. To import the hermit's poem, we first select the menu item **Insert, File**. A typical file dialog box opens up, and from there we navigate to the location of the poem. Alternatively, we can also drag-and-drop a file from the Windows desktop onto the **Select a File** dialog box.

Finding a file to import into our Web page. No duties or taxes required.

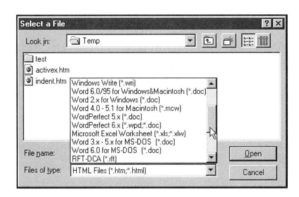

Because the poem file is a text file (e.g. ASCII format), the FrontPage Editor needs to know how to format it on the Web page. Thus, it pops up the prompt that appears in the next figure.

Selecting how to format an imported text file.

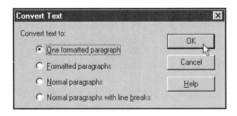

Consider each of the formatting options:

> **One formatted paragraph**: In this format, the entire text file is imported as a single paragraph. Any white spaces—such as spaces between characters or line breaks—are preserved as-is.

Formatted paragraphs: With this format, paragraphs are imported with a line break between them. Again, white spaces and line breaks are preserved.

Normal paragraphs: In this format, each paragraph is imported into the page as HTML text. This means that extra white spaces and linebreaks are removed, leaving formatting up to the individual browser.

Normal paragraphs with linebreaks: With this format, a compromise format, the imported text file is converted into HTML text (such that the browser formats it), however HTML line breaks are inserted wherever line breaks originally existed in the text file.

"Normal" versus "Formatted"

By its nature, the Web is supposed to be flexible. Originally, text on a Web page was supposed to conform to the size of the viewer's browser window. Thus, the Web designer did not determine where a line break occurred; the browser made this decision. In doing this, it was assured that each Web page would look "reasonable" on any browser.

However, sometimes a Web designer wants more control over how the text appears on a page. Exactly where line breaks occur, and so forth. Sometimes this is vital, as in poetry, for instance. Thus, two types of text have emerged: "Normal" text and "Formatted" text.

Whenever possible, it's best to use Normal text on a Web page to remain consistent with the flexibility of the Web. However, certain types of information, such as catalog listings, poems, and so forth, require precise formatting. In these cases, use Formatted text.

After selecting **One formatted paragraph** (because we want to insert the entire poem as-is), the text of the poem now appears on the Web page wherever the blinking cursor was last located. Note the little arrow marks beside each line of poetry; these represent a formatted line break.

The imported poem appears on the Web page, with formatted line breaks.

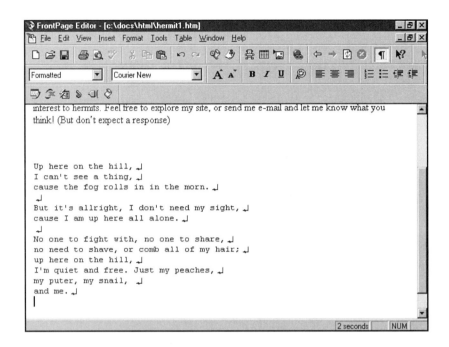

For Saving's Sake

Time to save our work of art so far. **File, Save** will bring around the save dialog box. If we're working within a Web site (meaning that we launched the FrontPage Editor from the FrontPage Explorer), we can choose a name for the page and click **OK**. If we are not working within a Web site, we click **As File** and save the page as a discrete HTML file.

With text on our page, we'll now fashion it. Size, colors, hyperlinks, the whole potato tamale. Mmm ... potato tamales ...

It's Not All About Size: Fonts and Colors, too

Being visual (and shallow) creatures, we respond to the look of text in addition to (and sometimes instead of) its content. Three quite obvious ways to dress up the text on our Web page are to change its size, color, and style. The extent to which any of these modifications succeeds depends in part on the reader's Web browser. Regardless of the font, size, or color we design into our text, the reader will only see these fashions if their browser is capable of handling such configurations.

Browser Bravado

Not every Web browser is created equal, despite Thomas Jefferson's best wishes. As with any set of competing products, some browsers possess capabilities that others lack. When it comes to fashioning text, one should keep in mind the fact that some browsers aren't capable of displaying some fashions.

For instance, if we select a special font for our text, the reader's browser may not be able to find that font. Thus, the reader will see the text rendered in a default, basic font. Similarly, some browsers may not understand the way in which FrontPage makes text larger or smaller. Rest assured, Internet Explorer and Netscape Navigator are running fairly neck-and-neck, and both can display the fashions which the FrontPage Editor can apply. However, less-commonly used browsers such as Opera and Mosaic may not enjoy such luck. Thus, keep your audience in mind, and use discretion when deciding whether to add that splash of color, or a fancy font.

For that reason, we must consider any dressing up as "best case scenario" design. Some readers may not see the colors, or font, although they'll still see the text itself (Which is fine, just something to remember as a Web page designer).

First things first, let's consider the page heading, "All About Me." As the banner of the page, we probably want this text to be large and eye-catching. On the FrontPage Toolbar, you'll notice two icons which represent text size (if you don't see these icons, be sure that the menu item **View**, **Format Toolbar** is checked):

 Increase Text Size

 Decrease Text Size

Highlight the text that we want to modify by holding down the left mouse button while dragging across the text. Now, if we click the Increase Text Size button, poof! text gets bigger. Click the Decrease Text Size button and foop! text gets smaller. For our page, we'll increase the text size three times by, not surprisingly, clicking on the Increase Text Size icon three times. Note that the exact size the reader sees will vary depending on his browser and screen size, but we can be assured that it will appear three sizes larger than whatever the reader's normal text size is. Of course, the text can't be increased or decreased in size ad infinitum. In fact, starting from the default size in which text appears before we modify it, it can be increased by up to five sizes or decreased down to three sizes smaller.

After inflating the highlighted text three sizes larger. Oooh.

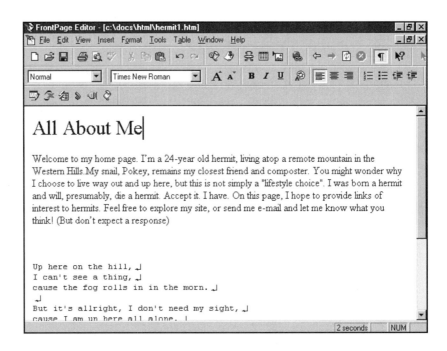

To the right of the text size buttons on the toolbar are three style buttons (bold, italic, and underline) as well as the Text Color button:

 Bold

 Italic

 Underline

 Text Color Button

Bold, Italic and Underline are typical styles, and clicking any of them will enable or disable that style on the highlighted text.

Beside those buttons is the Text Color button. We'll click this button, with the text "All About Me" highlighted, to change its color. If none of the offered colors pleases, clicking **Define Custom Colors** in the **Color** window allows us to create any color we want. Once we've created a custom color, either by entering RGB or HSL values, or moving the cursor around the palette spectrum until something pretty comes up, click **Add to Custom Colors** for future use. Choosing **OK** from the Color window will apply the selected color to the highlighted text.

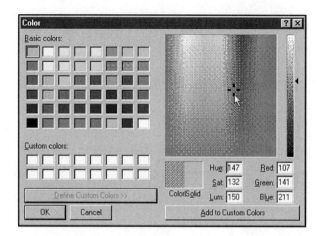

Defining a custom color with which to style text. Slide the crosshairs around the spectrum, or enter color values directly.

Although we can select any color for any bit of text on the page, keep in mind once again that not every user will have the same experience. A reader may have configured their browser to ignore our colors, or they may simply not have enough color capability to view them all. Color doesn't print well in this book, but imagine that we've changed the color of "All About Me" to a shade of purple.

Fonting Around

Changing the typestyle of our text is another way to modify its appearance. "Fonts" define the way text characters look, be they spacious and curvy, gothic and elaborate, or straight and narrow. However, it's worth repeating the caveat that some, perhaps many, readers of our Web page may not see our font choices. They may not have that particular font on their computer, or their browser may not support font changes within a Web page. Most browsers allow the reader to select which font to display text in, and that configuration may override the font choices we make in designing our Web page.

So, throwing browser caution to the wind, select **Format**, **Font** to display the Font dialog box (or right-click over the highlighted text and select **Font Properties** from the pop-up menu).

Changing the font and the type of selected text. Some visitors to our page may not see these improvements.

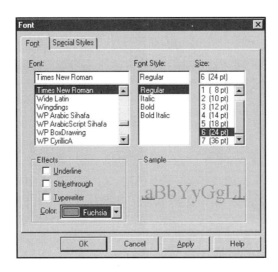

In the Font dialog box, we can configure several characteristics of the selected text. Choosing a different Font will affect the shapes of the letters (as pictured in the Sample box). We can then select a size, style (bold, italic, underline), color, and so forth for our font. Some of these options are redundant to similar options in the toolbar, but it makes no difference where you pick from. (In this example, we're not going to change the font from the default, Times New Roman).

The Font dialog box has another tab at the top marked Special Styles. Clicking this will bring up a set of additional styles which we may want to apply to our selected text. These styles are not frequently used, but most modern browsers should support them. Although entirely optional, the citation style is convenient when making references to a book, or other source of information.

Additional styles we might apply to selected text. So many choices!

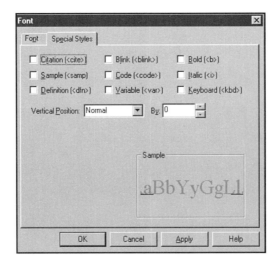

Similarly, the Code style helps represent the text of computer programs and other material which looks better when monospaced.

The Vertical Position menu allows us to set selected text as a superscript or subscript, while the by selector determines how many pixels high or low to position the superscript or sub-script. The Sample window displays the effect any of these styles will have, so we can experiment to see if any are suitable.

The other special styles are basically macros which apply a combination of styles (size and emphasis) to highlighted text—experiment with them to see their results. All are rarely used, but can be useful in special circumstances (such as including a citation). One note: when applied to selected text, the Blink style will cause that text to flash on and off when the visitor sees the page. Although this is meant to be an attention-grabber, it grows annoying quickly, and is considered a poor form of Web page design.

To recap, we've looked at three aspects of fashioning our text: changing its size, changing its color, and changing its style (font or affectation, such as bold or italic). Now that it's colorful *and* stylish, let's consider where the text is actually placed within the Web page.

Alignment Is More Than Cosmetic

The placement of text can influence its readability. While proper placement depends on the overall layout of the page, one wants text to flow in a manner that is comfortable with one's eyes. Obviously, there are exceptions, such as when trying to be "artsy" (meaning "difficult to understand by anyone other than the artist").

As fledgling Web designers, we'll choose to align our banner text, "All About Me," in the center of the margins. On the toolbar, we see three typical alignment icons:

 Left

 Center

 Right

Selecting the text "All About Me" and then clicking the centering icon on the toolbar will, not surprisingly, center the text as is pictured in the following figure.

Centered text. Notice how it's, well, in the center.

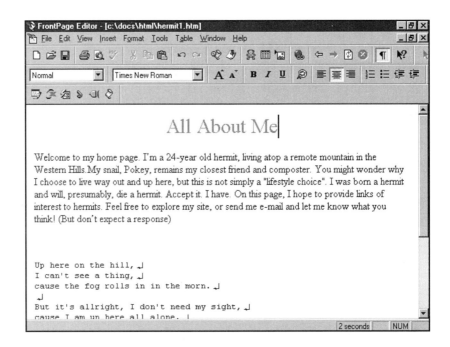

Predictably, clicking the left-align or right-align icons would move the text to the left, or to the right, margin of the page, respectively. While text alignment in the FrontPage Editor may seem as straightforward as with any word processor, there's one major caveat.

Recall our heart-to-heart about degrees of freedom. There are restrictions to where we can place text on a Web page, and one of them arises now. Imagine, for instance, that we want one line of text to contain "January 23, 1996" against the left margin, and "Volume 1" against the right margin, as in:

January 23, 1996   Volume 1

Well, we can't so easily do that in the FrontPage Editor. We can only align an entire paragraph of text at a time. By "paragraph," we refer to any text up until a line break (created by hitting Return key). Bummer, but rules are rules (there is a trick which conquers this obstacle, tucked into the end of Chapter 13, "Lights, Camera, Multimedia!").

Nudge Nudge Wink Wink

Two alignments allow us to move text by small increments to the left or right, without gluing it all the way in one direction or another: The Increase and Decrease Indent buttons, available at the rightmost edge of the toolbar:

Increase Indent

 Decrease Indent

Both of these icons apply to an entire paragraph, just as the left, centering, and right alignments did. After selecting the text to align, clicking the Increase Indent button will squeeze it closer into the center of the page. Clicking Decrease Indent will release the margins and let the text expand towards the edges of its bounds, like a Dad after a hearty Thanksgiving dinner.

Here is some basic text to type in for our example:

Welcome to my home page. I'm a 24-year old hermit, living atop a remote mountain in the Western Hills.

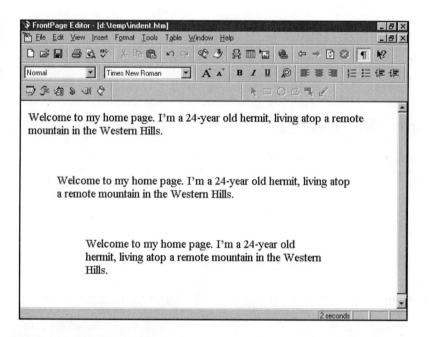

A sample line of text, first as it would normally appear, followed by the same text indented one time, and then indented two times.

Them's the Breaks

Margin-relative alignments are the three most common alignments we can apply to text. Another sort of alignment is the line-break, which determines where a line of text ends, and how much space there will be before the subsequent line begins. There are two types of line-breaks in the FrontPage Editor: A hard break and a formatted break. Remember that normally, the text on a Web page does not have line breaks built-in; the browser decides where to break the lines. If we move the cursor to a position within the text, and hit the **Return** key, a hard break will be inserted.

This is a line of text with a

hard break inserted

Notice that the hard break causes both advancement to the following line, and a big gap between lines. The hard break is considered the end of a paragraph by the FrontPage Editor. Thus, any styles which apply to a paragraph, such as alignment, apply up until a hard break is found.

The formatted break is used to move the text down one line, without a gap, and without closing the paragraph. We create a formatted break by hitting **Shift-Return** in the FrontPage Editor. By default, the FrontPage Editor will represent formatted breaks with a small arrow mark.

This is a line of text with a ↵
formatted break.

Any style which applies to the paragraph before the formatted break, such as centering alignment, will also apply to the text after the formatted break, because they are still considered as part of the same paragraph. Use the hard break to end a paragraph and its related styles.

Makin' a List, Checkin' it Twice

Although not commonly used, organized lists are another available form of text alignment. You will find two list icons on the FrontPage toolbar:

 Numbered List

 Bulleted List

For instance, consider that we wanted to list the chapters in this book. We could begin by typing each chapter name onto a line in the FrontPage Editor, following each list item with a hard break. Then, we highlight the entire list, and click either list icon.

If we hit Return at the end of a list item, a new, appropriately numbered or bulleted item will be created underneath. This allows us to set up the list alignment with only one item, and then type in the remaining items, while the list structure is automatically maintained.

Clicking the right mouse button on a portion of the list, and selecting **List Properties** from the pop-up menu, allows us to change the style of the list, or select different types of bullets or numbering schemes.

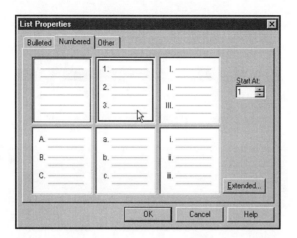

When creating numbered or bulleted lists, we can select from a variety of bullet styles, or numbering schemes, as pictured.

There are some other types of text alignment, which operate in relation to other elements on the page, such as an image or table. We'll consider these alignments when discussing the elements involved.

Making a Link: The Power of Connection

The heart, the power, the driving force behind all that is the World Wide Web is embodied in the hyperlink. A link, to recap, is any element on the page that can bring the user to another Web page, when clicked (or "followed," as is the more accurate term). Alternatively, a link may also bring the reader to a specified position within the current page, or a specified position on another Web page entirely.

First, let's consider the most common type of link: the link to another Web page. We call these hyperlinks in Web jargon, although many people merely call them "links," which means exactly the same thing. We want to select the text which will be the hyperlink. This text will appear as a different color than the rest of the text, and the user can click on it to be transported. For instance, consider the first sentence on the hermit home page we've been constructing:

Welcome to my home page. I'm a 24-year old hermit, living atop a remote mountain in the Western Hills.

The Western Hills, a fictional geographic region, has its own Web page, created by the Western Hills Chamber of Commerce. So, we think it'd be nice to provide a hyperlink to that page, should the reader be interested in more information about the Western Hills. To create this hyperlink, we begin by highlighting the appropriate text to appear as the hyperlink: Western Hills. Then, we begin creating the hyperlink by any one of these three ways: clicking the Create or Edit Hyperlink image on the toolbar, selecting **Insert**, **Hyperlink**, or hitting **Ctrl+K** on the keyboard.

Creating or editing a hyperlink. Transport readers around the Web.

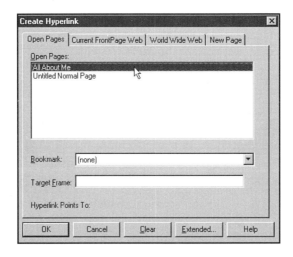

The Create Hyperlink window wants to know where to send the reader. We're provided with four general areas from which to choose a destination:

> **Open Pages**   A list of Web pages currently open in the FrontPage Editor.

> **Current FrontPage Web**   A list of pages which reside within our Web site.

> **WorldWideWeb**   Any Web page, anywhere in the world. This includes other pages on our own computer, assuming that we're running a Web server. If not, and we want to link to a page on our own computer, but outside the current Web site, that page would need to be imported into the current Web; see Chapter 11, "The Changing Shape of Your Web."

> **New Page**   A page which doesn't exist yet, but will exist eventually.

In some of the above tabs, we're also given the chance to specify these features:

> **Bookmark**   Specific location within a page. Created by adding an "anchor" or "bookmark" to that location (soon to be explained).

> **Target Frame**   If our page contains a frameset, which frame to load the hyperlinked page into (see Chapter 8).

Since this is our first page, we want to point the hyperlink to a World Wide Web page, that of the Western Hills, whose URL we happen to know is http://www.westernhills.net. To do this, we click the **WorldWideWeb** tab. Then, we enter **www.westernhills.net** into the URL box, and select **http:** from the Hyperlink Type menu.

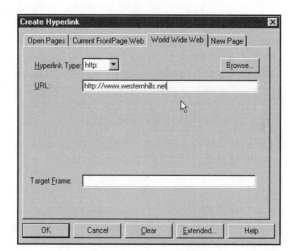

Pointing our hyperlink to a World Wide Web page. It's not rude in this case.

We don't need a target frame (see Chapter 8) for the Western Hills page, so we leave that field blank. Hitting **OK** completes the process, and our hyperlink now appears colored (default: blue) and underlined in the FrontPage Editor. Because hyperlinks are colored, be sure not to use that same color for other text on the page, lest the reader become confused about which colored text is a hyperlink, and which is merely aesthetic (You'll learn more about changing these colors in Chapter 10 "Behind the Scenes—Page Properties").

Bookmark the Spot or "Anchors Away"

As stated previously, a hyperlink may also point to a specific location within the current page, or a different Web page. We'll create another hyperlink on this page, which points to a specific location on the page. What's the point in doing this? Especially for long pages with a lot of information, using this type of hyperlink with, say, a table of contents, helps a reader easily jump from passage to passage, without having to scroll up and down.

First, we must define a specific location on the page, and assign it a name. This name doesn't appear on the page itself, but is used as a reference to that location. In the future, hyperlinks may point to this reference, to bring a user to this exact location on the page.

Bookmanchor

The folks at Microsoft have broken from tradition a bit, and possibly caused some confusion with their terminology. Commonly, marked locations within a page are called "anchors." When referring to an anchor in a URL, we use the syntax http://www.machine.com/ page.html#anchor1. That URL would take us not only to the page "page.html" but to the specific point in that page marked as anchor1. However, Microsoft has apparently decided to call these locations "bookmarks" rather than anchors. What's more, Netscape Navigator uses the term bookmarks to refer to URLs that have been saved by the user for future use (a "hot list"). Microsoft uses the term "Favorites" to refer to the same item as Netscape "Bookmarks." Confused yet?

In short: With FrontPage 97, a bookmark refers to a specific location within a page. In the rest of the world, this is called an anchor.

For our example, we want to make the first occurrence of the word "hermit" a hyperlink. That hyperlink will point to the poem further down on the page. For a user who has a small screen, or if our page had more information on it, this link would scroll directly to the poem in question, saving the user time and eye strain. Before we can create this particular hyperlink, we need to mark the location of the bookmark. Do this by selecting any portion of text where the bookmark should reside. For instance, we'll highlight "Up" the first word in the poem.

Once the text is highlighted, select **Edit, Bookmark** from the menu. It pops up with a small bookmark dialog box. Here, we choose a name for the bookmark (a default suggestion is given, but we'll modify that).Type **poem** for the name, and click **OK**. That's all; a bookmark now resides (quietly) at the location where the poem begins.

Moving back up the page, we select the text to hyperlink: "hermit." We bring up the Create Hyperlink window (**Ctrl+K** being the quickest way to do so), and we see a list of open pages. There will be at least one page in the list—our current page. Moving down to the bookmark menu, we can select a bookmark from the page. Of course, there's only one bookmark on the page now, so the only choice other than (none) is poem. Choose **poem**, click **OK**, and we're done. The Hyperlink is made, and it points to the location in the page where the bookmark named **poem** lives.

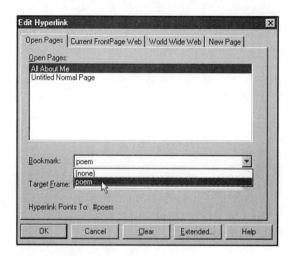

Pointing a hyperlink to a bookmark within the same page.

The Least You Need to Know

We considered quite a bit in this chapter, from how to place text onto a Web page, to how to customize its look and placement. Okay, that doesn't sound like so much, but it was. The highlights include:

➤ Text can be typed directly onto a page, or imported from a text, HTML, or word processing file (**Insert, File**).

➤ We can apply certain sizes and styles to the text, such as bold, italic, underline, superscript, and subscript.

➤ Text fonts and colors can be modified, but not all readers will see these effects, depending on the capabilities of their computer and Web browser.

➤ Paragraphs can be aligned to the left, center, or right of the page. Only hard returns, made by hitting the **Return** key, count as the end of a paragraph.

➤ Paragraphs can also be indented by small increments, towards the left or towards the right.

➤ Portions of text can be configured as hyperlinks, via **Insert, Hyperlink**, which can take the reader to other Web pages, or specific locations within the current Web page.

➤ Using the menu item **Edit, Bookmark** we can define bookmarks (also known as "anchors") on a page, to which hyperlinks can point to bring readers to that exact location on the page.

Friendly Forms

In This Chapter

➤ Wrapping our heads around forms

➤ Tapping away at text boxes

➤ Delicious menu forms

➤ Checks, boxes, and buttons, oh my

➤ Shipping and Handling: Form Processing

In everyday-speak, the notion of "forms" usually causes people to run, hide, spit, or parry. We've been conditioned to fear forms, as they stack up in our minds, pressing down a weighty sense of claustrophobia. Fortunately, in the world of the Web, forms are a *good thing*. In fact, they're the primary type of user interaction, and they greatly expand the Web page's capabilities.

The Idea of Form

To this point in the book, we've created Web pages which have showcased data as content. In many cases, this is fine and dandy, and it serves the mission of our page. But there's a whole other dimension to the Web that data-only pages are blind to: interaction. Let's consider a very basic and common example, the Guest Book.

Many Web sites offer a page with a forum for reader feedback, and this is known as a Guest Book. The idea is drawn from hotels and other tourist spots, where visitors are invited to scrawl their comments into a journal. On the Web, the Guest Book is a basic form of interaction, as the reader must be able to report information back to the Web page. For instance, the page might ask the reader to type a comment, along with his or her name or e-mail address. This requires a space for the reader to enter such information.

A Web page containing a Guest Book, which allows for reader interaction, feedback, and even insults.

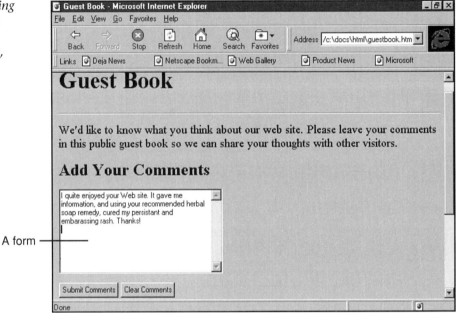

A form

Other interactions might involve selecting from a menu of choices, or clicking a check box beside desired options. In all of these cases, the basic principles of user-interaction are the same:

➤ To provide an interface where the user can report information

➤ To record this information in some manner

➤ In some cases, to process this information and generate new content.

In the case of the Guest Book, we might apply the first two principles, thus creating a private log which we, the Web owner, can read from time to time. On the other hand, we might also engage the third principle, creating a new Web page containing other readers' entries into the Guest Book.

The interface through which a user interacts and reports data to our Web page is known as a "form." In this usage, "form" is a general term, referring to any sort of interface through which interaction can occur. There are several specific *types* of forms which you can use on Web pages, and each one is individually known as a "form element" or "form field." One form may be made up of several form fields. The Guest Book form, for instance, would probably have used a "scrolling text box" form field, as well as two "push-button" form fields (Submit and Clear); each allows the reader to type information into the Web page.

In this chapter, we're going to look at using each of the basic form fields on our Web page. The basic set of form fields which all Web browsers should support are:

➤ **Text Boxes**   Both one-line and multi-line (scrolling), text boxes allow users to type information directly into the form.

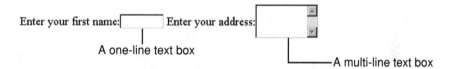

➤ **Drop-Down Menu**   Allows the user to select one or more items from a list of choices

➤ **Check box**   Often used to allow the user to select or deselect an option

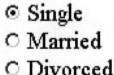

➤ **Radio button**   Similar to a check box, a radio button is a multiple-choice form, wherein the user exclusively chooses one choice from a set of several.

⊙ **Single**
○ **Married**
○ **Divorced**

➤ **Push button**   A clickable button image, clicking it will initiate some action, such as submitting the data entered into other forms.

The Form from the Field

Literally, a form is a collection of related form fields. Thus, one form might contain a one-line text box, two push buttons, and a set of radio buttons. However, in regular speech, we often shorten the form field reference to just "text box form" or "check box form." When "form" is preceded by the name of a particular type of form field, it's assumed we're referring to a "text box form field" or "check box form field."

Getting Personal: Text Forms

Perhaps the most common form, the text form provides an easy way to request information from the reader. Remember that implementing a form engages three principles: creating the interface, recording the input in some way, and possibly processing the input in some manner. We'll begin by creating the text form interface. For this example, imagine that we're inclined to ask some personal information about the reader. Perhaps we're compiling demographic statistics, which we hope to sell to a direct marketing firm for unethical sums of money.

We begin by locating the cursor in the FrontPage Editor to the position on the page where our form field should reside. In this case, we'll place it just below the text which explains the purpose of this page.

Position the cursor to place our text form.

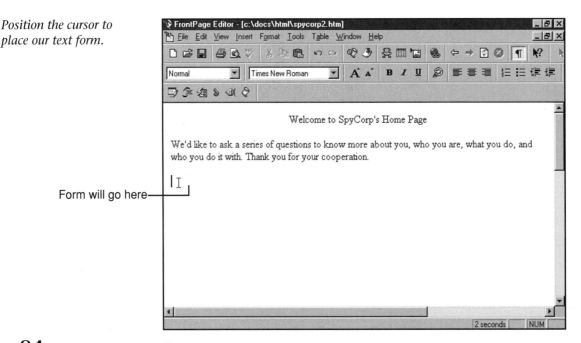

Form will go here—

Our first text box form on this page will request the reader's first name; the second text box form will request their surname. Keeping this data separate will help us manage any database we record this information in. Depending on the purpose of the page, using one form field for the whole name may be perfectly acceptable, as well. To create the first form field, we select from the FrontPage Editor menu: **Insert, Form Field, One-Line Text Box**.

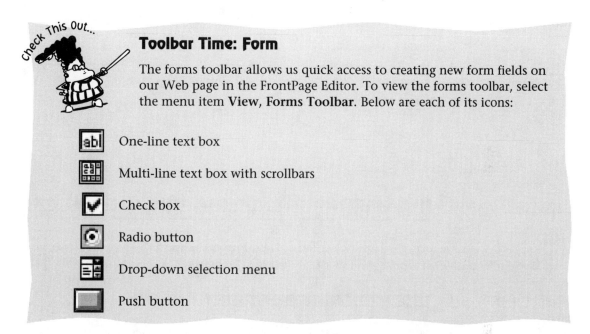

Toolbar Time: Form

The forms toolbar allows us quick access to creating new form fields on our Web page in the FrontPage Editor. To view the forms toolbar, select the menu item **View, Forms Toolbar**. Below are each of its icons:

One-line text box

Multi-line text box with scrollbars

Check box

Radio button

Drop-down selection menu

Push button

Magically, an empty text box appears on our Web page, with the cursor blinking to the right of it. We want to label this form, so the reader has some idea what it's purpose is. Because the label would look better to the left of the form, we'll click on the left side of the form to position the cursor, and then type **Enter your first name**.

Notice the dashed lines in the picture; they are FrontPage Editor markings defining the boundaries of this form. Recall that several form fields may reside within one form—any related form fields we wish to create later should be placed within these dotted lines. The form boundary is determined by the FrontPage Editor; creating a new form field outside the dashed lines will create a new form (Don't worry—these dashed line boundaries do not appear to the reader of our page). Now we've got a one-line text box form and a label. However, there's work yet to be done. We should configure a variety of properties which relate to this form and its behavior.

*Creating and labelling
the first form on our
page.*

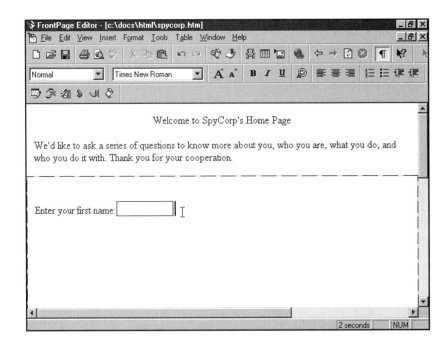

Right-click on the form field and select **Form Field Properties** from the pop-up menu.
We're now presented with a window titled Text Box Properties.

*Configuring some
properties of our new
text box form.*

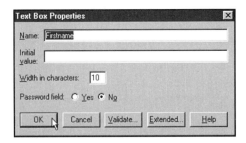

The first property of this form is its name. By default, because it's the first text-box on our
page, the FrontPage Editor has named this form T1. That's not such a nice name, so we
should choose a different one. This name never appears onscreen, but it will be used to
make reference to this form in certain circumstances. We'll name the form **Firstname**.
When choosing form field names, try to keep them short but comprehensible, and don't
use white space or punctuation marks. Thus, "Firstname" or "firstname" is a better form
field name than "First Name." Combinations of letters and numbers, as in "name1" are
good choices, as well.

Below the **Name** property is another marked **Initial value**. By default, this is blank. However, perhaps we'd like a default name to appear in the form, such as "Joe Q." In that

case, type **Joe Q** into the Initial value property. When the reader sees this form, it will already be filled in with Joe Q, although they may easily modify that to any name they like. The Initial Value property is useful for forms which we'd like to have a default value, but where the user is free to modify it.

The Width in characters property defines how many letters wide the text box form should be. Since most first names are shorter than 10 letters, we'll set this to **10**.

If the Password field property is set to No, then the user's typing will appear onscreen. If this field is set to Yes, an asterisk will appear on the screen for each character the user types. This hides the user's typing from anyone looking at the screen.

Whoa, Nellie—Restraining Wild Inputs

Once we're done with these Text Box Properties, we can hit **OK** to return to the FrontPage Editor. Right-clicking on the form field again, we'll select **Form Field Validation** from the pop-up menu. Note: if upon selecting **Form Field Validation**, an alert appears warning that this control's name is not a valid identifier for scripting languages. This means that the name you selected for the form field contains an illegal character, such as a punctuation mark or white space. Unless changed, this form field cannot be used in a script, as discussed in Chapter 16, "The Art of Script."

Validation is not something we'll always use when creating a form, but it can be useful, and it is worth a quick explanation. Using form field validation, we can constrain or restrict the data, or the data format, that the user may input. For instance, if we had a form requesting the user's age, we could assume it's not less than, say, 5, or greater than 120. To prevent out-of-bounds inputs, then, we could restrict that form to inputs between 5 and 120. Alternatively, we might ask for the person's surname, and we might designate to disallow any inputs other than alphabet letters. This is what **Form Field Validation** is for, and although it looks daunting at first, it's quite logical.

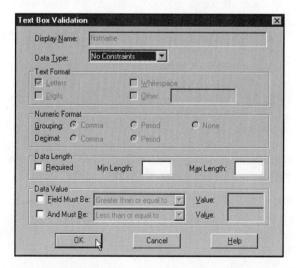

Configuring constraints and restrictions on the input allowed for a form.

87

By default, our form has no constraints, as it says in the Data Type selection box. Clicking on the **Data Type** selection reveals other constraints to choose from:

➤ **Text**   If selected, it restricts input to types of text specified in Text Format properties.

> Letters   Allows alphabet letters
>
> Digits   Allows numeric digits
>
> Whitespace   Allows spaces within input data
>
> Other   Allows any other character we specify, such as a decimal point or a pound sign

➤ **Integer**   If selected, it restricts input to integers of the format specified in Numeric Format Grouping.

> Comma   Allows use of commas for grouping (1,500,001)
>
> Period   Allows use of period for grouping (1.500.001)
>
> None   No grouping punctuation allowed (1500001)

➤ **Number**   If selected, it restricts input to numbers of the form specified in Numeric Format Grouping (see above) and Numeric Format Decimal.

> Comma   Use a comma to mark the decimal place (European style)
>
> Period   Use a period to mark decimal place (North American style)

Depending on what constraint we've chosen, we may be allowed to enter a value into the Display Name property at the very top of the Text Box Validation window. Should the user input data which violates the validation constraints, and alert box will appear, identifying the erroneous entry by the name configured in Display Name.

Regardless of which constraint we've chosen, we may set the Data Length property, half-way down the validation window. If we enable Required, we may then specify a minimum number of characters and/or maximum number of characters for the data input to this form field.

Lastly, we can set boundaries for the input by enabling either or both the Field Must Be and And Must Be properties, wherein we can set bounds for the input value. In the case of text inputs, they will be compared alphabetically against whatever bounds selected in these properties.

For our particular example, the surname form, we don't feel any constraints are necessary, so leaving Data Type set to No Contraints should be dandy.

Whew! Our first form field, created and configured. Although that seemed like a lot of work, with many options, the same basic steps are involved when creating any type of form, so we need not walk through them all again.

Recall that we wanted two one-line text box forms on our page; we've already made the one for a first name. Now let's create another for the reader's surname. Click the cursor to the right of the first text box (i.e. next to the first form field) and select the menu item **Insert, Form Field, One-Line Text Box**. Yet another text box will appear right beside our first one.

Configuring this one is exactly the same as for the first, except we want to remember to name this one **surname** rather than **firstname**. Clicking to the left of the new form, we can enter a label for the reader's benefit: **Enter your surname:** We'll right-click this form and return to the Form Field Properties settings, changing its name to **surname** and its width to **10** characters.

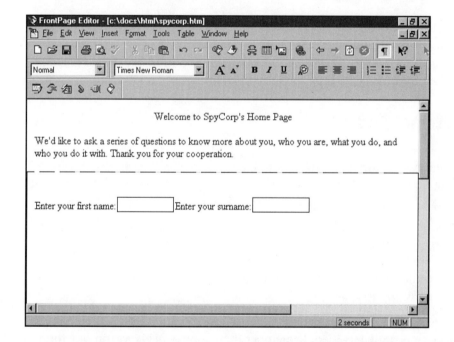

Two text-box form fields, side by side, in harmony.

In these examples, we used only one-line text boxes, but there's another text box form field known as the scrolling text box. The scrolling text box is basically just a very large text box. It allows the user to input multiple rows of text, and use scroll bars to navigate around his input. The scrolling text box has no differing function from the one-line text box, and only has one extra Form Field Property number of rows. In every other respect, both text-boxes are alike; simply use the one most suited for the type of data being requested; for example, for a person's name, a one-line text box is sufficient. When requesting a commentary, such as Web site feedback, a scrolling text box makes more sense.

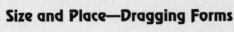

Size and Place—Dragging Forms

A shortcut to configuring the aesthetics of a form field is to resize and reposition it with the mouse. For instance:

To resize a form field, left-click it once. Sizing handles then appear: left-click one of the handles and, while keeping the left mouse button pressed, drag the mouse in a direction to resize the form field.

To reposition a form field, left-click over the field and keep the mouse button pressed. Then, slide the mouse left or right, and you can reposition the form field with respect to any adjacent text.

Note—in a scrolling text box, line breaks are not returned as input, so whether the user types his comments in one very long line, or breaks the lines to fit inside the text box, is no matter to the form processor.

À La Carte: Menu Forms

We all love choosing from menus. In fact, if I could go into restaurants merely to look at the menu, and then leave before ordering, I would, but for some reason the establishments around here frown upon that sort of thing. The menu form element brings all that excitement to our Web page: It presents the reader with a scrolling list of selections.

For instance, suppose that we'd like the reader to select which competitor's products he has tried. We could offer a menu form which lists each competing product, and the user can select one or more. Or, we might be selling travel tours, and would like to know which country the reader wants to visit. In that case, we might only allow one selection from the menu of many country names.

In our current example, let's go with the first scenario—querying the reader about which competing product brands she has tried. Remember that all form fields within one form are submitted for processing, so we'll create the menu form field within the same form boundaries as the firstname and surname text boxes.

Clicking to the right of the surname text box, we'll hit return to advance to the next line. Notice that the form boundary moves down, showing that we're still within the same form. Select from the FrontPage Editor menu **Insert**, **Form Field**, **Drop-Down Menu**, or select a form type from the Form toolbar.

A tiny empty menu form field appears on our page. Although we could resize this menu using the drag technique discussed in an earlier sidebar, we'll wait to configure its form field properties. First things first, we'll click to the left of it and enter the label **Which competing products you have tried at least once?** Following that, press **Shift+Enter** to create a formatted break, which will move the menu form field to below the label. Now we'll add an additional instruction label (**hold down the Ctrl key to make multiple selections**), and hit **Shift+Enter** again. Some readers may not know the technique for selecting multiple choices in a menu, hence the instruction in parentheses. The menu form will sit just below this label.

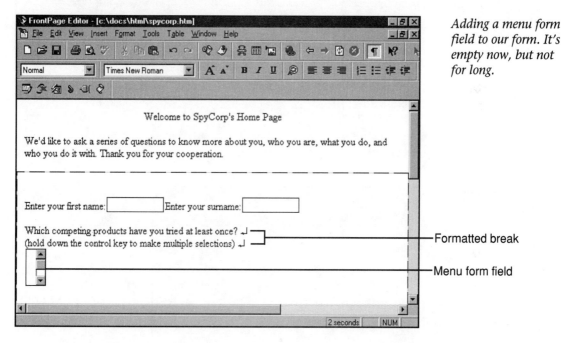

Adding a menu form field to our form. It's empty now, but not for long.

Right-click the menu form, and select **Form Field Properties**. Here, as usual, we configure the properties which are specific to this type of form field. First, we name it, in this case, **productmenu**. Now, we must add each menu item to appear in the list of choices. We do this by first clicking the **Add** button.

Configuring the menu form, adding items to the list.

Add a new item.

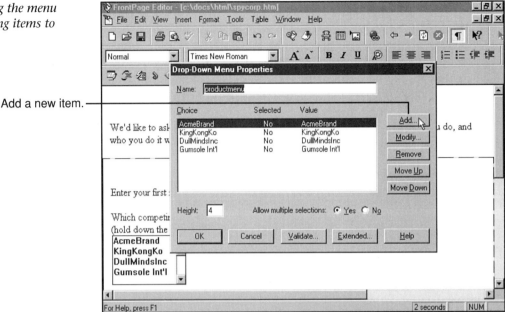

Defining the new item to add to the menu.

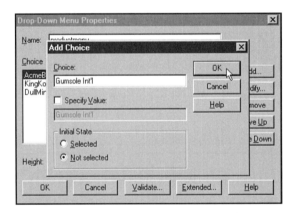

In the Add Choice window, we first enter the name of the choice. This name will appear in the menu. We'll enter **AcmeBrand**, as the first competing product name. Below is the Specify Value property. The value, in the case of the menu form field, is what data will be reported to the form processor. In many cases, this value will be the same as the choice name, hence Specify Value is disabled by default. When the form data is submitted, it may be processed by a "form processor," which may require certain types of values (for example, numbers instead of words). Thus, in some cases we might want to configure the value 1 to be associated with the first selection. Therefore, we may sometimes enable Specify Value, and specify which value to report for this selection.

Lastly, we can configure the Initial State property, to define whether this choice is selected by default for the user. In some cases we'll want to select one choice by default, in other cases we may not. In this instance, we can't be sure that the user has tried any competing products, so no choice will be selected by default.

Repeating the process above, we'll enter three more competing brands in the menu: **KingKongKo, DullMindsInc, and Gumsole Int'l.**

After we click **OK** in the Add Choice window, we are presented with the Drop-Down Menu Properties dialog box.

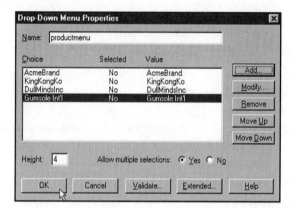

The properties of our menu form field, with four items created.

Using the buttons below **Add**, we can **Modify**, **Remove**, or shift items **Up** or **Down** within the list order. At the bottom of the window, the Height property defines how many items-tall the menu should be on the screen. If there are more items than what can fit in the specified height, a scrollbar will allow the reader to navigate the item list. We'll set a height of **4**, since that's not too tall, and it includes all of our items.

Lastly, we can configure whether to allow multiple selection. If we select Yes, the reader can hold down the control key while clicking on more than one item. If we select No, only one item can be selected at a time. We'll choose **Yes** for our example.

After clicking **OK** in the Drop-Down Menu Properties window, the new menu form field will appear on the page. Although the scrollbar is displayed here, it will not exist when the reader sees the page *if* the entire menu list fits within the height of the menu.

Right-click the menu form field again, and select **Form Field Validation**. The menu form field has its own set of validation properties, different from those available with the text box.

The few validation
properties of the menu
form field.

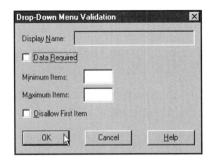

If we require that the reader select at least one of the menu choices, enable the **Data Required** property. By doing so, we can also enter a name for this form field in the Display Name property, for use in an alert box if the user violates one of the conditions.

In the case of multiple selections, we can also define bounds; a specified number of Minimum Items and/or Maximum Items. Lastly, the final validation property requires some explanation. Some Web designers like to use the first item in the menu as an instruction to the user, as in "Use the control key for multiple selection." Since this "item" is not truly a valid choice from the menu, enabling **Disallow First Item** prevents the reader from choosing that item.

Boxes and Buttons

A check marks the spot. We've seen a number of instances of check boxes, even while using the FrontPage Editor interface. The check box is typically used to enable or disable a selection. For our page, we'll use a series of check boxes, from which the reader can check off any or all options that apply. Posing the question, "Please check all products you currently own," we'll provide a list of products we're interested in tracking. The reader then places a check mark next to each one he owns, and leaves unchecked those he doesn't.

Begin by clicking to the right of the menu form element, so that we stay within the same form. Then hit **Enter**, and select **Insert, Form Field, Check Box**. A cute little check box pops onto our page. Clicking to the left of the check box, we'll type our label: **Please check each product you currently own:**, followed by Enter. Clicking to the right of the check box, we can enter a label for this specific box, such as, **Television**.

Creating a check box   ☐ Television
form field.

Clicking **Shift-Enter** beside Television will create a formatted break and move us down below the check box. Here, we insert another check box, type in another label beside it, and click **Shift-Enter** again. We keep doing this until we've created all the check boxes we want, as shown in the next figure.

☐ Television ↵
☐ VCR ↵
☐ Home Computer ↵
☐ Microwave Oven ↵
☐ Pet Tiger

Several check box form fields.

For each check box, we can configure its properties. Right-click any check box, and select **Form Field Properties**.

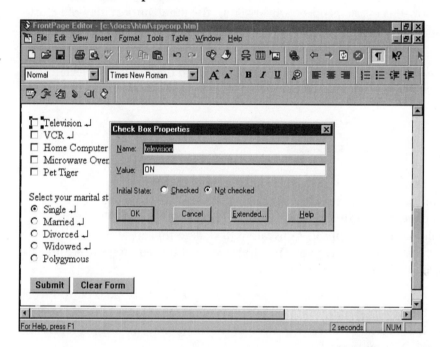

Setting the very few properties of our shiny new check box.

Each check box has a name, which we'll create as similar to its label. For the television check box, we'll assign the name **television** in the Name box. The Value represents what to send to the form processor (the program which interprets the data submitted from the form). Note that the value ON in this property window does not mean the check box is enabled, merely that the values ON or OFF is what will be sent to the form processor. It is the Initial State property that determines whether this check box is enabled or disabled by default.

The check box form fields have no validation properties, since they can only be ON or OFF. It is difficult to violate that condition.

Radio Friendly

"Friendly" might be the wrong word, as the radio button is the Web equivalent of that old academic nemesis: the multiple choice question! In recognition of the anguished memories this may bring many readers, we'll now pause for a moment of silence, wherein we can restore our composure.

Ahhh…that's better. As we were saying, the radio button is a form element which behaves like a multiple choice question. Usually, several radio buttons are used in conjunction, each being mutually exclusive of the rest—that is, only one of the buttons may be selected at a time. For instance, imagine we created a site which accepted pizza orders online. The customer has chosen to order a specialty pizza, of which we serve three: the HeartHappy Pizza (low-fat cheese, peppers, wheat germ), the RuralOutpost (day-old crust, V8 sauce, Velveeta), and the best-selling Pizzeriosclerosis (sausage, pepperoni, ham, meatballs, oil, lard, fried dough, triple cheese).

Thus, we would create three radio button form fields, of which one could be selected as shown in the figure.

> ⦿ HeartHappy Pizza ↵
> ○ The RuralOutpost ↵
> ○ Pizzeriosclerosis

In working with our current page, however, we'll use a more traditional set of radio buttons: marital status. Hitting **Enter** after our final check box, we want to stay within this form. Select the menu item **Insert, Form Field, Radio Button** (or use the forms toolbar), and a radio button will appear. As usual, we'll click to the left of the radio button to enter our instruction: **Select your marital status:**, followed by a **Shift+Enter** to move the radio button down one formatted break.

To the right of the radio button, we enter its label. In this case, the first radio button will be labelled **Single**. Press **Shift+Enter**, followed by inserting another radio button. We'll label this one **Married**. Repeat until we've created all five radio buttons: **Single, Married, Divorced, Widowed, Polygamous**.

> Select your marital status: ↵
> ⦿ Single ↵
> ○ Married ↵
> ○ Divorced ↵
> ○ Widowed ↵
> ○ Polygymous

Notice that only the first radio button, Single, is selected. Right-click this radio button and select **Form Field Properties**. Notice that the first property is Group Name. Unlike previous form elements, the individual radio button does not get a name. Rather, it is part of a group, and the entire group is named. Grouping is the way in which the browser knows which buttons must be deselected if one is selected. We'll name this group **marital**.

The Value property represents what the form processor will receive if this radio button has been selected. This depends on the form processor being used. We might send the value 1 for the first radio button, 2 for the second, and so on. By default, the FrontPage Editor sends the value V1 for the first, and so forth. Configure this to match the form processor.

The final property, Initial State, determines whether this radio button is selected by default. Of course, only one radio button within the group may be selected.

Push the Button, Frank

As a youngster, I thought the idea of pressing buttons was the highlight of life. Perhaps I shouldn't be telling that to others, but there's something appealing about a button. On, Off, On, Off. So nice. There are three types of button form fields in the FrontPage Editor:

➤ **Submit Button**   This button is used to submit the data in a form to the defined form processor.

➤ **Reset Button**   When clicked, this button resets the form elements to their default values.

➤ **Normal Button**   Undefined, this button can be used in a scripting operation, which we'll explain in Chapter 16.

Traditionally, a form contains a Submit and Reset button, conveniently located in relation to the other form fields. Seeing no reason to break with tradition now, let's create a Submit and Reset button for our current form. After the Polygamous label of the final radio button, we'll hit **Enter** to create a hard break. Create the first button by selecting the menu item **Insert, Form Field, Push Button**. By default, the FrontPage Editor creates a Submit button. With the cursor blinking to the right of the Submit button, let's choose **Insert, Form Field, Push Button** again, and add another button right beside it. Of course, now they're both Submit buttons, but that's soon to change.

Right-clicking the left-hand button and selecting **Form Field Properties** will bring up a familiar variation on this window. We need to name the button, so we'll christen this one **submit1** (in case we plan to have additional forms with submit buttons elsewhere on this page). The Value/Label property defines what text appears on the button. Normally, "Submit" is fine, but "Submit Data" would work, too. Anything we want to label the button is fine, as long as it gets the idea across. With respect to the Button Type property, this is already selected as a Submit button, so we're done.

Now we'll bring up the **Form Field Properties** for the right-hand button. Let's name it **Reset1**, and change the Value/Label to **Clear Form**. If the user clicks this button, anything they entered into the form will be erased without being processed. The form will revert to its original state, based on whatever defaults we programmed into the form fields. Lastly, we set the Button Type to **Reset**.

Processing...

We've now placed the form fields on our page, and configured their various properties. The reader comes along in a whistly good mood, sees our form, and happily punches his or her name in. He selects choices, checks boxes, and pushes buttons. Great, except, what are we going to *do* with the input?

Obviously, the input has to be *handled* somehow. Perhaps it will merely be saved to a file, perhaps it will be sent to a more sophisticated program. In either case, we must define *what to do* with the data which is input to our forms.

Right-click anywhere on the form, and select **Form Properties** from the pop-up menu. This is where we define how to handle the input.

Handling the form (Hot potato). Send it out for processing or develop in-house?

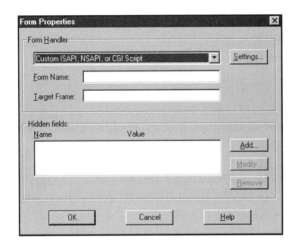

Not to "pass the buck," as they say in political circles (quite frequently, in fact); but the topic of form processing can be quite complex. The concept itself is straightforward enough: something needs to interpret and act upon the data submitted in the form.

In practice, form processors range from complex computer programs to automated WebBots (See Chapter 18, "Pump Up Your Page: Plug-Ins and WebBots" to learn more about WebBots, although not form processing ones in particular). Because this book's focus is on using FrontPage 97, a detailed discussion of processing Web forms is out of our scope. Readers who are already familiar with form processing will get the most out of this section; otherwise, you'll need to spend some time learning how to process forms before FrontPage 97's form processing configurations will make much sense.

Having said that, let's return our attention to the Form Properties window pictured in the previous figure. The first property asks us to select a Form Handler. The choices are as follows:

➤ **Custom ISAPI, NSAPI, or CGI Script** Form processing calls upon a custom computer program specifically written to interface with either ISAPI (Microsoft IIS Web servers), NSAPI (Netscape Web servers), or CGI (any advanced Web server). If you know how to use ISAPI/NAPI/CGI scripts, you'll understand what this option means. Clicking the **Settings** button allows you to select the action to trigger, and method for submitting the form (POST or GET). As it is, most form processing *is* done via the custom scripts above, which is why it's a complex topic. The majority of form processors are CGI scripts; if your service provider offers details on how to use specific CGI scripts with your forms, be sure to select this form handler in the Form Properties.

➤ **Internet Database Connector** Allows Web pages residing on Microsoft IIS Web servers to access live databases, such as Microsoft Access. This, too, is a very advanced topic; for details on connecting Web pages to live databases, consult the topic "FrontPage 97 Database Integration" in the FrontPage 97 manuals.

➤ **WebBot Discussion and WebBot Registration Components** These advanced processors allow forms to control on-line discussions or Web page access authentication. See the respective discussions in the FrontPage 97 manuals for further information.

➤ **WebBot Save Results Component** The simplest of the form processors, suitable for the novice form designer. However, note that because this form processor is a WebBot, it can *only* be used on Web pages which reside on Web servers with the FrontPage 97 extensions installed! If we select the WebBot Save Results Component, and then click the **Settings** button, a new window appears, as shown in the next figure.

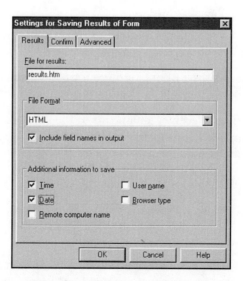

Configuring the WebBot Save Results Component, which saves the data from a form into a file.

The WebBot Save Results Component will save the submitted form data into a file. The data can be saved in a variety of formats, depending on what we select for the File Format property. The options range from HTML format to bulleted lists to plain text with white space separators.

In the File for Results property, we specify a filename to save the form data to. Selecting **Include Field Names** will specify the name of each form field, as well as its data, in the results file. Lastly, under **Additional Information to Save**, we can select any other information to include in the results file, such as the date and time of submission.

The **Confirmation** tab leads to features too advanced for our concern, but the FrontPage 97 Help files happily explain the details. Under the **Advanced** tab, we can specify a second file to which to save the results. This is useful for saving the results in a second format, such as "Formatted Text," other than that used for the first results file. We can also specify which form fields to include in the results data—leaving this property blank will include all form fields.

The Future of Forms

Quite a page we've created in this chapter. In a mock attempt to invade visitor's privacy, we have a page using several types of form fields, although only one form. The forms we've used in this chapter can be applied to many pages, in many circumstances. However, it doesn't stop here. When we discuss ActiveX, in Chapter 15, "How to Make Friends and Impress Enemies—Active X," we'll see the future of forms, and just how much more advanced and snazzy they can be.

The Least You Need to Know

In this chapter, we looked at adding user-interactivity to our Web pages via forms and form fields. Forms allow readers to enter information or select options, which we may process in any number of useful ways.

➤ A form consists of a set of one or more form elements. Each element may be a text box, menu selection, check box, radio button, or push button.

➤ Each form element receives a name, or in the case of radio buttons, each grouping receives a name. Other properties apply to each type of form field, such as default selections, and values returned.

➤ Form fields can be validated, such that user input is constrained within certain bounds.

➤ The check box is a true or false form element, while a set of radio buttons provides a mutually exclusive multiple-choice option.

➤ Form processors, or handlers, may either be computer programs which reside on the server, or WebBot components provided by FrontPage.

Chapter 8

"But Your Honor, I Was Framed!"

In This Chapter

➤ Frame it!

➤ Meet the Frames Wizard

➤ Filling the frames

➤ Framesets to inspire

A powerful metaphor in our language, the frame is a concept often invoked to define how we view a situation. Frames define perspective: "Such a lovely walnut frame"; "I resent how you framed that question"; or "But your Honor, I was framed!" However you frame it, frames are boundaries which select what we see, and what we don't see. On the Web, frames are used in a similar manner, to create pages-within-a-page. In this chapter, we'll look at how pages help improve content delivery, and how they don't. Of course, we'll spend the bulk of our time, and words, looking at how to implement frames in our own Web pages.

When Frames Are Good

We've all seen those fancy televisions with the "home theater" audio and picture-in-picture displays (usually in the home of someone other than ourselves). Although the picture-in-picture display is normally used to watch eight football games simultaneously, its purpose is more significant than that (although some would consider eight simultaneous footballs games quite significant, if not heavenly). Multiple sources of content are being delivered to the viewer, independently. In a sense, these picture-in-picture televisions are using a primitive form of Web frames.

Primitive? Note that we said the contents of each source were independent of each other. This has its uses, but so does interdependence. Frames, as they are used on the World Wide Web, may be independent or dependent, depending on how we choose to create them. In brief, a frame is like a mini-browser window within the main browser window. The contents of that frame can be viewed and navigated independently of the rest of the browser. In addition, and here's the key—actions taken in one frame can generate consequential actions in another frame.

Let's consider the most basic use of a frame, the table of contents. Consider the Web page below, which is the home page for a Web-based magazine:

Using two frames to create an independent table of contents.

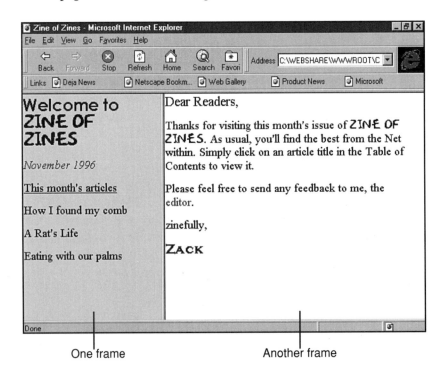

One frame   Another frame

The narrower, left-hand frame is the table of contents. It contains a list of each article available on this Web site. Of course, each listing is a hyperlink to that article. The wider, right-hand frame is where the actual article content is displayed. Thus, if we click any hyperlink in the table of contents, its article appears in the wide (or "main") frame. The convenience should be readily apparent—we can easily jump to any content on this Web site merely by clicking its hyperlink in the table of contents. Because the table of contents frame is physically independent of the main frame, the table of contents is always right there, easily accessible. No need to traverse back several Web pages to the main page.

For all intents and purposes, our Web page can contain as many frames as we want. Of course, if we have too many frames, they'll be so small that they will have no room for content. Most commonly, Web pages that use frames implement two or three, depending on the application and content.

Bad Frame, Bad Frame

Critical thought and technology sometimes do not go hand-in-hand. There's a compulsion in many people wherein the mere existence of a technology dictates that it be implemented. Merely because someone *can* dial up a friend on her cellular phone while sitting at a table in a quiet restaurant to see if she "got the tickets yet" doesn't mean she *should* (not that I'm naming names). Similarly, frames don't *have* to be used on every Web page. A number of Web pages have sprung up which use frames simply because, like Mount Everest, "they're there." Even when a page could use frames, some designers get carried away and create too many. Some browsers cannot display frames, and there's no reason to alienate readers. There are methods to create no-frame pages for readers without frame-capable browers, but why use frames at all if they serve no purpose?

Clearly, it is a personal judgment to decide whether one's site would benefit from having frames. Since we're not in the business of dictating what should and shouldn't be deployed on a Web site (we haven't been elected yet), we'll assume in this chapter that frames are a suitable solution in designing our Web page.

Your First Frameset

Nothing's more fun that a brief vocabulary lesson, so let's play. The term *frameset* is used to refer to the set of all frames within a Web page. A frameset can consist of any number of frames; in a table of contents scenario, the frameset could be said to contain two frames.

A Web page which contains frames is actually a composite of several Web pages. That is, each frame is composed as its own Web page. In addition, the definition for the frameset, (the number of frames on the page, what their sizes and orientations are, and which Web pages they contain) exists as its own Web page. Confused? Let's "frame" this concept in another manner: The Web page with two frames (a table of contents frame, and a main frame) is actually a conglomerate of three Web pages:

Web Page 1: A Web page containing the table of contents

Web Page 2: A Web page containing the main frame

Web Page 3: A Web page containing the frameset definition, which tells the browser about the layout of Web Page 1 and Web Page 2.

Of course, the above is all "behind the scenes." A visitor to our Web page merely sees one Web page, with multiple frames (they in fact visit Web Page 3 above). Why explain all this? When creating framesets with the FrontPage editor, we must approach each frame as its own individual Web page.

Although the above concepts can seem confusing at first, they will become clearer as we step through the process of creating a frameset. Let's consider the following hypothetical Web page: We're a Web-based retailer, selling a line of candies. We want to create a Web page on which the reader can click any candy product and view a description of the product, along with its price. Perhaps we will eventually include photos of the product and consumer testimonials, but we'll keep this site modest for now.

Your Own Personal Merlin: The Frames Wizard

This example calls for (surprise) the "table of contents" style frameset. We'll use one frame to list each candied product, and another frame to contain the product description. Thus, we will have a frameset consisting of two frames, vertically divided—one narrow and one wide.

To begin a frameset, we *must* be working from within a Web site. That means we've created a Web site using the FrontPage Explorer; it could be a completely blank Web site or any template. With the FrontPage Explorer running and our Web site loaded, we need to launch the FrontPage Editor. This can be done in any of the ways we've discussed, a simple method is to click the **Show FrontPage Editor** icon on the FrontPage Explorer toolbar.

Once the FrontPage Editor is running, we begin a new page by selecting **File, New**. As described in Chapter 3, we're asked what template or wizard to use for our new page. After selecting the **Frames Wizard** and clicking **OK**, the genie will be set free of its bottle.

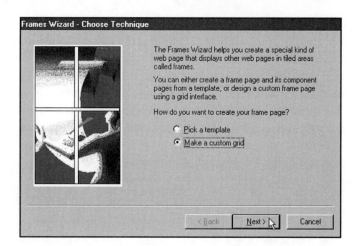

Beginning a dialogue with the Frames Wizard.

The Frames Wizard first asks whether we'd prefer to use a template frameset or whether we want to create a custom grid. The template framesets are predesigned framesets, although we can resize them, such as a table-of-contents arrangement. While these are fine for many tasks, we, being adventurous and with an avid thirst for knowledge, will create our frameset from scratch. Thus, we click **Make Custom Grid**, followed by the **Next >** button.

Next, the Frames Wizard presents us with the opportunity to visually design where our frames will reside. Doing so involves creating a grid, and sizing each tile within the grid. Besides being an easy way to see how our frames will relate on the page, it's fun!

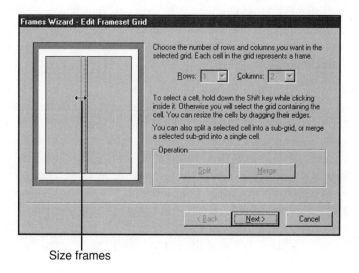

Adding and sizing frames in our frameset. Fun and easy!

Size frames

The Frames Wizard itself provides a good explanation of how to manipulate the grid. We select how many rows and columns we want using the respective selection menus. For the table of contents, we only want one row and two columns. Clicking on the dividing line within the frameset graphic, we can slide it to the left, so that the left-hand frame is narrower than the right-hand frame. The exact proportions are up to us. For our example, we'll make the left-hand frame about 30% of the width of the page, while leaving the remaining 70% to the right-hand frame. Admittedly, this is just an estimate; we might find that our table of contents elements are wider than we imagined. In that case, we can return to the Frames Wizard and adjust these proportions.

After sizing the frames, we have the basic table of contents frameset.

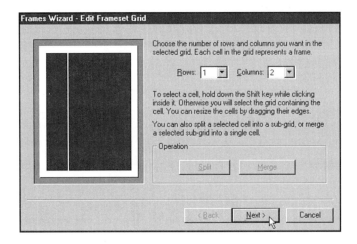

Note that by holding down the **Shift** key while clicking within a frame, we can restrict our actions to that frame only, and use the **Split** and **Merge** buttons to create more frames-within-the-frame. Doing this would lead to very complex Web pages, more so than we're going to detail in this book.

In our world, we have our two-frame frameset, and are ready to proceed. After clicking **Next >**, we are given the chance to edit certain properties of each frame. To do this, we must select which frame to configure by left-clicking within that frame on the graphic. We'll begin by clicking the left-hand frame. Notice that it becomes a darker color, so that we see which frame we're configuring. First, we must set the Name property. We'll need to reference this name from other objects on our Web page, although the name never appears on the reader's screen. In this case, *contents* seems like an apropos name for the frame. The Source URL property defines which Web page to display within this frame. In many cases, we may not have existing pages to include in the frameset yet; that's O.K. Simply enter a filename which *will* become the correct page once created.

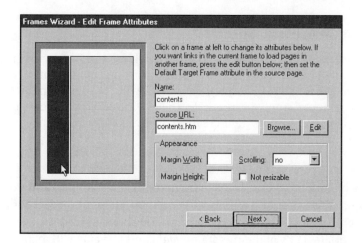

Configuring the properties of each frame.

Recall that our frameset, when completed, is made up of several Web pages. We'll need to create the table of contents as its own page—right now, it's merely a seed in our mind. Thinking ahead, we'll decide that when created, the table of contents page will have the filename contents.htm. Should the page we want to use in this frame reside in a different Web site than our own, we'll need to provide a full URL, such as **http://www.somesite. com/~mypages/contents.htm**. Assuming that we'll create the table of contents within the current Web site, we can simply type **contents.htm** for this property.

Several properties remain to be configured for this frame:

Margin Width   Specifies how many pixels of space to leave between this frame and any horizontally adjacent frames.

Margin Height   Specifies how many pixels of space to leave between this frame and any vertically adjacent frames.

Scrolling   If set to **No**, there is no scrollbar available for the reader. Only choose this option if the entire page fits within the frame size, even at low screen resolutions (otherwise the reader will have no way of seeing the entire contents of the frame!). If set to **Auto**, a scrollbar will be present *if* the page is larger than the frame, allowing the reader to move around the page loaded into this frame.

Not Resizable   If a check mark is not placed in this check box, the reader *can* slide the frame border, thus enlarging or reducing the frame. If there is a check mark in this check box, the user cannot move the frame border, leaving the frame a fixed size.

Frames Without Borders?

Both the current versions of Internet Explorer and Netscape Navigator support "borderless frames," or frames with no visual boundaries, such as vertical or horizontal lines. However, while borderless frames have become increasingly fashionable, the version of FrontPage 97 used at the time of writing does not support their creation. Perhaps this will change in subsequent updates to the product.

We'll set our table of contents frame to have no margins, no scrollbar, and no resizability. Before clicking **Next >**, we should remember to configure these properties for each frame. Clicking on the right-hand frame, we'll go through the above procedure again, settings its properties as appropriate. Let's name this frame *main* and leave its URL blank. Why blank? We don't yet know which page will appear in this frame; it depends on which link the visitor clicks in our table of contents. However, if we had a default page we'd like to appear in this frame before the visitor clicks any links, we could specify its URL here. Again, we'll leave the margins blank, and disallow resizing. However, we will set the **Scrolling** property to **Auto**, in case a product description happens to be larger than the frame (perhaps the reader will have a small browser window).

Beware of Frameless Browsers

Now that both frames have been configured, we can conscionably click **Next >**, thus advancing to the Alternate Page property. Some readers, as we've mentioned, might not have browsers which can view frames (such as the text-based browser Lynx, or less advanced graphical browsers). If we click the **Browse** button, we can select an alternate page for these users to see when they visit our Candy Catalog. This function is automatic—when the user's browser sees the frameset, knowing that it can't display it, it will attempt to open the alternate no-frames page (if we've defined one). If we choose not to provide an alternative, the readers will either see a badly formatted version of our Candy Catalog, or nothing at all, depending on how their frame-incapable browser behaves.

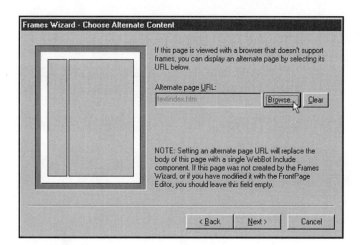

Choosing an alternate URL to display in frame-incapable browsers.

The Final Step to Frame Creation

Whether or not we configure an alternate page, clicking **Next >** brings us to the final step with our Frames Wizard, creating a title for the page. Remember that when a visitor opens our Candy Catalog, they're actually loading this page with our frameset definition. Thus, the title chosen here will be the title of the page including its frame. Selecting the title means following the same guidelines as when we chose a page title using the **Page Properties** settings in the FrontPage Editor. We'll go with **Candy Catalog**. Also, we must select a URL for this page; because it's residing within the current Web site, we can enter a name such as **candy.htm** in the URL box.

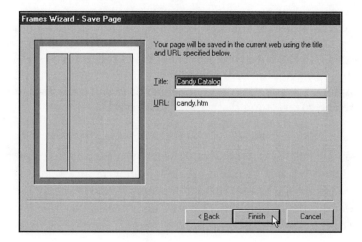

Finalizing the frameset with a title and URL.

After we select **Finish**, the Frames Wizard will sneak back into its bottle, leaving behind our new frameset, represented in the FrontPage Explorer:

The FrontPage Explorer shows our new frameset and frame page.

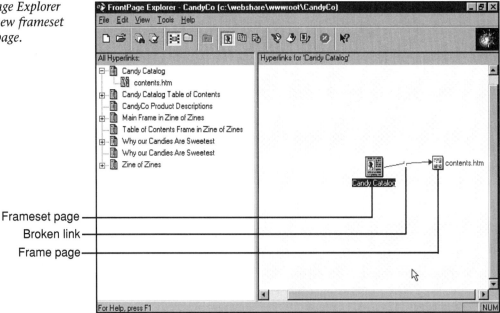

Frameset page
Broken link
Frame page

Ouch! Broken Links

A *broken link* is simply a hyperlink which leads to a non-existent page. Sometimes a broken link represents a problem with the Web page; other times, it simply means we have yet to create the page that the hyperlink points to. In the last figure, we have created the frameset, but not the pages which make up each frame. Thus, the broken link is merely a "reminder" that our job is incomplete. For more detail on understanding and correcting broken links, see Chapter 11, "The Changing Shape of Our Web."

At this stage, we've only created the frameset. Neither Web page containing the frame content exists yet. Before we dive in, one more note to prevent any possible confusion: If we click on the frameset page in the FrontPage Explorer ("Candy Catalog"), notice that in the graphic representation, both links are broken. That's because neither frame page has been created yet. These links will appear unbroken once we create those pages later in this chapter.

Editing Frames

Because each frame displays the contents of a specified Web page, creating the contents of the frames is merely a matter of creating some new Web pages. In our example, we have two frames—a table of contents frame and a main frame. For the table of contents, we'll create a Web page consisting of hyperlinks to each product in our candy line. This will function in the following way:

Our table of contents Web page is displayed in the table of contents frame. The reader will click on a hyperlink within the table of contents. As a consequence, a Web page containing the appropriate product description will be loaded into the main frame.

The product descriptions will derive from one of two actions we can take:

➤ Create a separate Web page for each product description. The hyperlinks in the table of contents will be designed (by us) to load the appropriate page into the main frame.

➤ Create one Web page containing all product descriptions, inserting bookmarks at the start of each. The table of contents hyperlinks will then load the product description page into the main frame, targeted at the appropriate bookmark.

The advantage of the first approach is that each description will appear in the main frame individually. Using the second approach, depending upon the length of each description, the reader may see partial bits of descriptions of other products above and below the product in question (because the reader is actually seeing one long page scrolled to a certain location). With the second approach we only need to create one Web page, rather than the many we will create if we take the first approach.

While both approaches would work, we'll primarily stick with the second method for our example. It's a more efficient use of computing resources (we only need to transfer the entire product description catalog once, rather than initiating a transfer for each description), and a more efficient use of the Web designer's time (that's us).

Blissful and Contented

To begin, we'll create the table of contents page. Selecting **File, New** from the FrontPage Editor menu, we select a Normal Page. Right away, let's name and save this page, even though it's currently blank. After choosing **File, Save As** from the menu, we're asked to enter a Page Title. **The Candy Catalog Table of Contents** has a nice ring to it. It also asks for a File Path Within Your FrontPage Web. Recall that we currently have our Web site loaded into the FrontPage Explorer, and we've previously decided (when working with the Frames Wizard) that the filename of this page would be *contents.htm*. Thus, we type that filename here, and click **OK**, returning us to the blank workspace.

The most natural question at this point, from someone older than a 5 year old, is "Why can't I see the frame on the page?" After all, the FrontPage Editor *is* supposedly a WYSIWYG interface, and it *would* be convenient to see the frame markings when designing the page which we hope to fit within the frame. The fact is, the FrontPage Editor does not feature any way to see the frame markings during design—a true flaw in its claim of WYSIWYG-ness. Alas, this is where previewing our page within a true Web browser takes on a crucial role. In a moment, we'll explore how.

Nonetheless, we must create our table of contents. We want to remember that it must fit in about a 30% width of the entire page, so we'll design it with that constraint in mind. Other than that, we create this page as if it were any other. Using basic text fashions, we've created a table of contents which approaches the one shown here.

Our lovely, and narrow, table of contents. We must design with frame in mind. (I believe Buckminster Fuller first said that.)

Keep it narrow—

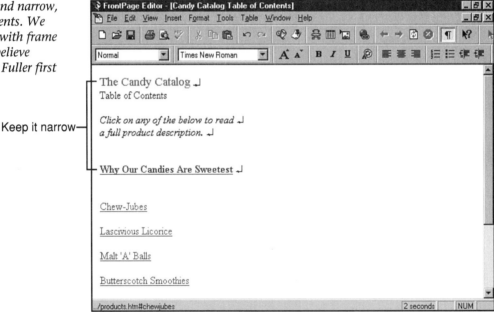

Time to preview and get a sense of how this page will look once it is framed. Normally, to preview a page, we'd select **File, Preview in Browser**. However, remember this isn't the page which will directly be opened by a visitor. That honor goes to the page containing the frameset, *candy.htm*. Thus, we must manually load the frameset page into our Web browser. For example, if our candy.htm frameset page resides within our Web site named CandyCo, we'll open a new URL in our browser to *http://www.oursite.com/CandyCo/ candy.htm*.

(Loading) Local Yokels

If creating our Web site on our local hard drive, opening a Web server based URL in our browser isn't the way to preview it, since the page doesn't reside on a server. For most pages this isn't a problem, because the **File, Preview in Browser** menu item within the FrontPage Editor works correctly wherever the page is stored (server or local). However, the FrontPage Editor doesn't know how to preview a frameset, which is why we must open it in our browser manually. Some browsers, such as Microsoft Internet Explorer, allow us to enter a local path into the **File, Open** menu, just as if we were entering a URL. Thus, instead of entering an http address, we might type c:\frontpage\webs\candyco\candy.htm. For other browsers, such as Netscape Navigtor, we must use the **Open, From Local File** menu, to distinguish a page on our hard drive from a page out on the Web.

After opening the frameset page *candy.htm* into our browser (Internet Explorer, in this case), we see that it looks a bit like the next figure.

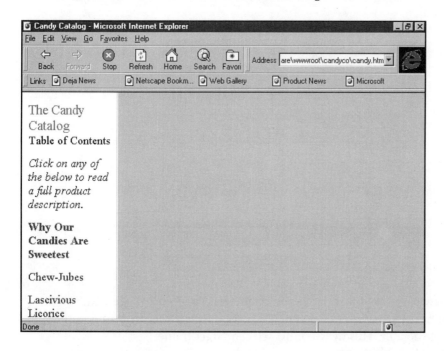

Our table of contents—squeezed a bit, but it looks good.

Notice that our table of contents page was squeezed within the frame, but it still looks reasonably attractive. Satisfied with this part, we need to create the hyperlinks for each product.

Whoops! Some Frame Considerations

Notice that although our Candy Catalog Table of Contents appears correctly within the Table of Contents frame, it is squeezed below the bottom border of the browser window. Therefore, we see that without adding a scrollbar to the Table of Contents frame, the user would not be able to access the additional products: Malt 'A' Balls, Butterscotch Smoothies and N & N's. To add the scrollbar to this frame, simply reload the frameset page into the FrontPage Editor; this will relaunch the Frames Wizard.

Manual Labor—Creating the Frame Content

Turning our attention back to the FrontPage Editor, we'll start by highlighting the text **Why Our Candies are Sweetest**, and then selecting the menu item **Insert, Hyperlink**.

The Create Hyperlink window appears, prompting us to select which page to open. Most likely, we haven't created this page yet. Thus, click the **New Page** tab of this window to yield the next figure.

Assigning a hyperlink to a new, unborn page.

Frame to open within

Edit Hyperlink

Open Pages | Current FrontPage Web | World Wide Web | New Page

Page Title: Why Our Candies Are Sweetest

Page URL: sweetest.htm

Target Frame: main

◉ Edit New Page Immediately

○ Add New Page to To Do List

Hyperlink Points To: sweetest.htm

OK | Cancel | Clear | Extended... | Help

In creating this new page, we'll first dance the traditional **Page Title/Page URL** two-step. The default Why Our Candies Are Sweetest makes a good title; **sweetest.htm** is perhaps a better URL than the default. Thirdly, we must select a target frame.

The Target Frame refers to which frame this hyperlink will open into. When a reader clicks a hyperlink within the table of contents, we want the resulting page to open into the *main* frame. Thus, we enter the name **main** (which we chose back during the Frames Wizard) into the Target Frame box. An important note: Sometimes, a hyperlink leads to a site which we don't intend to have displayed within a frame. Oftentimes, this is a site external to our own. When hyperlinking to a page external to our own site, consider specifying one of the following target frames:

➤ **_top** Specifying _top as the target frame will remove the frameset and load the new page into the browser window. This is used when leading the user to a completely new site. Failing to specify the _top target frame may cause the new site to be loaded within a frame on our page, leaving the user frustrated.

➤ **_blank** Specifying _blank as the target frame will launch a new browser window, into which the hyperlinked page will be loaded. This is a useful way of leading the user to a new site, without eliminating the view of our own site.

Lastly, we may either choose to **Edit New Page Immediately** or **Add New Page to To-Do List**. The former option would open the new, blank page into another FrontPage Editor window. The latter option would add an entry to the FrontPage Explorer's "To-Do" list for later attention. Let's choose to edit the new page immediately.

The FrontPage Editor asks us to select a template or wizard, as usual, and we go with **Normal Page**. Now, we begin creating the Web page we'd like to appear when the reader clicks Why Our Candies Are Sweetest. To save time, we'll create an extremely simple page right now. Type the text, **Because we use enormous amounts of sugar**, then choose **File, Save**. Choosing **File, Close** will close this page for now, or we can leave it open and switch between it and the table of contents under the FrontPage Editor's **Window** menu.

Next, we create the product description catalog itself. Remember that although we could create a separate file/page for each product, we'll create one long page instead. Unlike the Why Our Candies Are Sweetest page, we can't create the product description page from the **Create Hyperlink** window. Rather, we must use the menu command **File, New** (Normal Web) to create an entirely new page from scratch.

Techno Talk

FrontPage Glitch? When creating the new page for Why Our Candies Are Sweetest, we used the New Page tab from within the Create Hyperlink window. Why not use the same technique for the product description page? Answer: bookmarks. The hyperlinks for each candy in the table of contents will need to point to a bookmark. The New Page tab does not allow for creating a link to bookmarks which don't exist yet. Is this an intentional restriction or a lack of foresight on FrontPage 97's part? YOU make the call.

Descriptions Away

Creating the product description page is much like creating any other Web page. While we do have frame size-constraints, they're less severe than for the table of contents. Also, the main frame is scrollable, as we specified when using the Frames Wizard. Using all our creative energies, imagine that we hack together a product description page which looks somewhat like the next figure.

*Our product description
page, riddled with
bookmarks.*

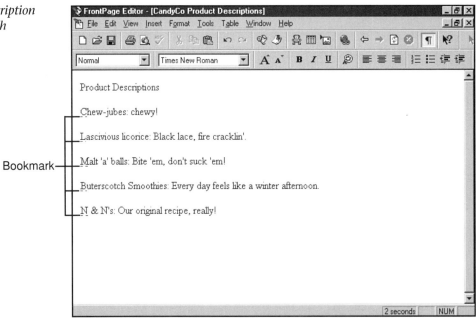

Before completing this page, we must remember to create bookmarks at the start of each product description. Following the technique described in Chapter 6, "The Joy of Text," we highlight a few characters at the start of each product description, and then select the menu item **Edit, Bookmark**. Choose a sensible bookmark name for each product, such as *chewjubes, licorice, maltaballs, smoothies, N&N's*. Once we're sure this page has been saved (we'll use the filename **products.htm** when prompted by the **Save** window) we can return our attention to the table of contents page.

Highlighting "Chew-Jubes," followed by **Insert, Hyperlink**, recalls the window in the next figure.

*Assigning a hyperlink to
our product description
page.*

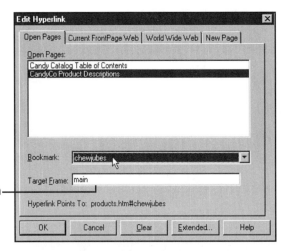

If our product description page is still loaded into the FrontPage Editor, it will appear listed under the Open Pages tab. If not, and it has been saved, it will appear under Current FrontPage Web, Browse. In either case, we select the product description page, and the bookmark appropriate for this hyperlink (*chewjubes*, in this case). Note that if we selected our page via the Current FrontPage Web tab, we must type in the bookmark, whereas it's available from a selection menu when using the Open Pages tab.

Had we instead wanted to create separate Web pages for each product, we could use the New Page tab when creating the hyperlink, and we would not need to specify a bookmark. We would, however, still need to specify the Target Frame as *main*. That is, if we want our frames to function properly. And we do.

Of course, be sure to enter **main** for the Target Frame, since that is the entire purpose of this chapter! Click **OK** and the hyperlink is set. Repeat the above process to create the hyperlinks for each product in the table of contents. Mix, stir, let chill for 10 minutes and serve!

Testing 1...2...4?

Due to the non-WYSIWYG nature of designing frames in the FrontPage Editor, it's super-extra-important (with sprinkles on top) to test our Web page in a real Web browser. Earlier in this chapter, we explained how to manually load the frameset page into our Web browser. Doing this periodically throughout the design process can help give us an idea how our page is progressing.

Using Microsoft Internet Explorer, we'll open our Candy Catalog to see how the frameset has fared. First, we launch the Explorer, if it's not already running. Select **File, Open**, and we're prompted to enter the URL. The proper URL, of course, depends on whether we're creating these Web pages on a server or on our local machine. Were they being created on a server, we'd enter a traditional URL such as http://www.machine.com/~myaccount/ candy.htm. If we've been saving these pages to a local hard drive path, we'd enter a pathname such as c:\frontpage\webs\candyco\candy.htm.

To test the frameset, we'll click each link within the table of contents, and be sure the correct product description appears in the main window.

After clicking the hyperlink, Why Our Candies Are Sweetest, in the table of contents frame. By the way, notice the fancy background graphic; you'll learn more about adding backgrounds in Chapter 10.

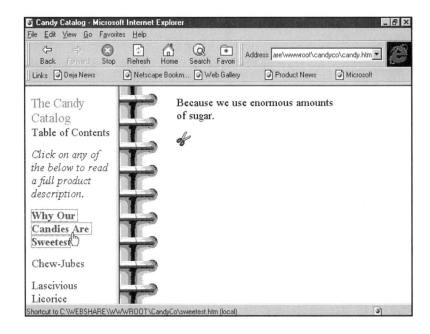

Future Frames

In this chapter, we constructed a simple frameset, consisting of two frames. Of course, you can design a frameset of as many frames as you want. Following are some candid photos of other common framesets which Web designers use. We can create any of the below using the same steps outlined in this chapter—use these samples as inspiration!

The home page of Auracom, an Internet service provider, utilizes a three-frame frameset (http://www.atcon.com).

Frame ——

Frame ——

Frame ——

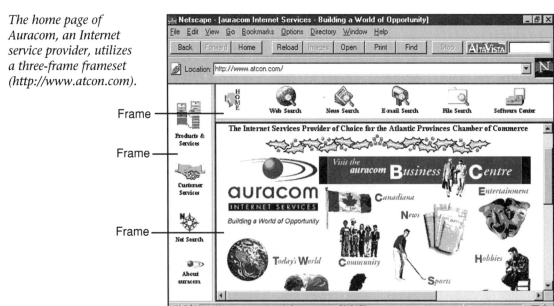

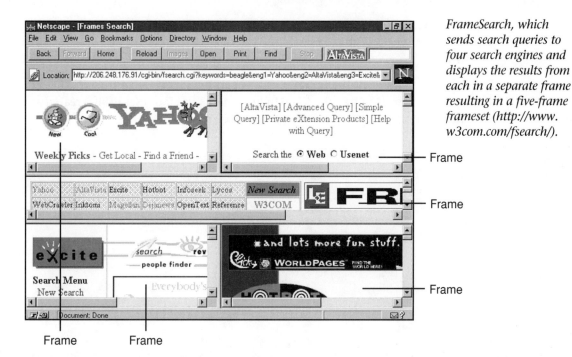

FrameSearch, which sends search queries to four search engines and displays the results from each in a separate frame resulting in a five-frame frameset (http://www. w3com.com/fsearch/).

The Least You Need to Know

This chapter has been obsessed with one concern: frames, Frames, FRAMES!

➤ A frame is a browser window within the main browser window. Each window contains a separate Web page, and may be independent of the other frames, or may affect the contents of another frame.

➤ To design a Web page with frames in FrontPage 97, we must use the Frames Wizard, available by creating a new page using the menu item **File, New**.

➤ The Frames Wizard is used to define the geometry of a frameset; that is, how many frames on the page, and the position and size of each. The Frames Wizard then allows us to configure the properties, such as which Web page to display, for each frame.

➤ Because the FrontPage Editor cannot display the frameset in a WYSIWYG manner, we must create or edit the Web page for each frame in its own FrontPage Editor window. Keep frame widths in mind when designing the pages.

➤ When creating hyperlinks, be sure to set the Target Frame property to the name of the frame in which the target of the link should appear. (The name of the frame was

119

configured when constructing the frameset with the Frames Wizard.) When hyperlinking users to Web pages external to our own site, specify the _top or _blank target frames.

➤ The only true way to test the frameset is by opening it manually into a Web browser. Remember to open the file which contains the frameset itself, created as the URL of the frameset on the final page of the Frames Wizard.

On the Table

Information makes the most sense when it's well organized. Like a graph or a spreadsheet, tables allow us to organize data into a defined structure. What's more, when used in Web pages, tables allow increased control in placement of page elements, be they text characters, form fields, or images. In this chapter, we'll look at creating tables and placing elements inside the table structure.

On the Table

The "table," as it is known in hip, goatee-wearing Web designer circles, is a rather complex beast. Tables have become quite common on Web pages, and rightfully so. They're a convenient and flexible way to organize text or data. In some instances, they can even help serve as workarounds to some traditional degree-of-freedom constraints. Creating tables, on the other hand, has traditionally been a difficult and mind-warping process.

Fortunately, we're in the world of WYSIWYG, and while tables are still complex, they're far easier to create than in the old days.

On a Web page, a typical table might look something like this:

The anatomy of a table.

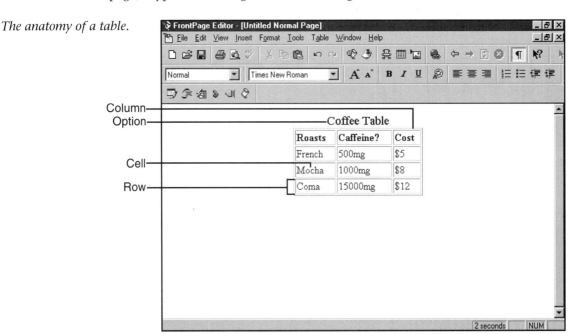

The basic building block of the table, as illustrated above, is the *cell*. A cell is one "unit" of the grid, and may contain any sort of data: text, an image, a Java applet, an ActiveX control, or even another table.

The table possesses a variety of properties that we can configure, including how many rows by how many columns it stands; the thickness and colors of its borders, the color or texture of the background, and the dimensions of its cells. That's a lot of properties, so we'll take it slowly. Let's begin with a simple table. It will be inserted where the blinking cursor currently sits on the page in the FrontPage Editor.

There are two ways to give birth to a new table. The first, and quickest way, is to left-click on the Insert Table icon in the toolbar and, while holding down the left mouse button, begin dragging the mouse down and to the left, until the desired table size is selected.

Insert Table

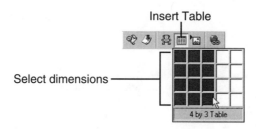

Select dimensions

Creating a new table the quick way—drag to the desired dimensions.

An alternative method is to select the menu item **Table, Insert Table**. It prompts us with a more sober window. This window allows us to choose the dimensions as well as some other properties in a more scientific manner than the drag-and-size method.

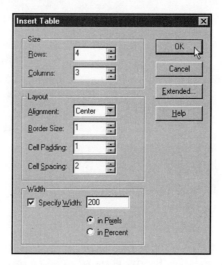

Starting a new table in a sanguine fashion. Numbers, numbers, numbers.

To start, we select the number of rows and columns we want in this table. Each of the remaining properties shown in this window may also be configured via the next table creation method, so we'll leave them alone for now. In the future, when the properties are more familiar to you, modifying them in the **Insert Table** window will save time. Also, rows or columns can be added to this table in the future, regardless of what initial dimensions we define; nothing's carved in marble, as they say.

After we have used one of the methods discussed to conceive our new table, it will be sitting happily on our Web page. Inserting content into the table is the easy part. Simply click in the desired cell and type. To insert anything other than text, click in the desired cell, and insert as appropriate for the desired page element; e.g. to insert an image into the cell, simply select the menu item **Insert, Image** (see Chapter 13 "Lights, Camera, Multimedia"). Alternatively, we can also drag an element from one portion of the page (by left-clicking on it and keeping the mouse button pressed) and drag it directly into the cell. The trick to creating tables is not entering content, but configuring the look of the table.

123

We will now take a (much) closer look at table properties by right-clicking anywhere on the table, and selecting **Table Properties** from the pop-up menu.

A whole smorgasbord of table properties.

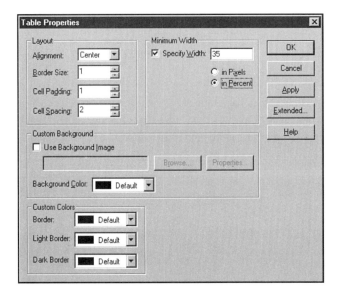

Keep the following in mind:

➤ Any of these properties can be changed any time.

➤ Experimentation is the spice of life.

Remembering these two general principles, let's go over the various table properties one at a time. In most cases, we'll only want or need to modify some of them from their defaults. In the upper-left-hand corner, we see the Layout properties:

Alignment   This property specifies where the table will appear on the page. Options are left, center, and right, and function just as the similarly named paragraph alignments.

Border Size   If this number is set to zero, there will be no visible border around the table when the reader views this page. If set to one, a 3-D border will appear around the table. If set to any number higher than one, a shadow that many pixels deep will be added to the 3-D border.

Cell Padding   This number determines how many pixels to leave empty between the content of the cell and the border surrounding it. A high number will yield a wide area of blank space between the cell's contents and the border of the cell.

Cell Spacing   This property affects how many pixels to leave between each cell border and the adjacent cell's borders.

Moving to the right-hand corner of the Table Properties window, we encounter the Minimum Width properties:

Specify Width   If enabled, this check box allows us to be specific about the width of this table in the reader's browser window. If disabled, the reader's browser will size the table however it sees fit. The latter option is more reader-friendly, but if the contents of our table depend on specific sizing, then we should enable Specify Width.

Width in Pixels   When we enter a number and select the in Pixels radio button, we define an absolute size for the minimum width of the table. For instance, if we enter 200 and click the **in Pixels** radio button, then the minimum width of the entire table (however many columns it contains) will be 200 pixels. It might grow wider if the contents of a cell are wider than its columnar width. Using this method will prevent the reader's browser from resizing the table to fit their screen. Usually, this method is used if the contents of the cells are graphic images, whose width is calculable beforehand. However, the next method is preferable for most tables.

Width in Percent: When entering a value, and clicking the in Percent radio button, we set the minimum table width to equal a percentage of the width of the reader's browser window. This allows the browser to customize the actual width to fit its size, yet allows us to retain our desired proportions for the table. For instance, if we enter the value **30** and click **in Percent**, the minimum table width will be 30% of the reader's browser window width. Using 100% would cause the table to be as wide as the reader's browser.

The Theory of Relativity

One of the challenges in designing Web pages is the fact that each user's screen may be different. It might have different dimensions or color depths than our own. When creating tables, we want to maintain certain proportions within the cells of the table, yet we want a variety of readers to be able to see the table. In this, and most other aspects of Web design, experimentation and variation is the key. When testing Web pages with your own browser, try resizing the browser to different common screen sizes (640×480, 800×600, 1024×768) to see how the page looks. In theory, Web page design should be so relative that the layout will look acceptable at any reasonable browser size. Although this is often difficult to achieve, we want to avoid, when possible, designing pixel-size-specific pages.

Moving down the Table Properties window, we reach the Custom Background settings. Here, we can select a certain color or graphic texture for the background of the table. Just as a Web page can have a background texture so can the table itself. Legibility is key, but we can select a suitable background texture by clicking the **Use Background Image** check box and selecting the file via the **Browse** button (more on this in the Chapter 10 "Behind the Scenes—Page Properties"). The **Properties** button can be used to alter properties of the image itself, as we'll discuss in Chapter 13, "Lights, Camera, Multimedia." Note: as of this writing, only Microsoft Internet Explorer 3.0 or greater supports background images within a table! Netscape 3.0 will not display the background image, although it will show the table itself. Perhaps future versions of Netscape will overcome this limitation.

Just like images, a background color can be an easy way to make the table stand out, visually, from the rest of the Web page. However, if we select a background color *and* a background image, the background color will only be visible through transparent portions of the image.

Finally, we can configure border colors. The first option in the Custom Colors section, Border, defines the color of the entire border. If we have a 3-D border, as a consequence of selecting a border size higher than 1, the Light Border and Dark Border properties define which colors in which to paint the 3-D effect. Usually, the light and dark borders should be shades of the same basic color, or else the 3-D effect won't appear as 3-D (of course, one may prefer it that way—we won't pass artistic judgment).

The Cell-ular Level

Hopefully, the above passages were fun and bemusing, because we're going to go through them again. This time, we will discuss properties with respect to an individual cell, rather than the entire table. Ahem— before you complain—you were warned that tables were complicated organisms.

Right-click a cell, and select **Cell Properties** from the pop-up menu. Easy enough. Note that these properties apply only to the specific cell that we right-clicked. We can configure a different set of properties for each cell (we don't *have* to, but we *can*, if, for example, we were locked in a small dungeon all day with nothing but a broken tea kettle and 12 hours before the guy with the key comes to let us out, and the only thing to give our attention to other than the deep meaningless void of our singular, isolated existence, is a 100 × 100 Web table the boss assigned us to create for the Donaldson account, due by Friday, no excuses, or it's back living at home with Mom and her cats, not that there's anything wrong with Mom, per se, but the cats are more than a little possessive of our old room).

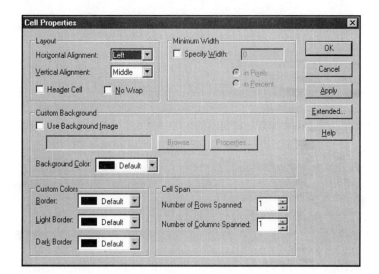

Déjà vu—a harvest of cell properties.

Starting again from the top ("take it from the top, boys!"), we see the Layout properties:

➤ **Horizontal Alignment**   This property determines where we align the content horizontally within the cell: left, center, or right.

➤ **Vertical Alignment**   Sounds like an overpriced chiropractic procedure, but actually this property determines whether we align the content of a cell near the top border, the middle of cell, or near the bottom border.

➤ **Header Cell**   Enabling this check box causes any text in the cell to be bold.

➤ **No Wrap**   If this check box is enabled, the reader's browser will not wrap text wider than the cell onto the next line. If the check box is disabled, text will be wrapped within the cell.

Moving to the right, we turn our tour to the Minimum Width properties for the cell. These properties function exactly like the Minimum Width properties for the table, except that they are only applied to the selected cell. For instance, selecting a minimum width for this cell of 10% will cause its width to equal 10% of the width of the table. We can use this property to make certain cells much wider than other cells (and vice versa).

Down further in the Cell Properties window, we re-encounter the friendly Custom Background properties. We can select a background image, or background color, which will apply only to this cell (for a full discussion of background images and background colors, see the preceding section).

Similarly, the Custom Colors properties allow us to select border colors that apply to the borders of this particular cell. Again, the properties apply in the same manner as

127

discussed for the Table Properties (see the previous section for a full discussion of Custom Colors properties settings).

Finally, a new property set, Cell Span, appears to the right of the Custom Colors:

➤ **Number of Rows Spanned**   This property allows one cell to take the space of one or more rows. Remaining cells are unchanged. This feature looks messy in a text description, but it will make sense when you try it. The bottom line is that it allows one cell to be extra roomy without pushing adjacent cells farther apart.

➤ **Number of Columns Spanned**   In a manner similar to the previous property this one allows the cell in question to reach across one or more columns, without pushing the adjacent cells away.

Cell spanning: the top-most cell in these tables spans 5 columns, while the left-hand "Arrive" cell and right-hand "Leave" cell span 3.

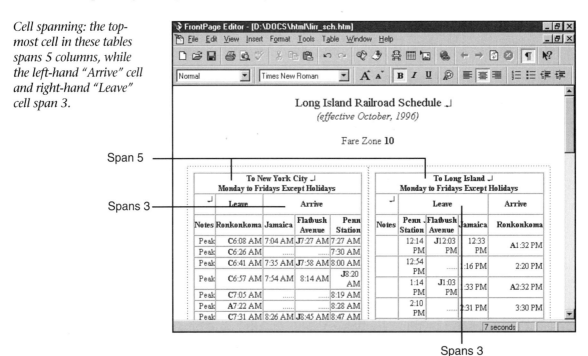

À La Carte

We are nearing the conclusion of our Table tour, and all that remains is the Table menu in the FrontPage Editor. We've already looked at the first item in this menu, Insert Table, which is how we created a new table in the first place.

*The Table menu in the
FrontPage Editor.*

The remaining items in the menu are either straightforward, or redundant:

Insert Rows or Columns   This command allows us to add a specified number of rows or columns to the table, relative to the currently selected cell.

Insert Cell   Adds a cell to the current row, thereby increasing the number of columns in the row by one. If there is any data in the cell, and the cursor is positioned to the right of the data *within the cell*, Insert Cell will add the new cell to the right of the current cell; if the cursor is positioned left of the current cell data, the new cell is inserted to the left of the current cell.

Insert Caption   Expects us to type a caption, or title, for the table, placed above the top row. Standard attributes may be applied as usual for text, such as size, font, style, color, and alignment.

Merge Cells   If we select multiple cells in a row (by holding down the left mouse button while dragging across several cells), this item will combine the contents into one large cell.

Split Cells   This menu option asks whether to split the selected cell into a specified number of rows or columns. If you confirm, the specified number of rows or columns is added, but the contents of the original cell are left untouched; for example the new cells are blank.

Select Cell, Row, Column, or Table   Each of these commands will highlight the respective part of the table (or the whole table, in the case of Select Table). Once selected, you might choose an operation to apply to the selected portion. For instance, to delete a table, left-click within any cell, choose Select Table, and then choose **Edit, Cut** (or hit the delete key).

Caption Properties   This command concerns whether to position the caption above or below the table.

Cell, Table Properties   Respectively, these lead to the same **Cell Properties** and **Table Properties** windows discussed in detail earlier in this chapter.

129

The Least You Need to Know

In this chapter, we focused on the table—not the piece of furniture, but a well-defined structure into which we place and align page elements.

➤ Tables are complex, so they get their own menu: **Table, Insert Table** creates a new table of specified dimensions. Alternatively, clicking the Insert Table icon on the toolbar allows us to drag the mouse and visually create a table.

➤ When configuring table and cell properties, pay attention to widths and alignments. Unless otherwise necessary, use relative measures, such as percentages, so that the table retains its proportions for readers with differing browser sizes.

➤ Any page element can be placed within a table cell, from text to an image to a form field. Simply create the element inside the cell as you would create the element anywhere else on the page. Alternatively, elements can be dragged-and-dropped from one portion of the page directly into a table cell.

➤ Tables and cells may have individually configured background colors or images. Note that background images in tables or cells are not supported by Netscape Navigator 3.0, although colors are.

➤ Once created, a table's dimensions can be added to and cells split or merged by using the items provided in the Table menu.

Chapter 10

Behind the Scenes—Page Properties

In This Chapter

➤ The Web page's inner self

➤ Mr. Dressup—background and color

➤ Our ding-a-ling (sounding off)

➤ Out from the margins

We're now ready to begin the wondrous journey into Web page design! Spelunking into FrontPage Editor, we begin designing some general characteristics of a Web page. As with the building of a house, we must decide the overall shape, colors, and so forth. While the FrontPage Editor allows flexibility in defining how our page will look (and sound), it cannot provide us with good taste.

Titles, Names, Places

Usually, we don't walk around the streets with every characteristic open to public display. Some properties, such as the color of our shirt, are immediately obvious. Others exist below the surface, but they are not less important. Web pages are largely vain animals, meant to be seen. But even they possess some characteristics that are beyond eye's reach.

A good Web page should have a title. In fact, two titles. One title is certainly visible—it's the text that we design, probably at the top of the Home Page. But pages also have an "internal" title, which readers may or may not see. For instance, the visible title on the Home Page of our WalNut-Mart Web site might read "Welcome to WalNut-Mart Web." However, we also should define a title for the computer's reference. To eliminate future confusion, it is best to choose the same title for both the internal and visible title properties.

To get rolling, in the FrontPage Editor, select the menu **File, Page Properties** (or right-click somewhere on the page itself and select **Page Properties** from the pop-up menu).

The properties of the current Web page.

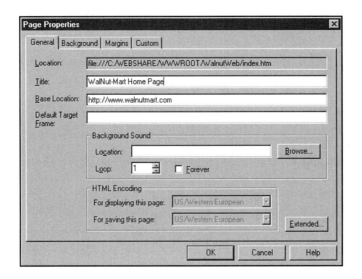

Notice the entry box labelled Title. This is where we enter an internal title for our page. There are two places in which a user might "see" the internal title, which is worth keeping in mind: Some browsers, such as Netscape Navigator, display this internal title in the frame of the browser window. In addition, some browers, Netscape Navigator again being one of them, use the internal title as the name of the bookmark if a user bookmarks the page. Thus, we want the title to be meaningful—a title such as "Hello" would not help a user who later searched his bookmarks for our site, and sees an entry called "Hello."

Nestled above the Title is a box marked Location. It's probably already filled in with a URL; this is where the file we're editing resides. For those of us who do not edit files directly on the server, the location is probably not the same URL as the one where the file is ultimately accessed by Web users. By and large, there isn't any need to change this location value, as it tells the FrontPage Editor where on the hard drive (or server) to save and retrieve the current page. If we move the Web site to a new location, such as a server, FrontPage will automatically update this location property.

However, note that just below the Title entry is a box marked Base Location. The Base Location is used to provide a reference point for any "relative" URLs in this page. A relative URL is a link which specifies a page, but not its full server and path location. For instance, the base location for this Web site may be http://www.server.com/WebSite/. This property is optional, and can usually be left blank.

Just below the Base Location property is another named Default Target Frame. You'll learn more about frames in Chapter 8, "But Your Honor...I Was Framed."

Finally, moving down to the bottom-most property setting, we see a section named HTML Encoding. (We discussed this briefly when configuring Web settings during the closing moments of Chapter 5.) While most Web pages are in English, some are not. If we want to create this Web page in a language other than the US/Western European alphabet, we should select its respective document encoding. Doing so will alert Web browsers to use a different alphabet if available. For instance, if we were creating a Web page in Russian, we'd select HTML encodings of Cyrillic (KOI8-R). This would prompt the reader's Web browser to use the Russian alphabet to view this page.

Background Candy: Textures, Colors, and Sounds

We've now molded some aspects of our Web page's personality—It has a name, a residency, and a language. Now it's time to get downright fashionable. Quite a few pages nowadays sport background textures. A texture is a repeated graphic pattern that covers the entire background of the page. All text and images on the page sit on top of this pattern.

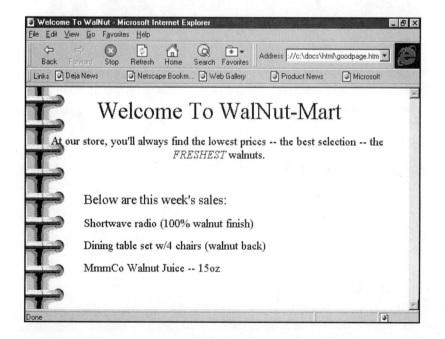

A Web page sporting an attractive background texture.

First, some cautionary words: Backgrounds are a privilege, not a right! (said in my best maternal voice). A page doesn't *have* to have one, and in some cases, they're best without one. Background textures can be an aesthetic pleasure or a painful nightmare. Always keep in mind that above all, our page should remain legible. A good texture will not only be one with an attractive graphic, but one whose colors contrast well with the text and images on the page. The earlier picture of a page with a background texture was a positive role model—cute concept, strong contrast. Contrast improves legibility.

Ouch! Either I'm going blind, or this background texture is causing me to.

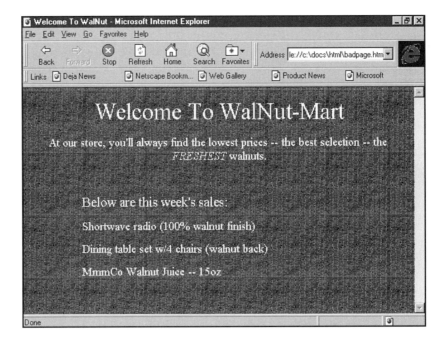

Similarly, when choosing colors for the background, hyperlinks, or foreground text, remember the contrast rule. Yellow does not look good on white nor does white on yellow.

Bodacious Backgrounds

Now, on our best behavior, we'll click the **Background** tab of the Page Properties window to configure our texture and colors.

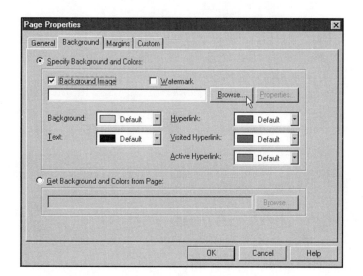

Choosing a backround texture and page colors. Sanely.

We can define backgrounds and colors for this particular page, or we can draw upon the settings defined in a different page. For instance, some people prefer to create a blank Web page which merely contains background and color settings. When creating additional content pages in their site, they simply choose **Get Background and Colors from Page,** and point it to their color settings page. As a result, we can quickly re-color all pages simply by re-configuring the single background/colors page.

On the other hand, we may want to define unique background and color settings for the current page only, thus choosing **Specify Background and Colors.**

Since we're feeling artistic, and do want to use a background texture, we click the box marked **Background Image.** This causes the location entry to wake up, wherein we may browse for the location of the image to use as our texture. When we click the **Browse** button, we are presented with several tabs from which to choose how—and where— to get a background for our page.

The first, and default, tab is Current FrontPage Web. Any images stored within the current Web site (if we've launched the FrontPage Editor via the FrontPage Explorer) appear. Should we want to use an image from elsewhere, three tabs remain:

➤ **Other Location**   By selecting this option, we have the choice of selecting a file from the hard drive or anywhere on the World Wide Web.

Selecting a background image from either a local file or the World Wide Web.

Selecting **From File** lets us choose the image file from anywhere on the hard drive. Choosing **From Location** requires a URL to the image file, assuming it resides somewhere on the World Wide Web. For instance, http://www.machine.com/ DogWeb/pawprints.gif

➤ **Clip Art**   When it was installed, FrontPage created a ClipArt gallery. We can browse this gallery here, and select the proper category of images (backgrounds, lines, bullets, and so on).

The Clip Art gallery.

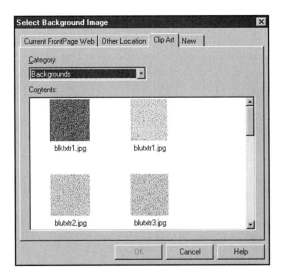

➤ **New Image**   If the image we want doesn't exist in the gallery, this option will help launch an image editor. After defining the filename and type of image (GIF or JPEG are good bets), the selected image editor (by default, Microsoft Image Composer, as defined by the associations in the FrontPage Explorer, explained in Chapter 4, "Discovering the Explorer").

Once we've selected an image for the background texture and clicked **OK**, its location will appear in the Page Properties window.

Once we've selected a background image, we have the option of enabling the property labelled Watermark. A watermark is a background image which does not scroll with the page. For instance, a corporate logo could be placed as a watermark background image. When the reader scrolls down the page, the logo will remain in place.

Tickled Pink

Selecting colors for the text on the page requires us to keep the rule in mind: Contrast, Contrast, Contrast. There are five different categories of colors that we may configure:

➤ **Background**   If there is no background texture selected, this color will appear as the background of the page. If a background texture has been selected, this color will not appear.

➤ **Text**   Any text that is not a hyperlink.

➤ **Hyperlink**   Text on a page that is a hyperlink to another page. It does not include a hyperlink which has previously been visited by the user, or a hyperlink which is currently being clicked.

➤ **Visited Hyperlink**   This is a hyperlink that has already been visited by the user. It's common practice to color it differently than unvisited links, so the reader knows if he's already been there.

➤ **Active hyperlink**   A hyperlink that is being clicked; that is, when the user presses the left mouse button on the link, we can define a new color to which it temporarily changes.

For each color category, we select a color using the selection menu to its right.

Selecting a color for a background or text on our Web page.

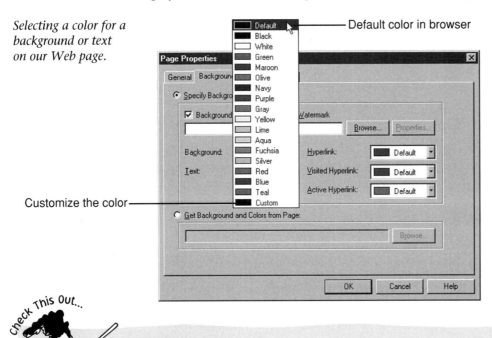

Default color in browser

Customize the color

Undefined Colors

The first color listed, "Default," is not really a color at all. Each Web browser is configured to a set of default colors to use for each category. Choosing Default means that no specific color will be imposed for this category, and the browser can use whichever color it has been configured to. This allows the person visiting our page to see the colors he wishes, but reduces our control in defining the color scheme.

A list of specific colors follows, ending with Custom. Choosing Custom will pop up a control window wherein we can find the exact color we want using RGB values or a color spectrum slider. This is probably necessary only if you're a true "artiste" and you know exactly what colors the page should have.

I Am Web Page, Hear Me Roar

Finally, some Web designers like to insert a background sound into their page. A background sound is usually a digitized sample (such as a .wav file) or a MIDI file (a musical score). If used, the sound will be heard by a visitor to our page, anytime she visits this page. One caveat—as of this writing, background sounds created with FrontPage only play when browsed with Microsoft Internet Explorer. They do not play with Netscape Navigator 3.0.

As with background textures, background sounds are not all good, and not all bad. A sound could enhance the atmosphere of a page, creating an effective "multimedia" experience. On the other hand, if a visitor needs to revisit our page frequently, hearing the sound or music each time may grow tiring, or irritating. Use background sounds judiciously.

The background sound configuration is in the **General** tab of the Page Properties window.

Sound file ──

Making our page sing, or scream. Wisely using (or not using) sounds will appease visitors.

When selecting the Browse button beside the Location property, a familiar window appears. We can either select a sound file from within the current Web site, or from another location on the hard disk or World Wide Web. When browsing for a sound file on the hard disk, be sure to choose the correct type of file. For example, if you're looking for a MIDI file, be sure to choose either **Midi Sequencer** or **All Files**; otherwise such files won't appear in the list.

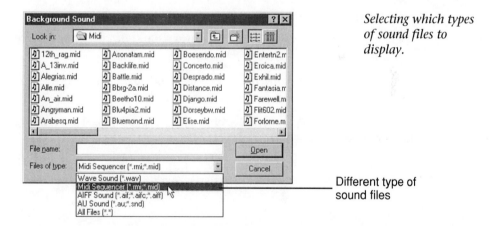

Selecting which types of sound files to display.

Different type of sound files

Returning our attention to the previous figure showing the Background Sound field we may configure it to play any number of consecutive times (by choosing a number beside the Loop setting), or for as long as the user is viewing this Web page (by enabling the box marked Forever).

Needless to say, repeating a sound several times, or indefinitely, may become extremely unpleasant to a visitor. It all depends on the sound in question, and the purpose of the Web page, but in many cases, people don't enjoy hearing the same droning tune over and over and over and over and... In addition, keep download times in mind. Small sound files are best—under 20 kilobytes for a WAV file. MIDI files are smaller by nature, and the preferred format for playing background songs (as opposed to sound effects, for which WAV is better suited).

Lining Up: Margins

Lastly, we can click the **Margins** tab to specify page margins when viewed in the Web browser. Measured in pixels, we can define how many pixels down (**Top Margin**) and to the right (**Left Margin**) to place the Web page in the browser window.

The Least You Need to Know

➤ Configuring Page Properties is done via the menu **File**, **Page Properties** or by right-clicking anywhere on the page and selecting **Page Properties** from the pop-up menu.

➤ Set the Title property so that user's bookmarks will seem meaningful, and set the Base Location property to reflect the official URL of this page.

➤ The Default Target Frame defines which frame, if this page has frames, will be the active frame upon visitation.

➤ Background textures are tricky beasts, and should be chosen with care. Contrast, Contrast, Contrast.

➤ Text colors go by the same rule: Contrast, Contrast, Contrast. Using the "Default" color allows the visitor to select her own viewing colors.

➤ Background sounds play when a Web surfer visits the page. Keep them tasteful and brief, lest guests be annoyed away from our site.

➤ Margins can be specified in pixels, to set the gap above the top of the page and to the left of it, when viewed in the Web browser.

Chapter 11

The Changing Shape of Our Web

In This Chapter

➤ Gonna wash that page right out of our Web

➤ New page on the block

➤ Oh, whatever shall we do... and when...by whom...

The Web is a dynamic structure—it is always changing. New connections are formed, while other connections crumble away. In this relatively short chapter, we'll look at some ways in which the FrontPage Explorer aids and abets the management of our Web's changing shape. Short, but sweet.

Elbow Room—Adding and Deleting Pages

In the old days (those described in Chapter 2, "FrontPage 97—A New Era in Easy Web Design"), a Web site was not unlike a house of cards. Links may fruitfully tie pages together, but remove one crucial page, and the link crashes down. The site falls down; goes splat. Although the Web designer can intervene, and adjust the hyperlinks which have changed, this can be a mind-consuming task. Fortunately, the FrontPage Explorer partly automates the changes associated with our Web's dynamism.

Bye-Bye Page

There are several approaches we can use to delete a Web page from our site. The most straightforward method is to use the procedure provided by the FrontPage Explorer itself:

In either the Hyperlink View or Folder View, right-click the Web page in question. In the pop-up menu which results, select **Delete**, and confirm this deletion in the dialog box which follows. That's it—the Web page is gone. Sort of.

In fact, the FrontPage Explorer deletes the .htm or .html file which contains the Web page, but it does *not* delete any of the files which are used within that Web page, such as images (either background or foreground), or sound files. This has its pros and cons. On the upside, at least these media files are still available within our Web site for use in other pages. On the downside, if we have no plans to use these files elsewhere in our site, they simply take up storage space (but they don't hinder the functionality of the site). To delete the stray files, should we want to, use the Folder View in the FrontPage Explorer, and manually delete each leftover .gif, .jpg, or any other files which we're sure are no longer needed. Just be sure that you don't delete a file which is also used in another one of the Web pages in this site, such as a background graphic or a logo.

When a Web page has been deleted from our site, any links to that Web page in other pages *do* remain in place. However, since their destination (the page we just deleted) has passed on, the FrontPage Explorer represents these links as "broken."

FrontPage Explorer representing broken links.

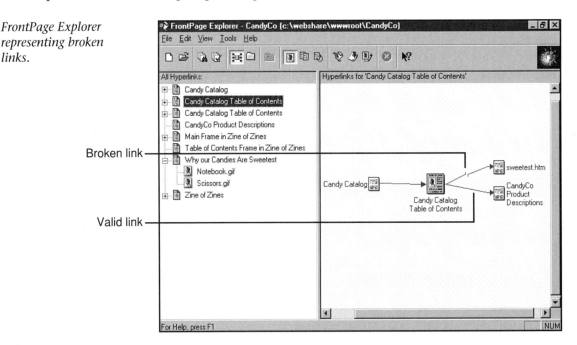

Now that we've deleted the page from our Web site, we probably want to change or eliminate the links-to-nowhere which are in our other pages. The workhorse solution to this problem is to open each of our Web pages into the FrontPage Editor and manually edit each old hyperlink. There is a more efficient way, however, courtesy of the FrontPage Explorer. Begin by selecting the menu item **Tools, Verify Hyperlinks**.

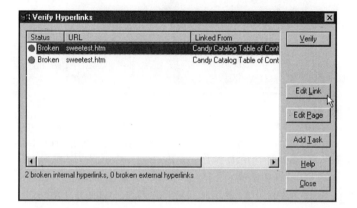

Adjusting old hyperlinks in the FrontPage Explorer. One-stop shopping for all our repair needs.

The Verify Hyperlinks function will examine each hyperlink in our Web site and determine which hyperlinks lead to invalid, or non-existent, Web pages. The invalid hyperlinks are divided into two categories: internal, which are hyperlinks leading to non-existent Web pages within our Web site, and external, which lead to non-existent Web pages outside our site.

By default, when we open the Verify Hyperlinks window, it automatically checks the validity of links which are internal to our site. As shown in the figure, there is a button marked **Verify**—clicking this button will check the validity of links that point outside our site. This process involves actually contacting those Web sites via the network, so our machine must be currently connected to the Internet before validation can be performed.

Notice in the previous figure that the hyperlink listed is marked as "Broken." That's because we've deleted the page the link pointed to. Now, we have three options to remedy the situation:

➤ **Edit Link**   Selecting this button will allow us to directly change the destination to which this hyperlink points. Furthermore, we can apply this change to one or all pages within our site that contain this invalid link.

Editing broken hyperlinks, we can specify a new destination for the hyperlink, and apply the change to one or all pages.

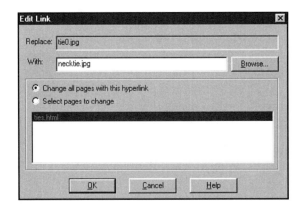

➤ **Edit Page**   This button will open the page containing the broken link into the FrontPage Editor. We can then modify the hyperlink there, by right-clicking the link and selecting **Hyperlink Properties** from the pop-up menu. Alternatively, if we leave a blank URL when editing the Hyperlink Properties, the hyperlink will be discarded entirely, and the highlighted page element will no longer be a link.

➤ **Add Task**   The procrastination button, clicking here will add an entry to the To-Do List (which we'll look at more closely later in this chapter); clicking this button effectively promises to fix this broken link at a later time.

What's in a Name?

There is another possibility, besides deleting a Web page. We can rename it. Doing so is a simple process in FrontPage Explorer. For some reason, we must select the Folder View to have the option of renaming a Web page file. Then, right-click the Web page file that we intend to rename, and select **Rename** from the pop-up menu. Once we've entered a new name, we'll be asked if all links within this site should be updated. Select **Yes**, and any links to this page on our other pages will be updated, preventing them from winding up broken.

Page + Page = Pages

Adding a Web page to our site isn't terribly difficult, although it's also not as flexible as one would imagine. A Web page can be added to our site via two methods: by creating it anew within the FrontPage Editor, or by importing it from somewhere else on our machine.

We've already enjoyed both methods of creating a new Web page from within the FrontPage Editor (Chapter 5, "Mission Statement: Editor at Large"). To recall, we can select **File, New**, followed by **File, Save As**, from where we select a filename for the page. The Web page will then be saved to our current Web site, assuming that we have a Web site currently opened in the FrontPage Explorer. Alternatively, we've used the New Page folder tab when creating a hyperlink, or editing hyperlink properties. This also adds a new page to our Web site.

Importing a page from elsewhere requires us to use the FrontPage Explorer menu item **File, Import**. A window appears, allowing us to select which files to import into the current Web site.

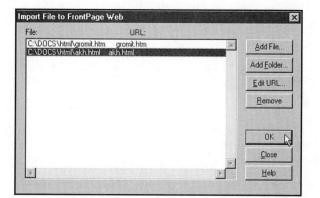

Make way—importing additional pages and files into our Web site.

The top-most button, **Add File**, will bring about a standard file dialog box requesting us to select which files to import. Multiple files can be chosen by holding down the control key while clicking on file names. Be sure to include all necessary files, if any, for a Web page, besides its .htm or .html file: images, sounds, etc.; FrontPage cannot automatically find them on its own. Alternatively, you can also drag files from the desktop and drop them onto the import window, rather than surfing through the file dialog box.

Selecting **Add Folder** will allow us to import the entire contents of a folder in one fell swoop. This is convenient if we want to import a batch of related files, all of which reside in the same subdirectory. This method is no different from selecting every file within a folder using the **Add File** button, but it is more efficient.

Clicking one or more of the entries in the **Import File to FrontPage Web** window, and then selecting **Remove**, will eliminate them from the import list. This does *not* delete the files from their original storage location, it simply tells the FrontPage Explorer not to import them into our current Web site.

The **Edit URL** button will, if clicked after we have selected a file in the import list, allow us to change its filename once imported into our site. Thus, if we're importing a Web page named "snap.htm," we could use the **Edit URL** button to change its name to "cracklepop.htm" within our Web site. This does not change its name in its original location, only its name in our Web.

Click **OK** to complete the process, and the new pages will appear in the FrontPage Explorer view. As we connect them to our other pages, by creating or editing hyperlinks and so forth, these new pages will be woven into our Web, as indicated by the graphical hyperlinks view.

To Do, or Not to Do...

Some people are list makers, some people are not—there are no in-betweens. Usually, these diametrically opposed people are paired in some relationship where the list-nots rely on the list-makers. In the case of oneself and FrontPage 97 (not that any romantic link is implied), we're freed from being the list-maker.

FrontPage Explorer recognizes that creating a Web site often leaves loose-ends. There are pages that need creating, or editing, images to add, links to update—without any form of organization, things could be a real mess. The To-Do List is a feature that aims to alleviate the mess.

Another complication is that many Web sites, especially the larger ones, are created by groups of people working together (with varying degrees of success). The To-Do list also provides a way to organize Web-related tasks and dole them out to specified individuals, with specified priorities. In these respects, the To-Do List is somewhat like a mini-scheduler, built-in and integrated into the operation of the FrontPage Explorer.

The To-Do List is accessed in the FrontPage Explorer via the menu item **Tools, Show To Do List**. Beside the item name in the menu is a number representing the number of tasks in the list awaiting completion.

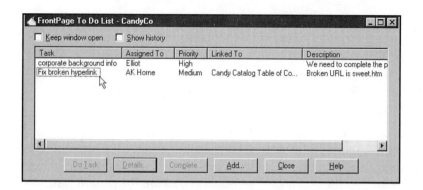

Ugh, Mondays! The To-Do List, helping to manage Web site construction.

Tasks are added to the To-Do List in one of two ways:

➤ **Automatically**   Via a wizard or configuration window within the FrontPage Explorer. For instance, when we created a hyperlink, and clicked the New Page folder tab, we were given the option to place the new page on the To-Do List. Alternatively, we can select the menu item **Edit, Add To Do List** in the FrontPage Editor to create a To-Do item for the current page.

➤ **Manually**   By clicking on the button marked **Add** in the To-Do List window. This will call up a window for defining the new task.

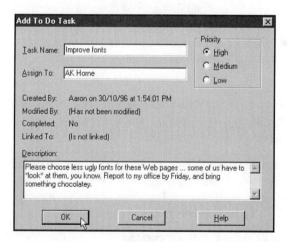

Adding and assigning a new task to the To-Do List. It's great being boss.

We first must fill-in a **Task Name**, something descriptive, such as, "corporate background info." We then enter someone's name to **Assign** this task to. There isn't any real checking done by the To-Do List to identify the user—the names assigned are for human reference only. No safeguards are in place to prevent Harry from completing a task meant for Sally.

147

For a **Description**, we can enter a more verbose instruction, such as, "We need to complete the page containing corporate background information by the end of this week...please include all text as per the memo, and use the logos provided by Markus in the art department...if there are any problems, you're fired." Lastly, select a **Priority** for this task, from **High** to **Medium** to **Low**. These priorities help everyone determine which tasks to attend to first.

In the To-Do List window, we can sort the tasks by any of the heading criteria. Thus, if we click the "Assigned To" heading of the list, the tasks will be sorted alphabetically by the names of the assignees. If we click the "Priority" heading, the tasks will be sorted by priority from high to low. Selecting any of the tasks and clicking the **Details** button will pop up an information window displaying the requirements of the task, including the full description.

Only tasks which have been generated by a wizard or the FrontPage Editor will contain a Linked To property. After selecting one of these tasks in the To-Do List, we can click the **Do Task** button, which will launch the appropriate application to work on the task (such as the FrontPage Editor, or an image editor). There is no way to automatically launch the applications for tasks entered manually into the To-Do List.

Once a task has been completed, we click the **Complete** button. This will ask whether we want to mark the task as having been completed, or delete the task from the To-Do List. In the former case, we can view old completed tasks by selecting the option **Show History** in the main To-Do List window. In the latter case, the task along with the completion history will be removed from the list, as if it were never there in the first place. (Hint to employees: click on task assigned to you, click Complete, choose Delete: "But that job was never assigned to me, really. You have no proof!")

Lastly, notice the check box labelled **Keep Window Open** in the main To-Do List window. If we check this, the To-Do List will remain open onscreen while we are working on other tasks.

Certainly, the To-Do List is not a vital component towards the functionality of our Web site, but it's a nice management tool which can benefit individuals or groups working on more complex sites, with many pages, links, and external objects.

The Least You Need to Know

On a diet from the girth of previous chapters, we've taken some time to consider some organizational issues concerning our Web site.

➤ Deleting a page from our site, from either the Hyperlinks or Folder View of the FrontPage Explorer, does not delete any of the graphics or files other than the basic .htm or .html file for that page.

➤ Deleting a page from our site will probably result in broken links on any of the pages in our site from which it was referred. Use **Tools, Verify Links** to quickly reassign those links to another page. Alternatively, open each page with a broken link into the FrontPage Editor, and enter a blank URL for the broken hyperlink, thus eliminating the link altogether.

➤ To add a page to our site, we can create and save a new page from within the FrontPage Editor, either via the menu **File, New**, or the New Page tab within certain configuration options for page elements, such as creating or editing a hyperlink.

➤ Alternatively, we can add an existing page to our site via the FrontPage Explorer menu item **File, Import**. Here, we can select files from other locations to import into our current Web site.

➤ When renaming a file in the FrontPage Explorer's Folder View, be sure to answer **Yes** to the question about updating links—this will prevent links on our other pages from becoming broken due to the new file name.

➤ The To-Do List, available from the Tools menu of the FrontPage Explorer, helps us manage loose ends when creating our Web site. It maintains a list of tasks to-be-completed, allowing us to assign priorities and people to complete them.

Chapter 12

If I Only Had a Crane—Hauling Your Web to a Server

In This Chapter

➤ Server science

➤ Publishing the easy way

➤ The (less than) Wonderful Wizard of Webz

➤ Disclaimers and coverups

There are the haves, and there are the have-nots. Fortunately, Web servers aren't required for any basic life functions, but nonetheless, some folks have their own Web servers, while others must rent server space elsewhere. The majority of us, in fact, probably don't own or run our own Web server—it's provided by our Internet service provider. In this chapter, we'll look at the crucial issues involved in moving our ready-to-go Web site from our computer to the server.

Where the Servers Are

Pages upon pages ago, in a time and a place known as Chapter 1, "Why We Web (and How!)," we talked about the role of servers, and Web servers in particular. Recall that for a Web user to read a Web page, he must access that Web page via a Web server. Therefore, for a Web user to visit *our* Web site, our Web site must be accessible via a Web server.

Surely, one way to accomplish this is to run the Web server on our own computer. In that case, we can create our Web site directly within access of the server. There are downsides to this, however. For one, running a Web server involves certain knowledge and maintenance responsibilities that may not interest us. Second, we may not have a fast enough connection to the Internet to handle a high volume of requests for our Web pages. Third, our Internet connection may not be in place 24 hours a day, 7 days a week, and a good Web site should be accessible to anyone at any time. If that's not daunting enough, then fine—be that way. Read Part 5, "Broadcasting from Bed: The FrontPage 97 Web Server" which delves into running our own Web server.

The bulk of Web designers, however, do not host their own Web server. In the case of private individuals and small businesses, the Web server is usually provided by an Internet service provider, who charges us a fee to store our Web pages there. In these cases, we design our Web pages on our personal computer, and then we must move them to the Web server. People in this boat will find this chapter the most helpful, and possibly even interesting.

Large businesses and organizations often have their own local area networks, on which a Web server resides. This server might be used to deliver organization-related Web pages to the outside world via the Internet, or it may be used to deliver pages throughout the organization, commonly called an intranet. In either case, the exact details of how to make one's Web pages available to the server will vary from organization to organization. Fortunately, these environments are usually headed by semi-friendly managers, who can explain the specific configuration of their network, and how to create or move Web pages to the server.

Moving on up...Moving Right in...

Before we look at the specific procedures for "publishing" our Web site (that is, moving its pages to a server), let's take a moment to consider what this involves. Whatever method is used, the same net goal is accomplished when we publish our Web site: All of the files which make up our Web pages are copied from our computer to the server's computer.

There are a variety of ways to copy files across the Internet, and thus a variety of ways to publish a Web site. FrontPage 97 includes two utilities for publishing our Web site, at least one of which should work for most users in most situations.

We'll consider two solutions to publishing our Web site: the Publish FrontPage Web feature of the FrontPage Explorer, and the Microsoft Web Publishing Wizard—a separate application included with the FrontPage Bonus Pack.

Publishing Solution 1: The FrontPage Explorer

Notice, under the **File** menu in the FrontPage Explorer, there is an item named **Publish FrontPage Web**. As the name implies, selecting this will walk us through the process of publishing the currently loaded Web site to a server.

Let's imagine that we still have our Candy Catalog Web site open in the FrontPage Explorer. Now, we select **File**, **Publish FrontPage Web**, and this dialog box appears:

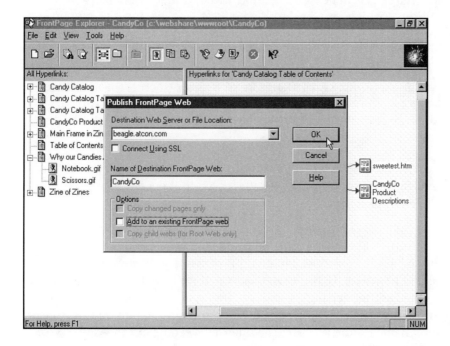

We are starting to publish our site via the FrontPage Explorer. Trickier than it looks, trickier than it should be.

In the Publish FrontPage Web window, the top-most option asks us to enter the Destination Web Server or File Location. If, for some reason, we wanted to move our Web site to another location on our local machine, we could enter a file location, such as *c:\otherwebs*. Assuming, however, that we want to publish this Web site to a server, we must enter the server's network name, such as *www.provider.com*.

Moving Day Hassles

Unfortunately, as simple a concept as Web publishing sounds ("moving our files from one location to another"), it turns out to be more complicated than that. Additionally, because of the way Microsoft has implemented FrontPage 97's publishing, it also turns out to be more complicated than it should be. So we begin with *caveat number one*:

The FrontPage Explorer publisher can only publish our Web site to Web servers which have the "FrontPage extensions" installed. *The whowhathuh?*

FrontPage 97 includes special features which most Web servers do not support. In an attempt to aid Web servers in being compatible with FrontPage 97, Microsoft has developed "extensions," which are added to Web servers, to allow them to support special FrontPage 97 features. Nice as that may sound, installing these FrontPage 97 extensions is entirely up to the Web server owner. If they don't want to, they don't have to.

Fortunately, those of you running on a Microsoft Web server (such as the FrontPage Personal Web Server, Microsoft Personal Web Server, or IIS Web Server) needn't worry, as the FrontPage extensions will already be installed.

If we enable the check box marked **Connect Using SSL**, then the Secure Sockets Layer protocol will be used when communicating with the server, thus encrypting the data from prying eyes while it is in-transit.

When it comes to the Name of Destination FrontPage Web, we want to choose a name of the Web site. We've probably already chosen a name, having been asked to do so when initially creating the site in the FrontPage Explorer, so we may as well stick with the same name (although we don't have to). In this case, *CandyCo*. If we leave this selection blank, our site will be published as the "default" Web; for example, a visitor will not need to specify a .htm or .html file when accessing our site. For more information on this issue of selecting a destination name for the Web, see the sidebar "Weeding out the <Root Web>."

Finally, there are three additional check box options:

➤ **Copy changed pages only** If we've already published this Web site to this server before, enabling this option will only copy pages which have changed since last publishing. This option saves time.

Weeding out the <Root Web>

In the field of Web publishing, there is a concept known as the "<Root Web>." The <Root Web> is the main Web on a server—the top-most Web of Webs. Other Web sites on the server are actually child webs, or subwebs, of the <Root Web>.

When selecting the **Name of Destination FrontPage Web**, a blank selection will attempt to publish the Web site as the <Root Web>. One advantage of publishing to the <Root Web> is that users can visit our site with a simplified URL, such as http://www.myserver.com/, without needing to specify an HTML file. However, we may not want to publish to the <Root Web> if our site is not the main site on the server. Secondly, we may not be allowed to publish to <Root Web> if we haven't been granted such permission by the server owner.

Thus, in most cases, we *do* specify a **Name of Destination FrontPage Web**, and the Web site is then published as a child web within the destination server's <Root Web>.

➤ **Add to an existing FrontPage web**   If this option is checked, our site will be stored as a subfolder of the existing FrontPage Web on that server. Use this if we have a main FrontPage Web site stored as the default Web on the server, and we want to store the current Web site as a site-within-the-main site. For instance, we might choose to store the full-blown Candy Catalog as a Web site within the main CandyCo Corporation Web site.

➤ **Copy child webs**   If we have published our site to the <Root Web>, enabling **Copy child webs** will automatically publish all subwebs of the <Root Web>, as well. For instance, one could use this option to copy *all* webs from one server to another. Provided, of course, that one has <Root Web> access on the destination server (see the sidebar above, "Weeding out the <Root Web>".

After clicking the **OK** button, the FrontPage Publisher will attempt to contact the Web server. If the Web server does not have the FrontPage extensions installed, an error message to that effect will pop up. The process halts there, so we must wait until the next section of this chapter, "Publishing Solution #2."

If, however, the Web server does have the FrontPage extensions installed, then we'll be asked to log in with a name and password. Here we enter whatever login and password our service provider has assigned to our account.

155

Logging into a Web server with FrontPage extensions installed.

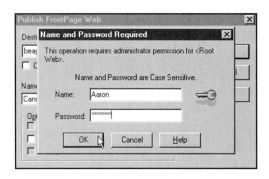

Assuming we enter this information accurately, the FrontPage Explorer will begin copying the relevant pages and files to the server. Once this process is complete, a happy window will appear informing us of its success. We might then test the site ourselves by launching a Web browser and connecting to the URL of our site (probably in the form of http://www.provider.com/~myname/somepage.htm).

Publishing Solution 2: The Web Publishing Wizard

The Web Publishing Wizard is a tool with which we can publish our Web site to servers which do not possess the FrontPage extensions. While not installed by default with FrontPage 97, the Web Publishing Wizard is included in the Bonus Pack which is bundled with the FrontPage 97 software. A further account of installing the Bonus Pack can be found in the Appendix, "Semper Paratus: FrontPage 97 Installation Tips."

Once installed, the Web Publishing Wizard is available via the Windows 95 **Start** menu, in **Programs, Accessories, Internet Tools**. Let's attempt to publish our server using this Wizard, after launching it from the menu just mentioned.

Employing the Web Publishing Wizard to succeed where the FrontPage Explorer cannot.

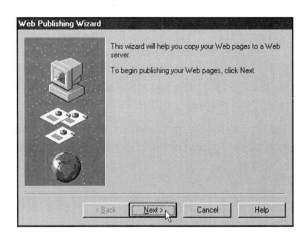

After clicking **Next** > on the initial welcome screen, we must select some files or a folder to publish. In good Web design form, we should have all the files that are related to our Web site in one folder. This is where we've been creating and saving the site when using the FrontPage Explorer. For instance, perhaps our site resides in c:\frontpage\webs\ candyco. In that case, we would click **Browse Folders** to find the folder containing our Web site. Of course, enabling **Include subfolders** will also publish any folders within the folder we've selected. If we only want to publish some of the files within a folder, we can use **Browse Files** to multi-select which files to publish (that is, hold down the **Ctrl** key while selecting multiple files). Perhaps we've only edited one file in our site, and thus only want to re-publish that one file.

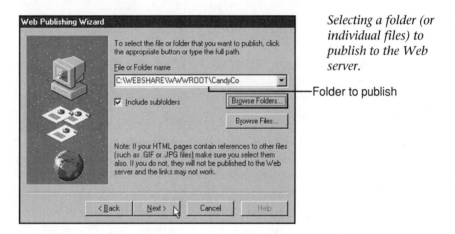

Selecting a folder (or individual files) to publish to the Web server.

—Folder to publish

Next, we're asked to select which Web server to publish to. A drop-down list is provided; this list includes any default servers included by Microsoft (such as Compuserve and Sprynet). Certainly, if your service provider is one of the included services, select it. More than likely, though, we'll need to create a new entry for our service provider, since only a very few major providers are included with the Wizard. For our example, in an attempt to represent the greatest number of readers, we'll imagine that our service provider is a local outfit named "Gramps' Olde Internet Shoppe." Their Web server is located at www. grampsnet.com.

We must create a profile of our service provider for the Web Publishing Wizard. Begin by clicking the **New** button. We're then asked to enter a human-friendly name for the Web server; this is the name by which we'll refer to the server when using the Wizard. For instance, "Gramps Server." Below that, we must select our Internet Service Provider. Again, a small list is provided of pre-defined providers—if one of those fit us, then we'd select it. But since none do, we choose <**Other Internet Provider**>. Click **Next** >.

Creating a profile of our service provider's Web server.

On the next page, after clicking the **Next >** button, we're asked for the URL of our Web pages on the server. In many cases, this will be in the form of *http://www.grampsnet.com/ ~myusername*. However, this may vary from provider to provider; it's best to check with one's provider to be certain of the correct URL.

Following the above, we're asked to select which network connection to use to contact the Web server. Users publishing within an intranet environment would select **Use Local Area Network**, while users publishing to a service provider's Web server on the Internet (most of us), will select whichever networking connection they normally use to contact the Internet.

Thus far, the Wizard has been a fairly straightforward sort of mystic. However, we now breach the Realm of Confusion. Let's take these next steps slowly:

The Wizard is now ready to perform certain queries of the Web server. It needs to know what method it should use to transfer our files to the server. Although it attempts to determine this method automatically, many times it will fail. Upon failing, the Wizard then asks us to tell it which protocol to use for file transfers:

Explaining to the Wizard which file transfer method to use.

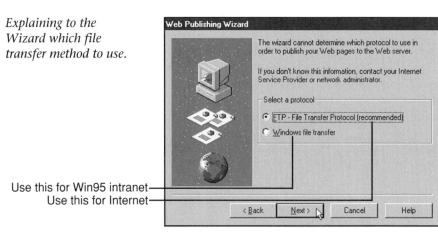

Use this for Win95 intranet—
Use this for Internet—

Anyone publishing to a Web server on the Internet (such as us) will want to select **FTP—File Transfer Protocol**. Only users publishing within a Windows 95 intranet should select **Windows file transfer**. After clicking **Next >**, we're then asked for the username and password of our "Web server account." This is information provided by our service provider—for most people, it's the same username and password they use to access their account normally, such as when dialing into the service provider. In cases of uncertainty, ask the specific provider.

Once the transfer method has been entered, we once again click **Next >**, and face the following prompt: FTP server name:.

The Explanation: The Wizard needs to use the File Transfer Protocol (FTP) to send our files to our service provider's machine. However, the Wizard does not know which machine to contact with FTP. It needs to contact a machine which stores our files where the Web server can reach them. We could try *www.grampsnet.com*, for instance, but that machine probably doesn't accept our FTP request. What FTP server do we enter, then? The service provider is the best source for this information: ask them, "What is the address where I FTP my Web pages to?" In most cases, it will be a machine named something like *ftp.grampsnet.com* or *users.grampsnet.com*, but we cannot predict that here. In this example, let's imagine that we either contacted Gramps' Net, or we learned the answer from one of their support files on the Gramps' Net Home Page. In any case, we found that we FTP our Web pages to *ftp.grampsnet.com*. Thus, we type that address into the FTP server name: prompt, and click **Next >**.

Ugh! The Wizard now asks another esoteric question: Subfolder containing your Web pages on your FTP server. Another explanation: Once logged into our account on *ftp.grampsnet. com*, the Wizard needs to know which subfolder to place the Web page files. Most providers require that we keep our Web page files within a specially named subfolder: oftentimes, that subfolder is named public_html. Again, this is information that only our service provider can confirm. For our example, we'll assume that public_html is the correct subfolder, as explained by Gramps' Net.

The Wizard then asks for the URL of our "home root" on the Web server; this will likely be the same URL we entered earlier in the Wizard, such as http://www.grampsnet.com/ ~myusername. Again, this may vary from provider to provider, although the above example is fairly standard.

At this point, after clicking **Next >**, the Web Publishing Wizard will attempt to contact our provider and begin the transfer. Assuming we entered the information correctly—most importantly, the FTP server name, username, and password—the transfer will begin, and our Web site is copied to the Web server.

Now, for an Interesting Fact

The Web Publishing Wizard is not as distinct from the FrontPage Explorer as it was portrayed in this chapter. In fact, once we've configured the Wizard to publish to our service provider, we can then use the menu item **Publish FrontPage Web** from within the FrontPage Explorer. Why?

Recall the configuration window from the FrontPage Explorer's publisher as shown in the next figure.

Using the FrontPage Explorer's publisher with a provider configured with the Web Publishing Wizard.

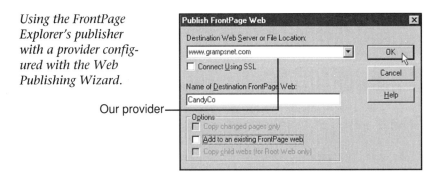

Our provider

When we enter our provider's address, the FrontPage Explorer will realize that we configured the Web Publishing Wizard to use this provider. Rather than reject us because the server does not have the FrontPage extensions, the Web Publishing Wizard will be launched.

Thus, from now on, when publishing to this provider, we can do so from within the FrontPage Explorer. The Web Publishing Wizard need only be launched manually when configuring it for a server for the first time. Convenient.

The Excuses

Due to the complexity and variation between service providers, and between servers, it's very difficult to write a step-by-step process which applies to all scenarios. The above procedures, as outlined, apply to the most common circumstances. However, any single service provider or intranet may have unusual configurations.

Therefore, if any problems are encountered publishing our Web site, the first and best place to go with questions is the organization who owns and runs the server. They're in the best position to know exactly what steps to take for their particular setup. Of course, always check for support documents and help files provided by the service provider before bothering humans (such documents are often available at the provider's home page). A good service provider will anticipate these questions, and provide readily accessible answers. Then again, if the provider has not offered any onscreen help or support, then feel free to bug 'em. They deserve it.

The Least You Need to Know

Publishing our Web site to a Web server is both a vital and potentially confusing process. There are many variations between servers and service providers, which make it difficult to account for every scenario. Nonetheless…

➤ Regardless of how or where we created our Web pages, they must eventually reside on a Web server for anyone to access them.

➤ Most Web servers are run by service providers or organizations, and we must transfer our Web pages to that server. (Running one's own Web server is the subject of Part 5 "Broadcasting from Bed: The FrontPage Web Server.")

➤ Some Web servers have "FrontPage extensions" (ask the server owner). Extensions make publishing easy, and with them we can simply select the menu item **File, Publish FrontPage Web** from within the FrontPage Explorer.

➤ Publishing to Web servers without the FrontPage extensions (ask the server owner) requires the Web Publishing Wizard, available in the Bonus Pack bundled with FrontPage.

➤ To use the Web Publishing Wizard for the first time with a particular Web server or service provider, launch it from the Windows 95 **Start** menu, in **Programs, Accessories, Internet Tools.**

➤ The Web Publishing Wizard can be confusing, so be sure to find out the following information from your service provider: your user name and password, the URL to your Web pages, the FTP server to store your pages on, and the subdirectory in which to store them.

➤ Once a profile for a specific provider has been created in the Web Publishing Wizard, future publishings to that server can be initiated from within the FrontPage Explorer's **File, Publish FrontPage Web** menu.

Part 4
It's Alive! Advanced Web Tactics

Ah, the dessert; we sprinkle our pages with a fine selection of sweet goodies. Graphics and animations add visual appeal. ActiveX and Java open up whole new worlds, allowing us to add a wide variety of fancy flavors. At our most advanced point, we construct scripts with the FrontPage Editor Script Wizard, where our page elements become fully interactive. Web pages never tasted so good.

OK PEOPLE, LET'S TRY TO GET IT IN ONE TAKE...

Chapter 13

Lights, Camera, Multimedia!

In this chapter

➤ Imagespotting

➤ GIF versus JPEG

➤ Sheer and natural—transparent images

➤ Not-so-stupid layout tricks

➤ Visual cartography, aka image maps

What a buzz word—"multimedia." Everyone and anyone with a tie to the computer industry practically has this word stamped on their head. They mutter it at night. Marketing departments convulse with pleasure at every instance they can shout it. So along we come, arriving upon the densely rich fauna of Part 4, with every intent to extinguish the buzzword of its marketable prowess, and expose its true self. Which isn't half bad. Simply realistic.

A Picture's Worth a Thousand Bytes

Nearly every Web page contains graphic images. That's a simple fact. Of course, as with frames and background textures, not every Web page *needs* graphic images, but they seem to have them nonetheless. Not to begin this chapter on an entirely dour note, plenty of Web pages use graphics to great effect. Images can simply be attractive to look at, they can serve to format the rest of the page's content in a more facile way, or images can be content in and of themselves.

Graphics have been used for a variety of purposes in Web pages. Consider the following examples:

➤ Formatting elements, such as horizontal lines, can be more attractive when replaced with a suitable graphic, such as a stylized line.

➤ Promotional campaigns, such as the placement of corporate logos or related imagery on Web pages.

➤ Hyperlinks—also known as *image maps*—graphic images which can be clicked to lead the reader to another Web page.

➤ Action buttons—graphic images which can be clicked to cause certain actions to occur, such as submitting a form. We'll cover this topic more closely when we chat about ActiveX in Chapter 15.

➤ Pure aesthetics—A pretty picture or two, in the right spots, can make a Web page more pleasing to the eye. Eyes like to be pleased.

➤ Content—In some cases, graphic images may serve as content itself. For instance, images of products for sale, or photographs from last year's family vacation to Tuktijuktuk.

Brushing Up—Adding an Image

In this chapter, we'll be working to spruce up a sample personal home page. The original version has plenty of text, but looks a bit drab:

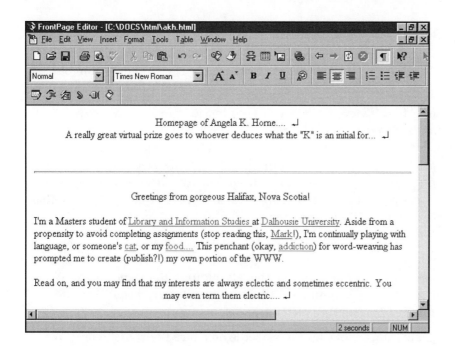

A text-only home page. The content is there, but the presentation is lacking.

This page could use some tasteful graphics. Let's begin with a replacement for that straight-laced horizontal line which appears just below the "Homepage" heading banner. First, we'll delete the existing line by left-clicking and dragging the mouse over it, so that it becomes highlighted. Then we hit **Ctrl-X** to cut it from the page. To insert an image in this spot, we can either select the menu item **Insert, Image**, or click the Insert Image icon on the toolbar.

Inserting an image in the FrontPage Editor.

A window pops up, from which we must select the image file to insert. We're given three main locations from which to find the image file:

Current FrontPage Web   Here we see any images currently residing within our Web site.

Other Location   In this view, we may select our image from a source external to our current FrontPage Web. **From File** allows us to select or browse for the image from somewhere on our hard drive, while **From Location** will let us enter a URL to specify an image that resides somewhere on the World Wide Web. As we'll see later, when we choose to save our Web page, FrontPage will ask if it should save these images to the local Web site. We should always answer **Yes** to that question, so that the images will be automatically imported into our site.

Clip Art   FrontPage 97 includes a number of predesigned images, which were installed with the entire FrontPage suite. Selecting this tab will allow us to browse any of the images in any of the categories (bullets, buttons, lines, and so on). While this is basically the same as choosing the image from a file outside our Web site, it offers the advantage of previewing each image before inserting it.

After browsing the Lines category of Clip Art, we settle on a nice horizontal scrawl. We click **OK**, and the image appears before us on the Web page. Easy enough, for a start.

Poof! The selected image leaps onto our Web page. A nice horizontal dividing line. We've also spruced up the text a bit using basic text formatting techniques (Chapter 6).

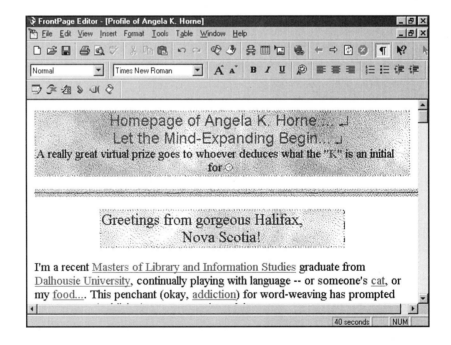

A Room with a Preview

There's a simple way to include any image files we want in the Clip Art gallery. When we installed FrontPage 97, a subfolder named *clipart* was created inside the *Microsoft FrontPage* folder. The latter folder was created wherever we instructed FrontPage to install to; by default, the full path would have been *c:\Program Files\Microsoft FrontPage*. Within the clipart subfolder are additional subfolders; one for each of the categories which appear as a selection in the Clip Art browser. To create an additional category, simply create a new subfolder inside the clip art folder. Copy or move any image files you want into either the existing subfolders, or new ones, and they'll then appear in preview form when you use the Clip Art browser while selecting images in the FrontPage Editor.

Apples and Oranges, GIFs and JPEGs

Graphic images are saved in computer files using different schemes. Each scheme has its own reasons for existence, but suffice it to say, the program that displays the image must know how to decode the scheme it's been stored in. The two most common schemes, or "image file formats" as they're more commonly known, are GIF and JPEG. Image files saved in the former format are usually named something like picture.gif, while images in JPEG format are named picture.jpg.

While other image formats do exist, such as BMP (common in Windows) and PICT (common on the Macintosh), the reader's browser may not know how to decode images saved in such file formats. For this reason, the FrontPage Editor will automatically convert such images to either GIF or JPEG format. We'll encounter this issue again when discussing the Image Properties settings a few paragraphs from now.

Confounded Configurability

As is the case with virtually every element on our Web page, the image can be configured to reflect a variety of properties. First off, it was placed onto the page against the left-hand margin, but we'd prefer that it be centered, to align more pleasingly with the banner text above it. We'll click the image to activate it, and then select the centering icon from the toolbar. Voilà—image centered, same as if we were centering a line of text.

The remaining image properties lie within the associated properties window; they are available by right-clicking on the image and selecting **Image Properties** from the pop-up menu.

Stepping into a pile of image properties.

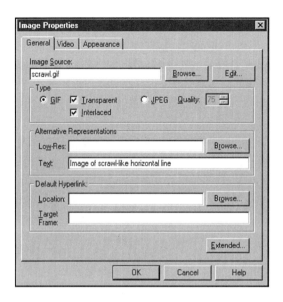

The General Tab

Under the General tab, we're presented with a number of properties:

Image Source   The filename and location of the image file. No location is shown if the file was selected from within our Web site. Clicking the Browse button allows us to select a different image; clicking **Edit** launches our image editor (as defined in the FrontPage Explorer menu Tools, Options, Configure Editors), in case we want to make any modifications to the image.

Type   Either GIF or JPEG will be selected, depending upon which format the image was saved in. In the case of images which were in some other file format, the FrontPage Editor will have converted them to GIF or JPEG. Choosing the unselected format will convert the image into that format. Thus, if GIF is selected, and we click JPEG, then the image will be converted into a JPEG image. In most cases, we won't need to change the image format. However, keep in mind the following rule of thumb: GIF is a better format for images containing line-art or a lot of text, but GIF produces larger file sizes. JPEG can produce very small, highly compressed files, but can lose some image quality. Use JPEG with images that are more complex, such as photos, where minor losses in quality are less noticeable.

If GIF is selected as the image **Type**, two additional variations on the GIF format may be selected:

➤ **GIF—Transparent:** This option reflects whether a transparency color has been selected for this image. We'll discuss transparency in detail in the next section of this chapter.

➤ **GIF—Interlaced:** This option reflects whether the image is in an interlaced format or not (an older style of the GIF format). In truth, it shouldn't matter to us one way or another because modern browsers can decode any GIF variation, so this property can simply be left alone, whether it is checked or unchecked.

➤ **JPEG—Quality:** This number defines how tightly the image file should be compressed, and how much quality to lose (assuming that the JPEG option button has been selected). Between 1 and 99, the higher the number, the higher quality the image (and the less compression); the lower the number, the lower the quality (and the more compression). Quality loss and gain is very dependent upon the particular image in question: Certain images can be compressed down to, say, 5K in size and appear only marginally worse off than the same image at 20K size. Experiment with each image to see what the optimum balance is.

Alternative Representations   The next pair of properties allow us to customize "contingency plans" in case the reader's browser cannot handle our graphic images.

➤ **Low-Res**   Some browsers can display a small image while the larger image is downloading. If we have such a small image, we can select it here. Most Web designers don't do this, and in most cases, it's not necessary.

➤ **Text**   While some browsers cannot display images at all (such as the text-only Lynx), some users choose to disable graphics to shorten download times. In both cases, any text we enter here will be displayed instead of the image. This text might be informative or instructional: For instance, if our image was a decorative puppy, we might enter "Cute puppy image." If our image was some sort of content, such as "Choose an item below," then we would enter that same text here, so that non-graphical readers don't miss out on content. In our example, we've inserted a horizontal line image, so we'll type in "horizontal line scrawl" as the alternative text representation.

Default Hyperlink   Images can also behave as hyperlinks, when clicked, leading the reader to a new page.

➤ **Location**   If we enter a URL here, the image becomes a hyperlink. Clicking the image will lead the reader to wherever the URL points. See the section in this chapter on image maps for more on this feature.

➤ **Target Frame**   As usual, this specifies in which frame to display the hyperlinked page, if any.

171

The Video Tab

For now, we'll skip over the Video tab of the Image Properties window, because we're inserting a still graphic, not a moving video. That'll come in Chapter 14, "...Action! Movie Magic!"

The Appearance Tab

The Appearance tab, however, is quite important now.

Squeezing, squishing, and measuring the dimensions of our image.

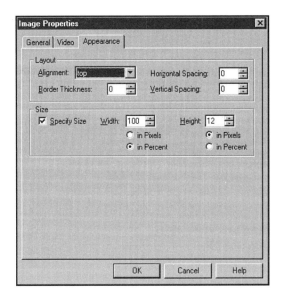

The first set of properties, Layout, defines a number of position-related characteristics:

Alignment   If there is any text adjacent (on the same line as) this image, we must define how to align the two with respect to one another. The popular choices are:

➤ **bottom, middle, top**   Align the respective (bottom, middle, or top) part of the image with the text.

➤ **absbottom, absmiddle**   Aligns the image with the bottom or middle of the current line, rather than the text itself

➤ **left, right**   Image appears against left or right margin, text is wrapped around opposite side. For instance, if we select left, then the image will appear against the left margin, and any text will be wrapped along the right side of the image.

With so many alignment options, words fail to describe the subtler distinctions. Clearly, until one has an innate feel for them, experimentation with each option is the quickest way to see how each alignment fares.

Border Thickness   If set to any number greater than zero, a rectangular border that many pixels thick will be drawn around the image. Usually the result is quite ugly.

Horizontal and **Vertical Spacing**   Respectively, the amount of pixel space to leave between adjacent text or images either beside (horizontal) or above and below (vertical) the image.

Specify Size   Selecting this check box enables the width and height measurements, while unchecking it disables them. It is considered proper Web design etiquette to always enable these size specifications. Doing so allows the browser to know ahead of time the dimensions of each image, thus text can be displayed on the page properly while images are downloading. If the browser does not know each image's size, it must wait until the image is downloaded before any text is displayed, leaving the irritated reader staring at a blank Web page.

By default, the **Width** and **Height** options will be set to the pixel size of the image based on the original image file. Modifying the pixel size in **Width** or **Height** will cause the image to be scaled to fit. Note that scaling an image to dramatically different dimensions than the original dimensions will cause it to look stretched or squished, both of which can be quite ugly.

Stretching by Percent

If we set the **Width** and **Height** options in percentages, then the image will be scaled relative to the browser window. Thus, an image set to 70% width will be stretched horizontally to 70% of the current width of the browser. In the case of our horizontal line image, we want to stretch it to 100% of the browser width. However, we should preserve its original height of 12 pixels. While stretching images too much is generally a bad idea, after clicking **OK** and seeing the results, we decide that this particular scrawly line looks acceptable.

David Copperfield Move Over—Transparent Images

A transparent image is an image which contains one color defined as "transparent." Wherever that color appears in the image, a transparent spot appears, allowing the background to show through. Only GIFs can contain a transparent color; JPEGs are always opaque, and therefore they are not a good format choice for images which require the background to show through.

An opaque image, which covers up the background. Transparency would cure this eyesore.

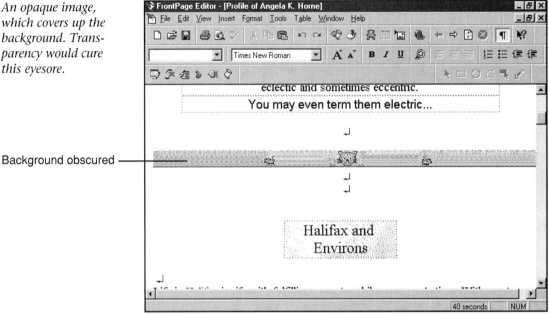

Background obscured ———

Many GIFs created for Web design already contain the transparent color. However, we may have an image that is not transparent, but should be. Imagine that after inserting our image, it appeared opaque (as pictured above). Fortunately, the FrontPage Editor provides an easy way to make an image transparent. First, be sure that the image is configured as a GIF in the **Image Properties** settings. Then click the Make Transparent icon on the image toolbar (be sure the menu item **View, Image Toolbar** is checked). The mouse pointer then turns into an image of a pencil eraser—simply click on the opaque color in the image. It will then become transparent, and the background will shine through. Hint: If the Make Transparent icon is not available on the image toolbar ("ghosted"), be sure the image has been selected by left-clicking the pointer on it once. If the Make Transparent icon is still disabled, the image is probably not in GIF format. Correct this in **Image Properties**, as described earlier.

Transparency Truth

Transparencies only work well with images with large amounts of "blank" space, which is all one color. Therefore, when we are creating or modifying our own images in an image processing application such as Microsoft Image Composer or Adobe Photoshop, we must remember to use one particular color in any place that should become transparent.

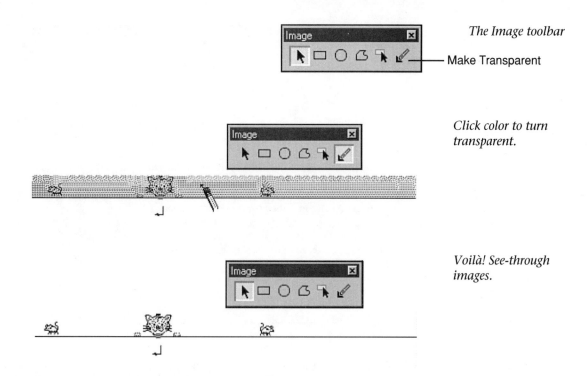

The Image toolbar

Make Transparent

Click color to turn transparent.

Voilà! See-through images.

(The Art of) Creative Artistry

Considering the plethora of image alignment options, text alignment options, and so forth, it's hard to believe that Web pages have any layout restrictions. Earlier in this book, though, it was alleged that there were numerous degree-of-freedom constraints in Web page layout. That remains true, in-so-far as we cannot simply plop any image or textual passage anywhere on the page. However, by using some creative command of the subtle layout options for text and images, we can increase our layout freedom.

Let's consider a couple "tricks of the trade" to achieve fanciful layouts: wrapping a paragraph around an image and using tables to create a flexible layout structure.

The Wrap-Around

Consider the common newsletter/magazine layout style, wherein a paragraph of text "flows" around an inset picture. It might look something like this:

Like a gentle brook, the paragraph flows around the banks of the inset image.

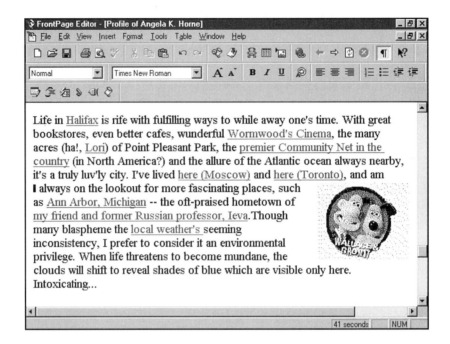

To create this wrap-around effect, we'd use the following steps:

1. Locate the FrontPage Editor cursor in the spot where the text paragraph should begin. At this point, either type in the text, or insert it from an external file (**Insert, File**). If the external file is a plain text file (.txt), choose **Normal Paragraphs** as the formatting option when the Convert Text window pops up.

2. Locate the exact spot within the text where the image should reside. This may be at the end of a sentence, or the end of a single word within a sentence, whatever is most appropriate. Click that spot to locate the FrontPage Editor cursor there. Do not include an extra space; e.g., if we want the image to be inserted following the word "dog," locate the FrontPage Editor cursor in the space immediately following the "g" in "dog."

3. Insert the image, either via the image toolbar, or the menu item **Insert**, **Image**. Once the image has appeared, right-click it and select **Image Properties** from the pop-up menu. Then click the **Appearance** tab of the Image Properties window.

4. In the **Layout** area of the **Image Properties** window, select either a **Left** or **Right** alignment, depending upon which way the paragraph should wrap. If the image should appear on the right side of the page, with the text flowing around its left side, select a **Right** alignment. And vice versa.

5. Now make any final adjustments, such as adjusting the **Horiztonal** or **Vertical Spacing** properties of the image, to determine how much of a gap to leave between the image and the wrapped paragraph.

In our sample home page, we've used a variation on the above trick to align a bulleted list to the left of a lighthouse image. While the text doesn't wrap above or below the image, we've still used the **Right** alignment setting in the lighthouse's Image Properties to keep the bulleted list to the left.

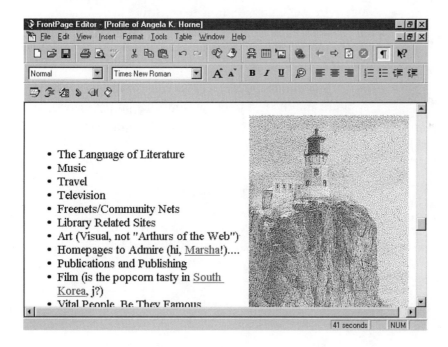

A bulleted list beside a lighthouse image. We've set the lighthouse to be right-aligned with respect to the text, as defined in its Image Properties.

Table Tricks

Sometimes, when we just can't figure out how to layout several elements the way we want, a table might be the answer. Although we've previously looked at the table in the traditional manner—a textual way of laying out information—the table can also be seen as a layout tool.

Consider that when we make a table on a Web page, we're essentially creating a custom bounded area, within which we can layout elements with certain freedoms. For instance, consider a simple example, albeit one without any graphics at all. Remember when we discussed the left and right text alignment tools, there was no way to left-align one phrase of text, while right-aligning another phrase, with both residing on the same horizontal plane; for example,

Some text here   Some more text here

Using a table, we *can* achieve this effect. Simply create a one-row, two-column table (see Chapter 9, "On the Table," for a refresher course on how to construct tables). Then, in the Table Properties, be sure that the table has a width of 100%, that it is left-aligned, and that it has a border size of 0 pixels.

Next, type in the text to appear left-justified in the first column, and the text to be right-justified in the second column. Right-click each cell to adjust its **Cell Properties**, and set the first column's cell to be left-aligned, and the second column's cell to be right-aligned. Ta-da! Because the border size has been set to 0 pixels, the reader doesn't even realize this is a table. Impressive! We can apply any fashion to text within a table cell that we can to regular text, allowing us to use colors or fonts, or even make these cells into hyperlinks (simply highlight the text in the cell, and select the menu item **Insert, Hyperlink**).

Check This Out...

Image Precision

Because images can also be placed into a table cell, we can use a table structure to layout the placement of images with more precision than when inserting them directly onto the page. For instance, we could create a table of one row and five columns which is the width of 75% of the page, and a border size of zero pixels. Then, images can be placed in certain cells, allowing us to place images on the page with increased precision. The widths of individual blank cells ("padding") could be adjusted to nudge the cells with images.

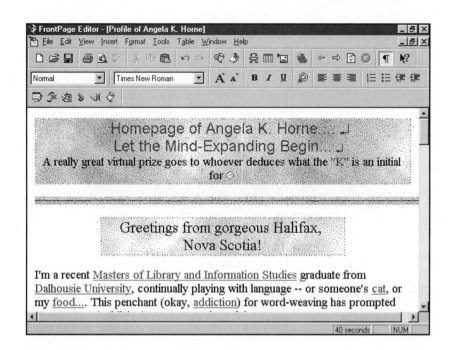

*Using borderless
tables to create a
standout heading.*

To create these headings, which stand out from the background texture, we simply
created a one-by-one table, which contained the text of the heading. Then, we configured
the Table Properties to contain a background image of our choice, with a border size of
zero pixels. Voilà! Ici! Comme ci comme ca! Note, however, that at the time of writing,
Microsoft Internet Explorer is the only Web browser which can display background
images within a table. However, both Internet Explorer and Netscape Navigator do
support background colors within cells and tables, so we could still use this trick to make
text standout, by using a different background color for the table.

Mapmaker, Mapmaker, Make Me an Image Map

Image maps have become an increasingly common design element for Web authors. They
can add to the aesthetic experience of navigating a Web page, or they can be a waste of
time. First, let's consider what an image map is.

An image with multiple, clickable "hotspots." Each hot spot is a hyperlink.

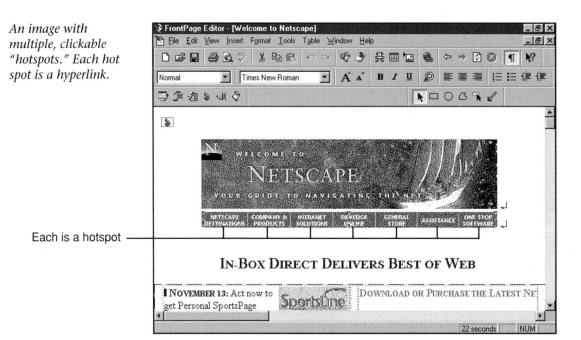

Each is a hotspot ——

While the above is one graphic image, it's been designed to invite the reader to believe that clicking different portions of the picture would yield different results. For instance, if the reader clicks on the portion of the image which reads, "Company & Products," they'll be taken to the Company & Product Information page. In short, this image contains multiple hyperlinks, each bound to a different portion of the image.

Toolbar Time: The Image Toolbar

When designing an image map, we define "hotspots" (a region within the image which stands as its own hyperlink). If the reader clicks within that region, or hotspot, the defined hyperlink will be followed. Image maps have become a popular way of simulating navigation toolbars or graphical "menus" on Web pages. Creating one with the FrontPage Editor is quite easy, in fact.

Imagine that we've inserted the image pictured earlier into our Web page. The image was a typical GIF or JPEG file, which we created in an image processing application, such as Microsoft Image Composer. First, be sure the Image Toolbar is in view, by enabling it under the menu item **View, Image Toolbar**.

➤ The arrow pointer is used to select a whole image on the Web page. Once selected, we can resize it by dragging the sizing handles, or copy/paste/cut it. We must also select an image before applying the other image toolbar functions to it.

➤ After selecting this rectangle icon, left-click the image and drag the pointer to define a rectangular hyperlink area within the image.

➤ Use this circular icon to define a circular hyperlink area within the image.

➤ The polygon icon allows us to define a custom-shaped hyperlink area within the image. Left-click on the image to anchor the first side of the polygon, let go of the left mouse button and drag the mouse to another anchor in the ploygon shape. Click the left mouse button to anchor the line, then let go and drag to the next anchor point. Repeat until you've drawn a polygon and have returned to the original anchor point. This process takes some practice.

➤ To select a hotspot or hyperlinked region within this image, use this icon. Once a hotspot is selected, its hyperlink can be altered by right-clicking the hotspot and selecting **Image Hotspot Properties** from the pop-up menu. Pressing the Delete key on the keyboard with a hotspot selected will remove that hotspot from the image.

➤ This icon is used to define a transparent color in a GIF image, as described earlier in this chapter.

Forming the Hotspot

We must now decide whether our first hotspot region is best bounded with a rectangle, circle, or free-form shape. In the image we're using, each region is designed in a rectangular manner, so we can use a rectangle to define each hotspot. Simply click the rectangle tool on the image toolbar, and then drag the mouse pointer over to the image. Left-click the image wherever one corner of the boundary should be, and then drag the visual rectangle to encompass the desired hotspot region. Once we let go of the left mouse button, a Create Hyperlink window will appear, with which we can create the hyperlink for this graphical region, just as we did when creating text hyperlinks in Chapter 7, "Friendly Forms."

After defining the hotspot region in the image, the familiar Create Hyperlink window appears, where we set the destination link for this hotspot.

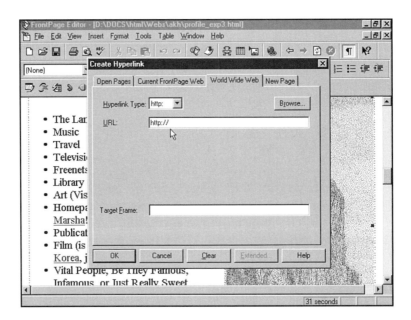

Should we choose to use the polygon tool in the image toolbar, we can define any free-form shape. Simply click the left mouse button on a variety of points that bound the desired hotspot region, and lines will appear, thereby "connecting the dots." We continue doing this until the entire hotspot region has been bounded, and when we click on the point we began with, thus closing the polygon, the Create Hyperlink window will appear.

Using the polygon tool to define a free-form hotspot.

Left-click to create free-form boundary

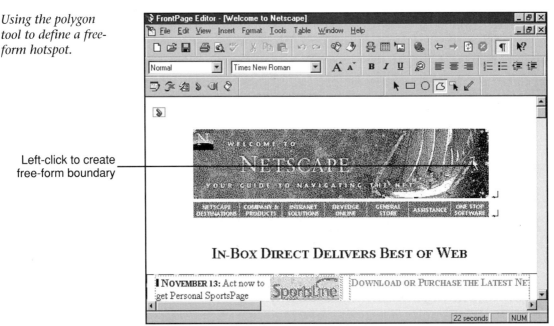

Image Map Ethics

Although image maps are a nice touch, you should never rely on them solely. If, for instance, we use an image map as a navigational tool, be sure to provide those same hyperlinks in text form somewhere on the page (either directly below the image map, or at the bottom of the Web page). Not all users can or wish to see graphics, and not all browsers support image maps (although, yes, Internet Explorer and Netscape Navigator do support image maps). Providing no alternative hyperlinks to the image map is considered poor Web design.

Of course, the boundaries defining each hot spot only appear in the FrontPage Editor for our sake; the reader will not see them in his Web browser. It's up to the design of the image to communicate which regions will lead to which pages.

Recall from Chapter 4, "Discovering the Explorer," we looked at the Tools, Web Settings menu item in the FrontPage Explorer. There was a tab labelled **Advanced**, under which we defined the behavior of image maps. Be sure that setting is configured properly (as explained in Chapter 4) for these image maps to function properly on our Web page.

The Least You Need to Know

Placing an image on the Web page is the easy part; simply select the menu item **Insert**, **Image** or click the Insert Image icon on the toolbar. It's what happens behind the scenes that really matters.

➤ Although we can import many image file formats, the FrontPage Editor will convert them into either a GIF or JPEG. When saving the Web page in the FrontPage Editor, we should answer **Yes** when it asks whether to save the image into our current Web.

➤ We should always define a meaningful alternative text representation for the image, found in the Image Properties window (right-click on the image, select from pop-up menu). This allows readers without graphics enabled to have a sense of what the image's purpose was.

➤ Always specify a size for the image, in the **Appearance** tab of the **Image Properties** window. Whether we choose to scale the image or not, defining its dimensions helps the browser layout the page more quickly for the reader.

➤ A transparent GIF contains one color which is invisible, thereby allowing the background to show through. JPEG format images cannot contain transparency. To make a portion of an image transparent, be sure it is set to GIF (**Image Properties**), and then select the **Make Transparent** icon on the image toolbar. Click on the color within the image to become transparent.

➤ Placing text and images within cells of a table can provide more flexible layout options. Be creative.

➤ Use the Rectangle, Circle, or Polygon icons in the image toolbar to define hotspots within an image. Each hotspot can then be defined as a hyperlink, thus creating an image map. Always provide alternative text hyperlinks in case the reader cannot use the image map.

Chapter 14

...Action! Movie Magic!

In This Chapter

➤ An abridged history of motion pictures

➤ The spinning GIF

➤ AVI video Vérité

➤ It sure is quiet...*too* quiet

As the story goes, the first time a motion picture was played to an audience, they ducked when the train steamed toward the camera. Whether or not that actually happened, it seems that people are still fascinated by moving pictures. Perhaps because they match our daily perceptual experience more closely than still pictures, and thus carry a greater perception of reality. In any case, moving images are still somewhat rare on Web pages, but in this chapter, we'll look at how to incorporate some modest animation into our Web pages. (Modest is the key word here.)

For the Love of Movies

As Web pages have become increasingly complex and capable in their presentation of content, the tools available to the Web designer have multiplied in kind. From text alone, to frames, to images, Web pages can either deliver content in meaningfully improved ways, or become an even harsher attack on the senses. Moving images, also known as animation or videos, can contribute to both ends.

If a picture *is* worth a thousand bytes, or several thousand bytes as is more commonly the case, a moving image is worth several times that. Which is a problem. The amount of data required to represent a small, several-second long video can reach into the hundreds of kilobytes, and usually megabytes. This makes most videos unfit for Web pages, because most Internet connections cannot transfer data fast enough to make such videos worthwhile.

Therefore, only two types of animation formats are directly supported by the FrontPage Editor: animated GIF files and AVI video files. ("Directly" means that these animations are displayed within the Web page itself.) However, implementing each type of animation is slightly different.

Common Video Formats Found in the Wild

As with still picture images, there are a variety of file formats used for storing videos. Common formats include:

➤ **AVI**   Video for Windows, the most common format for videos played in Windows 95.

➤ **MPEG**   The most common cross-platform format for videos.

➤ **MOV**   QuickTime video format, created and supported by Apple computers, can also be played on Windows computers with proper QuickTime software.

➤ **GIF (89a)**   Not a "true" video format, but it can be used to store moving images. Commonly used for small animations found on most Web pages.

Most AVI, MPEG, and MOV videos are very large files, and thus not suitable for appearing within Web pages. Although one could create hyperlinks that point to these types of files, the Web user would need the appropriate viewing software, and the connection speed to download them quickly (otherwise the user would wait a long time). AVI files can be played within a Web page by Microsoft Internet Explorer, and both Explorer and Netscape Navigator can play GIF (89a) animations within the Web page.

The Many Faces of GIF

As stated, because moving images require lots of data, most animations on contemporary Web pages are rather brief—perhaps a twinkling star, or a spinning arrow. Anything more complex would take too long to download.

The GIF image format, while traditionally used to represent a single image, can contain several images (see Chapter 13 "Lights, Camera, Multimedia!" for a refresher on GIF). A GIF file that contains more than one image is known as an *animated GIF*. These animated GIFs can either be found in clip art collections, or they can be created in image processing applications.

Inserting an animated GIF into our Web page is, in fact, exactly the same as inserting a typical single image GIF. The procedures described in Chapter 13 apply in just the same way. In fact, neither the FrontPage Editor nor the Web browser considers the animated GIF to be any different than a single image GIF. It can be aligned in the same ways as a still image, it can be made to have transparent portions, and so forth. Of course, the animated GIF won't *appear* animated in the FrontPage Editor—you'll have to preview the page in a real Web browser to see the GIF dance on its toes.

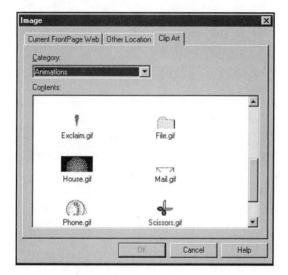

FrontPage includes a small set of animated GIFs in the Clip Art gallery under the category heading "Animations." In real life (as opposed to this printed page), these images would be animated.

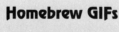

Homebrew GIFs

If creating an animated GIF using image processing software, be sure to save it in "GIF89a" format, which is the necessary variant of GIF for saving multiple images into one file. The older GIF87 format cannot be used to create animated GIFs. Although most modern software will automatically default to GIF89a format, this point is worth keeping in mind in case a GIF doesn't seem to animate.

When the reader's Web browser loads the animated GIF, it will simply cycle through each frame of the GIF. By creating a clever series of images, such as an arrow that changes position slightly in each frame, the image appears to be animated in the Web browser.

Animation doesn't print very well, but in real-life, some images in this Web page would be animated.

Spinning

Moving

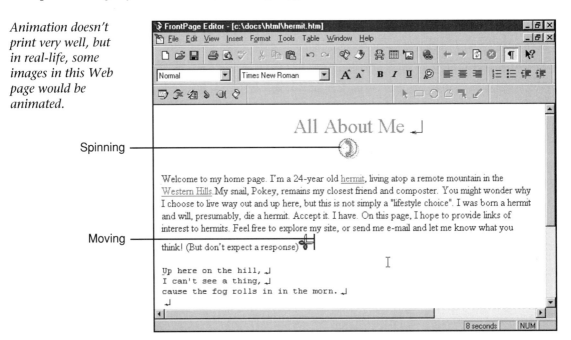

While it is a simple way to insert small bits of movement into a Web page, the animated GIF does have its drawbacks. There is no way to control how it is played by the browser; it cycles repeatedly, forever, until the reader moves to another Web page. A more advanced video format for Web pages is the AVI animation...

One Step Forward, One Step Back: AVI Animation

The AVI format is also known as "Video for Windows." It's a full-fledged video format, which can be used to store anything from brief animation to television-like video with sound. Of course, the latter would require large amounts of disk space, and thus has no place on a Web page. (Consider, for instance, one of the AVI demonstration videos included with the Windows 95 CD. A four minute music video by the band Weezer, the AVI file that contains the graphics and sound is 30 megabytes in size! On a 28.8kbps Internet connection, such a file would take at least five hours to download).

However, daunting as the above may seem, a very brief, small AVI animation could reside in just a few kilobytes. A small arrow bobbing up and down might take up 5K—just a few seconds to download. With the FrontPage Editor, we can insert AVI animations (whatever their size) into our Web page.

Bobbing for Arrows

Imagine, for instance, that we do want to insert the arrow that bobs up and down. We've acquired that particular AVI from a collection of free animations offered on someone else's Web site. We'll then create a text hyperlink adjacent to the video, thereby using the video as an attention getter for that particular hyperlink.

We begin by selecting the FrontPage Editor menu item **Insert, Video**. Using the now-familiar file browser, we either select the AVI file from within our current Web site, or from another location. A small box then appears on our Web page, representing where the AVI video will be played.

The FrontPage Editor cannot animate the video within the editing canvas, and so the box shape is used as a placeholder (another lack of true WYSIWYG implementation). We may now configure certain characteristics of how the AVI video will play. Right-click the AVI placeholder and select **Image Properties** from the pop-up menu.

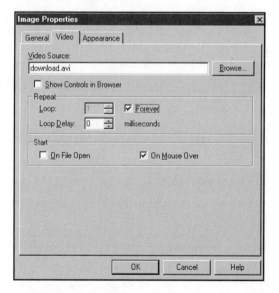

Configuring how the AVI video will play. Let it roll...

If we enable the property **Show Controls in Browser**, then clickable buttons will appear on our Web page that allow the reader to control the play of the video. The reader could then stop, pause, play, or position the video at any point they want. Disabling this property will leave video playback entirely up to our settings. Note that if we decide to enable the playback controls, they will only appear if the video image is wide enough to accommodate them. For our bobbing-arrow example, we will not enable the **Show Controls in Browser** property.

The Repeat properties box allows us to select how many times the video should **Loop**, and how long of a Loop Delay to allow before re-playing the video. Enabling **Forever** will loop the video indefinitely. We'll select **Forever**, which combines well with the next option.

Lastly, we can configure when to start the video playback. **On File Open** causes the video playback to begin immediately once the AVI file has been downloaded by the Web browser. **On Mouse Over** will start playing the video anytime the reader's mouse pointer passes over it; the video stops playing once the mouse pointer moves away. This can be a nice way to use the video as an attention getter—a sort of, "Hey, look at me" whenever the reader wanders by it. In fact, we'll enable **On Mouse Over** for our example. Because we've told the video to loop **Forever**, it will loop as long as the mouse pointer stays over it.

After clicking **OK**, the video playback is now configured. We click the FrontPage Editor cursor to the right of the video placeholder, and enter text for our hyperlink: **Click here to see What's New in our Product Line.** We configure that hyperlink as usual (highlight and select **Insert, Hyperlink**), and that's that.

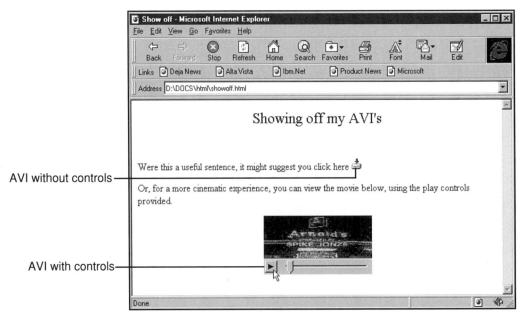

AVI without controls

AVI with controls

Browser-Friendly Animation

In many respects, our AVI example could have been done just as easily using an animated GIF instead. Of course, using the GIF we wouldn't have been able to control playback. However, the animated GIF has one quality that the AVI doesn't: cross-browser compatibility. At this writing, only Microsoft Internet Explorer supports playback of AVI's within the Web page. However, both Internet Explorer, Netscape Navigator, and other Web browsers support playing animated GIFs. Thus, what we lose in GIF configurability, we gain in a wider audience. And vice versa. Life's full of tradeoffs that way.

Gimme a Beat!

All right, so we've covered text, and still images, and moving images. The eyes are happy. But the ears feel so left out. To be fair, we did look at inserting a background sound to the Web page in Chapter 10, "Behind the Scenes—Page Properties."

How, though, to add sounds to other interactions? For instance, perhaps we want to play a certain sound when a reader clicks a button, or a hyperlink, or an imagemap. All very reasonable requests—with one minor problem: there's no basic way to do so.

Text and images were straightforward, because the FrontPage Editor provided simple ways to add them, via menu items. Interactive sounds, however, are a more complicated game. A game we will learn, fortunately, when we learn how to construct scripts in Chapter 18 "Pump Up Your Page: Plug-Ins and WebBots."

The Least You Need to Know

We finish up our chapter on visual multimedia with a look a little teeny animations which can add pockets of zest to any Web page. Shaken, *and* stirred.

➤ Due to the large file size of any substantial animation, only small animations are suitable for Web pages.

➤ The FrontPage Editor can insert either GIF or AVI animations on a Web page.

➤ Animated GIFs are inserted in exactly the same way as non-animated GIFs. There is no way to configure their playback.

➤ The Video for Windows file format, or AVI, can be inserted directly into a Web page using the FrontPage Editor menu **Insert, Video**. We can then configure its playback, such as how often to loop, and when to start and stop.

➤ Although it is less configurable, the animated GIF is supported by more Web browsers than AVI.

191

Chapter 15

How to Make Friends and Impress Enemies: ActiveX

In This Chapter

➤ Meet ActiveX

➤ Control-ling our Web pages

➤ Button Up

➤ I spy with my little eye—more controls!

➤ Legal Consulting (please remit $200/hour to cashier)

If this book were a sort of therapy, which it is not on account of lack of qualifications and several federal and local laws, the next three chapters would represent what is commonly touted as a "breakthrough." To this point, we've looked at designing Web pages using the tools that are made available, and are directly supported by, FrontPage 97. Now, though, we're ready to expand our focus. By incorporating premade modules of computer code into our Web pages, we can greatly expand their functionality. In this chapter, we'll take a look at the opportunities available to us by using ActiveX technology to break the Web page possibilities wide open. By and large, however, this is not a thorough tutorial on ActiveX itself—that would require a book in and of itself. Rather, our focus is on ActiveX using with FrontPage 97.

The Skinny on ActiveX

As a child, before it was unanimously agreed upon that I was irreparably mechanically inept, family members would gift me with boy-appropriate construction toys, such as the infamous Erector Set. Full of youthful optimism, I'd build a variety of minor creations, none of which would have contributed to a promising civil engineer's portfolio, but were mine nonetheless, in their skeletal way. Ambitions grew, and I set my sights higher. I wanted my crane arm to *move*. Without the know-how to build my own motor from scratch, there was little I could do — that is, until I found out about the motor kit add-on!

ActiveX can be broadly defined as the motor-kit add-on for Web page design. Not because of the motor analogy, per se, but rather because ActiveX provides the opportunity to add premade components to our Web page. These components come ready-to-work at a variety of tasks, just as the Erector Set motor kit was a ready-to-install motor. As Web page designers, we still retain some say in how to configure the ActiveX add-on, just as I still had to decide where and how to connect my motor kit; but the bulk of the job comes pre-packaged.

ActiveX components are called *controls*, and an ActiveX control is a computer program which we download and install on our computer. For instance, there might be an ActiveX control which allows us to scroll a text message in a horizontal fashion. By installing that control on our computer, we can then incorporate its capabilities into our Web page.

When a visitor comes knocking on our Web page, their browser will notice that we've used an ActiveX control. It will then check to see if they have the same control installed on their computer. If not, it will automatically be downloaded and installed for them, so that viewing the Web page may proceed. Of course, this raises some security and copyright issues, which we'll address towards the end of the chapter.

Additionally, using more advanced techniques, we can cajole ActiveX controls into interacting with each other, or other events on the page, depending on reader activity. This is the stuff of Chapter 18, "Pump Up Your Page: Plug-Ins and WebBots," but it begins with controls

There are many ActiveX controls available for our use, and their capabilities are wide ranging. They vary from small and simple enhancements, such as more attractive form fields, to complex functions, such as sending an e-mail message to a mail server. We'll look at some simple controls in this chapter, which are included with FrontPage 97 and Microsoft's Internet Explorer, and close with an overview of where to find other ActiveX controls on the Internet.

One important caveat before we proceed: As of this writing, the only Web browser which supports viewing pages with ActiveX controls is Microsoft Internet Explorer. However, after some initial hesitation, Netscape recently announced support for ActiveX controls in an upcoming update to Netscape Navigator. Perhaps, by the time you read this, a version of Netscape Navigator greater than 3.0 will support ActiveX.

Adding the Motor: Inserting a Control

Behind-the-scenes, when FrontPage and Internet Explorer were installed, a set of ActiveX controls were also installed. These make up the base set of controls which are provided by Microsoft, and owned by anyone who is using the Internet Explorer as their Web browser. We'll focus on these controls for our examples, although the concept and process behind using any control is the same, even if we obtained it later from some other source (as explained in "Sniffing Out Controls" near the end of this chapter

Some of the simpler controls mainly provide us with aesthetic options. This is a good place to start, because once we understand the concept and procedure behind inserting ActiveX controls, the basic rules apply to any control, however complex. Let's imagine that we're creating a page which allows the user to try different combinations of background and foreground colors. When we're done, the page will offer a series of buttons, one row representing background colors, and one row representing foreground colors. We'll start building this page slowly.

Thus far, our page contains only the design elements which we've learned so far, but the active parts—the selections of colors and the buttons—we'll start building in this chapter.

Properties Aplenty

Recall that we looked at creating a button in a form in Chapter 7 "Friendly Forms," but this time, we'll use an ActiveX control to create the button. To create our button, we first position the FrontPage Editor cursor at the desired location. Although we haven't created the color selection menus yet, we'll plop the button further down the page, and insert our other controls later.

Now, we begin the process with the FrontPage Editor in one of two ways:

➤ Choose the menu item **Insert, Other Components, ActiveX Control**

 ➤ Select the ActiveX icon from the Advanced Toolbar)

Either option will yield the ActiveX Control Properties window, within which we click the **Pick Control** arrow, to select our desired control.

Each computer will have a differing set of available ActiveX controls, depending on which software applications have been installed. We're most interested in those controls whose names are preceded with "Microsoft Forms 2.0," because these controls were installed with FrontPage and/or Internet Explorer. In the future, however, we'll want to select whichever control we desire, and whichever control we know how to use.

195

Locating the spot where our ActiveX control will live.

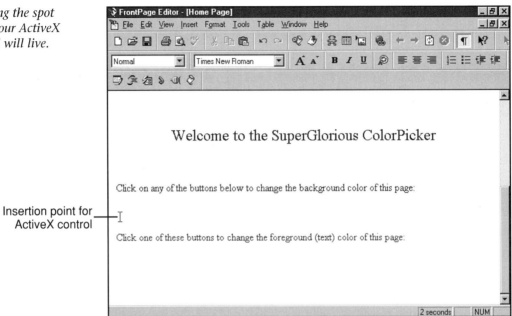

Insertion point for ActiveX control

List of available ActiveX controls to choose from, mmmmm, good.

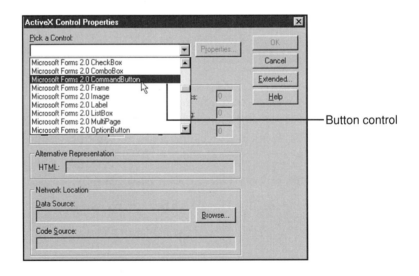

Button control

To create the clickable button, we select the control named **Microsoft Forms 2.0 CommandButton**. Now, we are entitled to a number of configurable properties for this control.

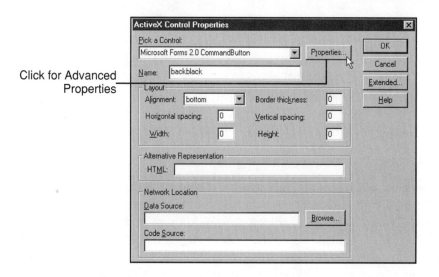

Click for Advanced
Properties

A cornucopia of properties to configure for our ActiveX control. "Have it your way!"

For the **Name** field, we may enter an internal name for this control. This name will not appear to the reader, but will be used to reference this control in any scripts we create later on (Chapter 16 "The Art of the Script," specifically). We'll call this control *backblack*, because it will be clicked by the reader to change the background color of the page to black.

The Layout Properties should seem familiar by now; they are the same as those available when inserting an image onto the page (see Chapter 13 "Lights, Camera, Multimedia!"). **Alignment**, **Border Thickness**, **Horizontal** and **Vertical Spacing** all work in the same way as when inserting an image. The Width and Height properties determine the visual dimensions of the control. Depending upon the control, we might leave these properties unset. For now, we'll only set the **Horizontal Spacing** to 3 pixels, to leave some space between adjacent buttons. We can tweak these later, if necessary, for improved layout. Keep in mind that only some controls are graphical, and, obviously, these properties are less effective for controls which don't actually appear. (For instance, our commandbutton is graphical, and so layout properties may apply; on the other hand, a control which communicated with a POP mail server may not have any graphical representation; it's actions work within a script created for it.)

For the sake of readers whose Web browsers don't support ActiveX controls, we're asked to enter Alternative Representation HTML tags to display. However, because we're not learning direct HTML tags in this book, we may need to leave this property blank. Of course, readers who are familiar with HTML tags may insert any alternatives to the control in this property.

In the Network Location properties section, we may configure certain pointers to external files. For instance, some ActiveX controls require data from an external source. Consider the Marquee control (named MarqueeCtl in the list of controls), which displays a scrolling message on the Web page. The control needs to know what message to scroll. Thus, we'd enter the location of the filename whose contents to scroll in the Data Source property. We can enter the filename either as a file path on the same machine as the Web page (for example, c:\docs\message.html) or as a URL (http://www.server.com/~me/message.html), depending on where the file resides. The commandbutton control doesn't require any external data, so we can leave this property blank.

The Code Source property allows us to define where the computer code for this ActiveX control resides. This way, if the reader of the page does not have the control already installed, the browser knows where to download it from. In many cases we might not know the URL of the original control. Fortunately, most standard controls have their default location built in, so even if we leave this property blank, the reader's browser may still be able to locate the control. However, when using new controls obtained from other sources, it's a good idea to see if they include any documentation about their code source, allowing us to properly fill in this property. Because the commandbutton is a standard Microsoft control, we don't need to specify the code source.

Customize that Control!

Perhaps the above seemed easy. *Too* easy. True enough, these properties are only the beginning, and less influential, in some senses. To *really* configure the ActiveX Control, we must forge ahead to its advanced properties, available by clicking the **Properties** button which is beside the Pick Control menu at the top of the **ActiveX Control Properties** window

After some thrashing about of the hard drive, two new windows pop up: **Edit ActiveX Control** and **Properties**.

First, let's turn our attention to the **Edit ActiveX Control** window. Here, we see a graphical representation of the control; in this case, it's a typical button. (Which makes sense, since we're inserting a commandbutton control!) Despite more advanced appearances, there are basically two modifications we can make using this window. If we click once on the control, it becomes active, with handles on each side.

Although we can move the entire control to a different location within the window, it's not advised to do so—repositioning the control in this manner doesn't seem to affect where it ultimately winds up on the Web page. However, if we click a second time on the control (that is, one click after it's already been selected), a cursor appears, allowing us to enter a text caption. This caption appears on the face of the button, so we should enter something meaningful, such as, "Click here to change colors." Don't worry if the text is wider than the control, we'll fix that in a moment.

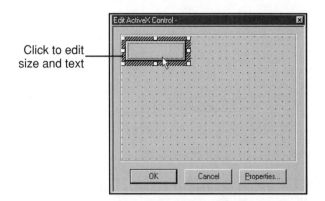

Click to edit
size and text

*The real deal;
configuring the
precise properties of
this ActiveX control.*

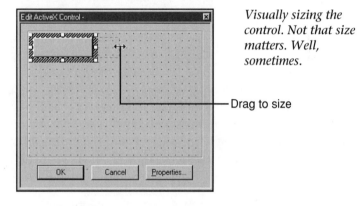

*Visually sizing the
control. Not that size
matters. Well,
sometimes.*

Drag to size

Don't Move That Control!

The **Edit ActiveX Control** window contains a small grid pattern, in which the control appears. Everything about this window implies that we can select the control and reposition it within the window. And we *can* do so—but it doesn't change anything about where the control winds up on the page. What's going on?

Placement of the control on the page is determined by the standard factors which apply to all page elements—alignment settings and the like. The presence of the tempting grid seems to be a holdover from another Microsoft application—the ActiveX Control Pad (freely available from the Microsoft Web site)—which contains a special control known as the "HTML Layout Control." That control allows us to specifically position several controls within a grid—however, the HTML Layout Control is not directly supported in the FrontPage 97 Editor. Thus, the grid is a vestige, like the human appendix, which doesn't truly serve a function. Like the appendix, it's best not to play with it.

Custom Control Properties

Having exhausted the usefulness of the Edit ActiveX Control window, we now turn to the **Properties** window.

The many technical properties which apply to this control. Some are more obvious than others. When in doubt, leave it out.

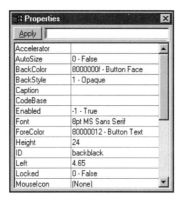

The **Properties** window consists of two columns, the left-hand listing property names, and the right-hand listing each associated value. For instance, the second property listed for this commandbutton control is named Autosize, and looking to its right, we see its value set to 0 - False. This means that the button will not automatically adjust its size to fit the caption we've defined. If we click anywhere on the Autosize row, it becomes highlighted, and its value appears in the entry at the top of the window, beside Apply.

Modifying the value of a property for this control.

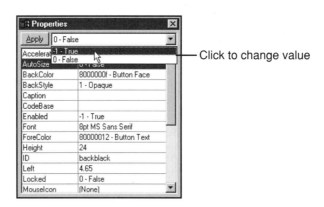

— Click to change value

If we click on the down-arrow, as pictured above, a list of other possible values appears. In this case, only two possible values exist for this property: True and False. We'll select True, thus allowing this commandbutton to automatically change size to fit the caption.

200

Let's take a tour of several more properties for this control:

➤ **BackColor**   The background color of the button, we can either select a different color style from the drop-down list, or click the ellipses which appear to the right of the drop-down list to select a custom color from a palette.

➤ **BackStyle**   The background style of the button, either opaque or transparent.

➤ **Caption**   The text to appear on the face of the button. If we enter new text beside the Apply button, we should be sure to click the **Apply** button to make the new value take effect. Entering a caption via this property is exactly the same as entering it directly onto the button in the Edit ActiveX Control window.

➤ **Font**   The font style in which to display the caption. Click the ellipses to the right of the value entry area to select a different font.

➤ **ID**   The name of the control, as we specified earlier in the ActiveX Control Properties window.

So Many Properties!

Clearly, there are quite a number of properties. Furthermore, each control has its own set of properties, some of which are common from control to control, others which are specific to a particular control. While some of the properties define obvious characteristics, such as Font and BackColor, some are less obvious. Because there are so many properties, and so many controls, we can't list the meaning of each one in this book—that would require a book solely dedicated to the topic of ActiveX. Specifications for each of the Microsoft controls can be obtained through the Microsoft Web site (http://www.microsoft.com) which contains an ActiveX Control Gallery, including property definitions for each control.

In this case, other than the AutoSize property, we'll leave the others alone, and click **OK** in the Edit ActiveX Control window to close both it and the Properties window.

We can now hit **OK** on the initial ActiveX Control Properties window, and return to the FrontPage Editor. It will display the control on our Web page within the Editor—of course, to see the control in action, we'd need to preview the page in a real Web browser (one which supports ActiveX controls!).

ActiveX control ——

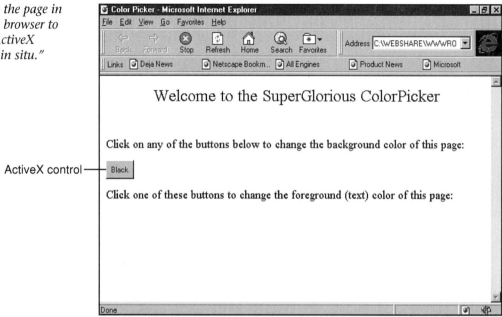

Cranking Out some Examples

Now, we'd like to create four more of these commandbuttons to complete the background color choices: one for White, Red, Blue, and Green. Thus, we position the immediate cursor to the right of the ActiveX control placeholder in the FrontPage Editor, and repeat the previous procedure, inserting another commandbutton control. For each control, we want to modify the property Name, to reflect our naming scheme, such as *backwhite* for white, *backred* for red, and so on. We also need to modify the advanced property Caption to reflect the correct color name on the face of the button.

Not to sound repetitive, but now we need to create another set of five commandbuttons to represent the foreground color options. Obviously, this example is somewhat poorly designed from an efficiency point of view (why not design an interface with drop down lists and fewer buttons?), but this is done purposefully to highlight the use of ActiveX controls. After creating another row of commandbuttons, each appropriately Named and Captioned (*foreblack/Black, forewhite/White, and so on*), our page has advanced to this minor masterpiece, when viewed in the Web browser:

Of course, as moderately attractive as our current page looks, it doesn't actually *do* anything yet. Sure, we could (and should) load it into our Web browser, but clicking the buttons doesn't yield any results. To cajole the control into *doing* something—interacting in some way—we must employ scripting. Scripts are behind-the-scenes elements of a Web page which instruct various elements of the page, including ActiveX controls, how to behave and when to act. Thus, we explore the truth about scripts in the following chapter, where we'll make this page come to life.

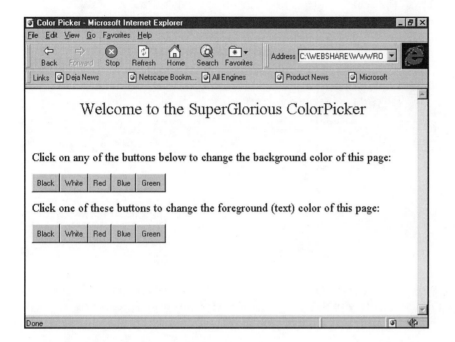

Page o' many buttons, each one an ActiveX control.

Sniffing Out Controls

Because ActiveX controls are self-contained computer programs, they can be created by any individual with the proper know-how (that is, the ability to write computer programs). Many companies create and sell or distribute ActiveX controls suited for a variety of tasks.

Microsoft, of course, is a major supplier of ActiveX controls, and their offerings are available from Microsoft's ActiveX Control Gallery, available at their Web site. The simplest way to find the Gallery is to open the Microsoft web page, at **http://www. microsoft.com**, and enter the **Products** area, where ActiveX is listed. This will lead to the Gallery.

Viewing a demonstration of any control in the gallery will automatically download and install the control onto our own computer. Therefore, if we've seen a control we like — we've already acquired it! Of course, by the same logic, if we see a control that doesn't inspire us, we've already acquired that one, too.

*The Microsoft
ActiveX Control
Gallery; one stop
"shopping" (actually,
the controls are free).*

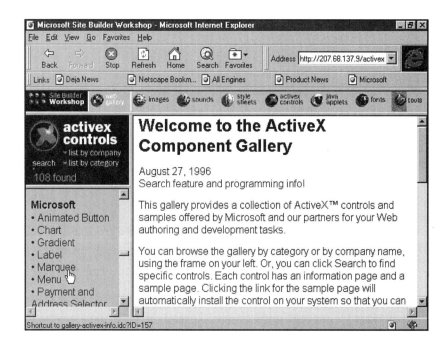

CNet, a major presence on the information Web that offers software, news, and reviews, has also set up an ActiveX gallery of its own, including controls from Microsoft and many other companies. Find it at **http://www.activex.com**.

Ideally (and necessarily), the creator and distributor of the control should provide the necessary information on its properties and their effects, as we encountered when configuring the advanced control properties earlier in this chapter.

Advanced Discourse: Out Damned Control!

While installing ActiveX controls onto our computer is a nicely automatic process, removing them is quite a bit less so. The following is a general guideline for removing controls, which may not apply to every control. In such cases, contact the creator of the control for further help.

Most controls are installed into the directory C:\WINDOWS\OCCACHE, and their filenames end in the suffix .OCX. However, do not merely delete the file from this directory to delete the control. Because the controls are registered with the Windows 95 registry, removing a control requires us to unregister it. To do so, we use the program named regsvr32, which was installed into the directory C:\WINDOWS\SYSTEM with Windows 95.

Thus, to remove a control from our system, we'd need to execute the following sort of command from the MS-DOS shell:

regsvr32 /u controlname.ocx

Depending on our path and the global paths specified on our computer, we might need to use more explicit paths for the above command, as in:

c:\windows\system\regsvr32 /u c:\windows\occache\controlname.ocx

Messy looking, but as of this writing, it's the only way to remove ActiveX controls from one's machine.

Security, Copyrights, Licenses, and All the Fuss

Because ActiveX controls are programs which execute on our own computer, potential security issues arise. Microsoft's resolution to this has been to implement what they call "Authenticode" technology, which is a form of encrypted digital signatures.

In brief, when the creator of the ActiveX control is ready to distribute it, he or she "digitally signs" it with a specially encrypted code. If anyone should tamper with the control, such as trying to infect it with a virus, the signature becomes invalid. When the reader's Web browser attempts to download a control, it checks the signature for validity, and if it has any doubt, it can either prompt the user whether to continue downloading the control, or automatically abort downloading the control. (Microsoft Internet Explorer is configured by default to abort downloads of any control which has an unverifiable signature, although the user can override this security setting if he desires.)

Although there is some debate over the protection that Authenticode provides, many agree that it is the equivalent of "shrink wrap." That is, it does ensure that nobody has tampered with the product since it left its creator. However, neither shrink wrap in a store, nor Authenticode in a computer program, can guarantee against an "inside job" (someone within the original organization tampering with the product). Obviously, this is not a common phenomenon, and thus carries low risk.

If you obtain an ActiveX control from a major distribution site, such as Microsoft's or CNet's, and it fails the Authenticode test (as reported by the Web browser), report this fact to whoever supplied or created the control. Sometimes an unsigned version of a control is simply distributed by mistake, in which case, a properly signed version can be supplied.

Aside from criminal deviousness, licensing issues also apply to ActiveX controls. While many controls are freely distributable, some are commercial products which must be purchased. To prevent illegal distribution of these controls to people who didn't pay for them, some controls come with built-in license privileges. For instance, many controls allow us to both view pages using that control, or create pages using that control. However, some controls are more limited: We can use them to view pages created with them, but we cannot create a page with that control itself. Make sense? Let's re-explain:

Company X sells an ActiveX control called ZippyDooda Control. We must pay $50 for the control, which we can then insert into our Web page, modify its properties, and so on. However, someone comes along to view our page, and they need ZippyDooda Control. Rather than freely handing them what we just paid $50 for, they are given the "read-only" version of the control. With it, they can view our page containing ZippyDooda, but they cannot insert that control into their own pages. To do so, they'd need the ZippyDooda control with the appropriate license, which they must buy from Company X.

While many freely available controls can be used for authoring as well as viewing, some of the controls available from Microsoft or CNet are read-only, and attempting to insert them into our page with the FrontPage Editor will result in an error message. In such cases, if we truly want the control, we'd have to return to the gallery we obtained it from and find further information on obtaining the fully-licensed version of the control.

The Least You Need to Know

ActiveX itself is a technology which allows preprogrammed modules to be "inserted" into Web pages, offering a vast array of new possibilities. While ActiveX is a book-length topic, we looked a bit at ActiveX, and focused on how to use ActiveX controls with FrontPage.

➤ ActiveX controls are automatically downloaded and installed on our computer anytime we visit a page containing controls with an ActiveX compatible browser (such as Microsoft Internet Explorer).

➤ From within the FrontPage Editor, the menu item **Insert, Other Components, ActiveX Control** allows us to use an ActiveX control on our page, chosen from the set of controls currently installed on our computer.

➤ Although not always necessary to worry about, many controls have advanced properties which can be manipulated to give the control more power and functionality on your Web page.

➤ Additional ActiveX controls can be found at Microsoft's ActiveX Control Gallery (**http://www.microsoft.com**) or CNet's ActiveX site (**http://www.activex.com**).

The Art of the Script

In some movies, the actors and actresses follow a "script," although this apparently does not apply to any films released lately. In theory, then, the script provides instructions to the actors, detailing what to say, where to walk, who to talk to, and so forth. Similarly, we can write scripts for our Web page, wherein elements of the page—such as form fields and ActiveX controls—are the actors. Thus, a script determines the behavior of the elements of a Web page. By authoring these actions, reactions, and so forth, we can enhance a page's functionality. In this chapter, we'll look at a simplified form of scripting as provided by the FrontPage Editor's Script Wizard. Keanu, watch out.

Benefits of Script

The introduction of scripting to Web page design is a recent development, but it's caught on like Raisinettes at a Chocolateer's Anonymous meeting. As described in the introduction to this chapter, a Web page script, like a film script, provides instructions to the elements of the Web page. For instance, let's consider a conceptually simple script idea: We have a Web page with a check box, and if that check box is enabled, we'd like to change the text caption on a certain button.

The above example represents the interaction between page elements, and that's largely what scripting allows us to design. Imagine, then, that some elements of a Web page are actors, and the script tells the actors how and when to react to the other actors. However, not every element of a Web page is a actor that can be scripted. For our purposes, the following Web page elements can be directed with a script:

➤ Form fields, such as text boxes, radio buttons, check boxes, and images

➤ ActiveX controls

➤ Page properties, such as background colors, foreground colors, and link colors

➤ Browser window characteristics, such as size bar and status bar messages

We cannot script tables, Java applets, or images which are not form fields. Scripts *can* direct these elements, but the type of scripting we're using in this chapter cannot direct them. For further clarification on scripting , read on.

VBScript, JavaScript, and the Script Wizard

In reality, a Web page script is a sort of computer program. It consists of instructions to the computer that are organized according to certain syntactical specifications. For readers who are familiar with computer programming, Web page scripts are similar to a combination of BASIC and Pascal. Briefly, an excerpt from a "real" script might look something like:

```
function evalform (address)
{ crucial = address.indexOf ("@") ;
  //the above uses a method of the string object to locate an at-sign in
  //the submitted form
  if (crucial == -1)
   { window.alert ("Your e-mail address is invalid! You are an abject liar!") ;
     return false }
  else
   { return true } ;
}
```

Yikes! Fortunately, this chapter is *not* a guide to authoring scripts—that would require a whole book, and in fact, there are whole books on the topic (Check out *The Complete Idiot's Guide to JavaScript,Second Edition* . However, the readers of this book may fall into two categories: those who are familiar with scripting (to whom the above excerpt would actually make sense), and those who are not.

To Those Already Familiar with Scripting

The FrontPage Editor supports two different scripting languages: VBScript, a Microsoft variant on Visual Basic, and JScript, which is Microsoft's emulation of Netscape's JavaScript. Readers of this book who are familiar with either scripting language need only select the FrontPage Editor's menu item **Insert**, **Script** to add script code to the Web page. Doing so brings up a window in which you select which scripting language to use, then type in the script to insert.

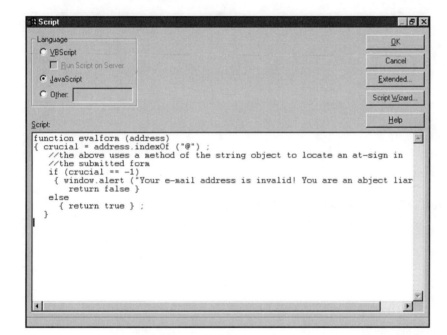

Readers who know how to write scripts can insert them into a page with the FrontPage Editor.

Again, because we are not teaching full scripting in this chapter, the above is all that needs be said about writing script by hand in the FrontPage Editor. For readers who know little to nothing about scripting, the FrontPage Editor offers the Script Wizard.

The Script Wizard

Because scripting requires specialized programming knowledge which many FrontPage users may not have, the Script Wizard can be used to create scripts in a graphical, point-and-click manner. Using the Script Wizard, we can visually select which "actors" to direct, and define the conditions under which they should act. Actual script is generated behind-the-scenes by the Wizard, leaving our hands free of the dirty work.

Still, although the Script Wizard simplifies script creation, it requires a bit of explanation to use. As is often the case, learning by example is the best recourse at this point, so let's get up close and personal with the Script Wizard. Bring a breath mint.

Start Yer Scripting!

First, we'll recall our ColorPicker Web page created with ActiveX controls in Chapter 15, "How to Make Friends and Impress Enemies: ActiveX."

Yanked from Chapter 15, our ActiveX control-riddled ColorPicker Web page.

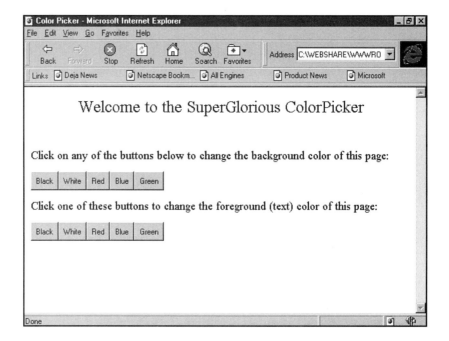

When we last left the intrepid Web page, it was riddled with ActiveX control commandbuttons, but none of them generated any results. Now, then, we call up the Script Wizard, and begin work on our "screenplay." To conjure the Script Wizard, we right-click any scriptable page element, such as one of the ActiveX controls, and select **Script Wizard** from the pop-up menu. The result is represented in the next figure.

Since the Script Wizard is a complex fellow, let's take a guided tour of the window in the previous figure. The top border of the window reads: **Script Wizard - Home Page (JavaScript)**. This means that the Wizard will generate the script code in the JavaScript language. Because JavaScript is more widely supported than VBScript, we should use JavaScript unless we have a particular reason to do otherwise. If the Script Wizard claims to be using VBScript, then we can change this by selecting the FrontPage Editor menu **Insert, Script**, and a window will appear allowing us to select which scripting language to use.

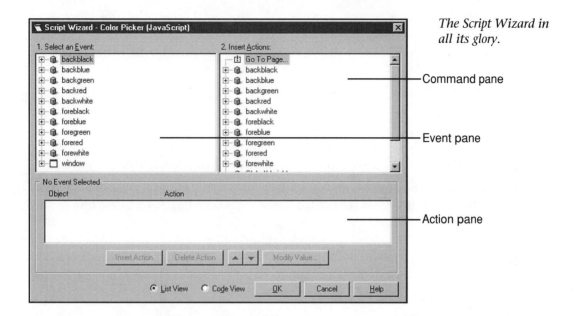

The Script Wizard in all its glory.

Command pane

Event pane

Action pane

Looking at the overall Script Wizard now, we can see that it is composed of three main panes. The upper left-hand pane, marked with the heading 1. Select an Event, we will call the Event Pane. Similarly, we'll call the upper right-hand pane the Action Pane, because it is labelled 2. Insert Actions. The wide bottom window displays the script commands which we've created; thus, we'll refer to this window as the Command Pane. Lastly, in Script Wizard vocabulary, a page element is known as an Object.

Scripting Linguistics

The script is the "director" of a Web page, instructing which elements to act or interact, and how to do so. Scripts have a long history in computing, also known as "programming languages", although scripts tend to be simpler than more advanced programming languages.

There are multiple scripting languages to choose from, however, and that can confuse the scene. These days, Microsoft's VBScript (based on their Visual Basic programming language) and Netscape's JavaScript (which isn't directly related to Java, despite the marketing-friendly name) are the main scripting languages of choice. However, JavaScript is more widely supported, both in Microsoft Internet Explorer 3.0 and Netscape Navigator 2.0 and 3.0. While Internet Explorer's JavaScript support is not 100% compatible with Netscape's, it's certainly a better choice than using VBScript, which isn't supported at all by Netscape.

Crafting the Script

Now that the nomenclature is settled, let's consider the overall logic behind each of the Script Wizard's panes. In creating a script, we author on the following logic:

> An Event occurs at one of the Objects > As a result, we select an Action to occur at an Object.

For instance, consider two page elements: a check box form field and an ActiveX commandbutton control. We might create a line of script which behaves thusly:

> The reader enables the check box (the Event) > As a result, the caption on the commandbutton changes to Click to see this week's Low Fat specials (the Action).

The action may be performed on any object, including the same one which experienced the Event. Keeping in mind the above logic, let's recall the Script Wizard window. Both the Event Pane and the Action Pane contain a list of each scriptable object on the page.

Clicking the plus sign (+) beside an object in the Event Pane will expand its list of possible events. For instance, if we click the plus sign beside the object Backblack in our example, it expands to reveal the event list in the following figure.

Expanding the event list for an Object (these are the events which could possibly happen to this object).

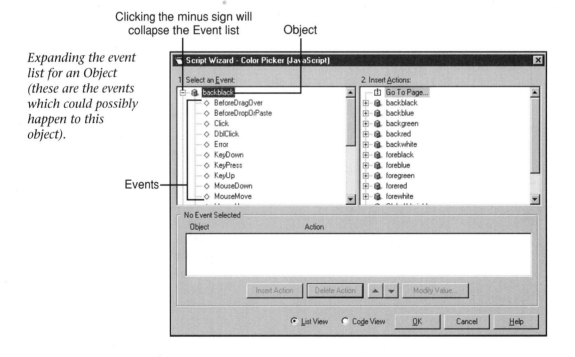

Many of the events have names which are suitably descriptive; for example, the Click Event would occur when the user clicks the mouse on this object. The DblClick Event occurs when a user double-clicks the mouse on this object. Because each ActiveX control has its own set of Events, we cannot define each one here. This is why one needs to refer to the documentation for an ActiveX control when inserting it into a page, as explained when discussing control properties in Chapter 15. For our example, we'll click on the **Click** event, to choose this event for our first script command. Notice that after clicking this Event, the label above the Command Pane changes to On Backblack Click Perform the following Actions. This indicates that we must now select an Action, or Actions, to trigger as a result of this event.

Turning our eyes to the Action Pane, we can similarly click a plus sign to expand the list of possible Actions for an Object.

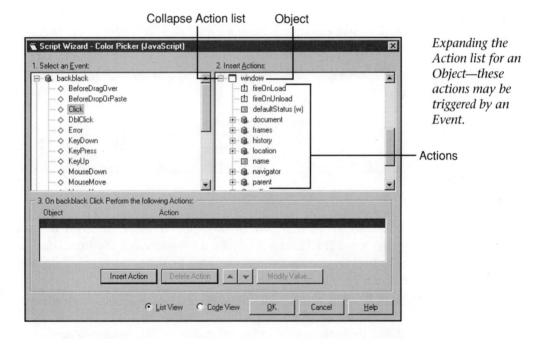

Expanding the Action list for an Object—these actions may be triggered by an Event.

In the above picture, we've expanded the Action list for the Window Object. This Object controls many properties relating to the page properties and other characteristics of the browser window. Every Web page contains this Object, regardless of what other elements are on our page. Remember our example: When the user clicks the backblack command-button, we want the page's background color to change to black. We've already defined the first half of this logic by selecting the Click Event in the previous paragraph. Now we must select the Action to trigger. Within the list of Actions for the Window Object, there are other Objects. In this case, we want to expand the list of Actions for the Document Object. Herein we find the Action named bgcolor, which determines the background color for the current page.

Objects within an object

After expanding the Document Object, which resides within the Window Object, we find the bgcolor Action, which determines the current page's background color.

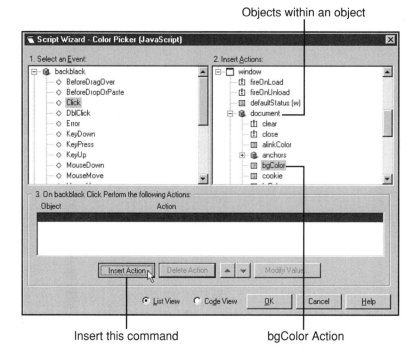

Insert this command   bgColor Action

Notice that some Actions are preceded by exclamation points, while others are preceded by a small cube, or other icon. The latter will require us to add some additional data, such as what color to set the background to. Actions preceded by the exclamation point need no additional information to operate, such as the clear Action, which simply clears the current page in view, or the close Action, which closes the page from the browser.

Check This Out...

Where the Actions Are

If it seems unclear how we knew where these Actions were in the Object list, and their functions, that's because we read the scripting documentation provided by Microsoft at their Web site. Alternatively, one can also experiment and play around with different Objects and Actions to learn their effects. Hopefully, these details will be provided with the FrontPage manuals, but we can't be sure, since this book is being written prior to FrontPage's completion.

Because we want to trigger this page's background color to change, we click the **bgcolor** Action. Next, we must click the button marked **Insert Action**, which is just below the Command Pane. We're then asked to enter just a bit more information.

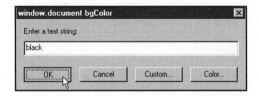

After selecting our desired Action and clicking the Insert Action button, we're asked to provide the Action with a value. In this case, the color to which we want to change the background.

A window appears asking us to Enter a Text String. Here, we enter the name of the color to which we'd like to change the background. Note that there is a set of pre-defined colors, which we can reference by name, such as *black, white, red, green*, and so on. In this case, we'd type black and click **OK**.

Color Coding

For more advanced users, we could have entered the value for our desired color in hexadecimal triplet form, as in FF10A1. In addition, if we want to specify a variable rather than a literal for this Action, we should click the **Custom** button when asked to Enter a Text String.

In our example, after we click **OK** we see the following command added to the Command pane:

```
window.document                              Change bgcolor to "black"
```

Another note: Clicking the radio button marked **Code View** will display the JavaScript or VBScript code for the command. In addition, we can manually edit or add to the code shown by clicking in the Command Pane (Readers who aren't learned in the details of scripting languages should stick to the radio button marked List View, because it displays the most English-friendly forms of our script commands).

To recap, we've completed one script command thus far: when the reader of our page clicks the background black commandbutton control, the background will change to black. Nice work! It's Miller Time.

Adding More Action(s)!

If we wanted, we could certainly add another Action for this Event. Any single Event can trigger any number of Actions; we simply click on some other Action under any desired object in the Action Pane, and then Insert Action. For example, let's imagine that after changing the background to black, we want to display a message in the status bar of the browser, reading "Background changed to black". We find that there is an Action named Status within the Window Object. Thus, we click the **Status** Action, followed by **Insert Action**, and enter **Background changed to black** when prompted to Enter a Text String.

After adding another Action to be triggered by the Click Event, both commands are now shown. We can also modify or re-order them.

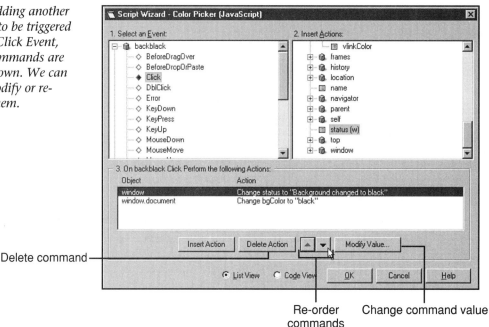

Delete command

Re-order commands

Change command value

As pictured above, the new command has been inserted just ahead of the previous command. The order in which the commands appear in the Command Pane determines the order in which these Actions will occur—if we'd like to change this order, we simply use the up and down arrow buttons to the right of the Delete Action button. Speaking of the Delete Action button, it functions as advertised—deleting whichever Action we've highlighted from the Command Pane. Lastly, selecting a command and clicking **Modify Value** will allow us to change the value we chose for the action. For instance, if we select the Change bgcolor Action and click **Modify Value**, we could change the value to white, for instance. Note that we should not erase any quotation marks (if any) which appear around our value in the Modify Value window. However, we'll leave our commands as is; they're fine for now.

Although we've only scripted two commands, both for one event (the Click Event of the backblack commandbutton), we should load this page into our browser to make sure it works. We'll close the Script Wizard for now by clicking **OK**. Notice that a small script icon appears on our Web page in the FrontPage Editor. This merely means that a script lives there, and it does not truly affect the positioning of the elements on the page, although it may appear to in the Editor. To prove this, and test our current script, we select **File, Preview in Browser** from the FrontPage Editor menu. Our Web page appears in our browser, and we click the Black background button to see the results.

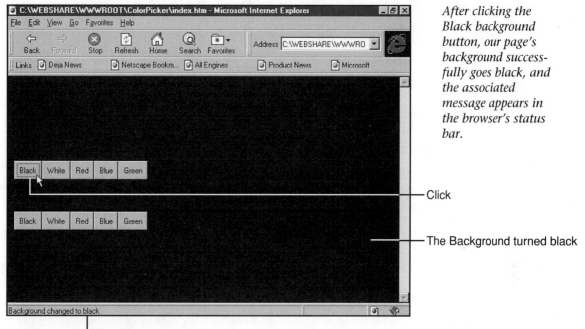

After clicking the Black background button, our page's background successfully goes black, and the associated message appears in the browser's status bar.

Click

The Background turned black

A Message in the status bar

Success! Our modest script works like a charm. To complete this page, then, we need to re-open the Script Wizard. Right-clicking any scriptable page element, such as a form field or ActiveX control, will let us recall the Script Wizard. Now, tedious though it may be, we must create similar event/action commands for each of the buttons on our page. For instance:

Expand the Event list for the backblue object, and select the **Click** Event > expand the Action list for the Window Object, expand the Action list for the Document Object, select the **bgcolor** Action > click the **Insert Action** button > enter **blue** for the text value. Select **status** Action in **Window** Object > click the **Insert Action** button > enter **Background changed to blue** for the text value.

217

When repeating the previous process for each foreground button (the Objects named **foreblack**, **forewhite**, etc), remember to trigger the **fgcolor** Action within the **Document** Object (which resides within the Window Object), rather than **bgcolor**. Otherwise, the procedure remains the same.

Once we have done this, we should test our page again. This time, clicking any of the background or foreground color buttons should change the page appropriately, and display the respective message in the browser's status bar.

Caveats and Further Information

In this chapter, we've used the Script Wizard aimed at the novice reader. In doing so, we assume no prior scripting or programming experience. However, we've also sacrificed a certain amount of capability—scripts can be made far more flexible and powerful than the Script Wizard allows for a novice designer.

Readers who have some experience in Web scripting, or any form of computer programming experience, can squeeze more utility out of the script wizard by taking advantage of some its more advanced capabilities. These advanced users might be interested to know:

➤ Clicking the **Code View** button beneath the Command Pane allows us to view the actual script as the Script Wizard intends to write it. In doing so, we can manually modify or add to this script. Advanced users might prefer to always remain in Code View mode

➤ Right-clicking on either the **Global Variables** or **Procedures** Object in the Action Pane allows us to add global variabes or new procedures to our page script. We may then use these global variables as values for Actions, or write new procedures from scratch, which we can call Actions for an event. Again, both of these features will only make sense to the ears (err, eyes) of a reader who is already familiar with computer programming.

As it stands, scripting is a flexible, but semi-advanced technology. Web designers who only intend to author basic scripts can live quite happily with the FrontPage Editor's Script Wizard. On the other hand, anyone who is serious about making more complex interactive Web pages should pick up a good book on JavaScript or VBScript. Those new skills can be applied to your page using some more advanced features of the Script Wizard.

The Least You Need to Know

Because scripting is a high-concept topic, readers who are unfamiliar with it should read this whole chapter—summaries would be no help. Readers who are experienced with Web page scripting might find the following useful:

➤ The FrontPage Editor supports VBScript and JavaScript, selectable by choosing the menu item **Insert, Script**.

➤ True scripting pros can manually enter script directly into the Web page from the **Insert, Script** feature.

➤ The Script Wizard is a quick way to create event scripts, even for those with scripting experience. To create script commands, one selects the desired object in the Event Pane and associates them with desired Actions for Objects listed in the Action Pane.

➤ Global variables and new procedures can be created for the page's script by right-clicking either the **Global Variables** or **Procedures** Objects in the Action Pane.

➤ To pass variables as values to an Action, after clicking the **Insert Action** button, click the **Custom** button when prompted for a text value.

➤ Select the **Code View** radio button to view the Script Wizard's output in its true VBScript or JavaScript form. Click within the Command Pane to manually edit or add to the code.

Java (I Simply Refuse to Make a Coffee Joke)

Just as we viewed ActiveX as the Erector Set "motor kit" for our Web pages, Java is another example of the same idea. In a sense, Java and ActiveX are competing technologies, although in truth, their differences are such that in advanced use, each is better suited to certain types of tasks. In this chapter, we'll look at using Java in our Web pages, which, it's nice to say, is fairly straightforward. Full steam ahead.

The Point of Java

What makes Java different from its predecessor programming languages (Pascal, C, C++) is that it's tailored for the Web. Java programs reside in Web pages, and therefore they can greatly extend the possibilities of Web page design.

Sound familiar? It should. That echo ringing in our ears from Chapter 15, "How to Make Friends and Impress Enemies: ActiveX," reminds us that ActiveX and Java are similar technologies. Both allow us to "insert" pre-made modules into our Web page, which we can configure to some extent, in order to customize their behavior. Java, developed by Sun Microsystems, strives to be the "Web extension technology" of choice with ActiveX, which was developed by Microsoft. In reality, both technologies can be used in harmony, and ActiveX controls provide us with some features which Java does not.

From a more advanced point of view, Java applets are highly portable, but somewhat limited as they cannot directly access hardware features of your computer, such as the hard drive, sound card, and so on. While there are some indirect ways in which to achieve these goals in Java, ActiveX is much better suited to accessing the user's hardware and operating system. On the other hand, this raises security concerns for some people, and is less portable than Java. Since Java is more widely supported in Web browsers than ActiveX, when compatibility is at stake, many Web authors still stick with Java.

In ActiveX, the pre-made module was known as a "control." In Java, we call it an "applet" (meaning "small application"). Apparently, Java's creators had a bit more flair for language than the folks at Microsoft. Thus, a Java applet is analogous to an ActiveX control; we acquire applets on our machine, we can insert them into our Web pages, and configure their properties.

The Real World, Starring Java and ActiveX

In practice, Java applets are used for somewhat different tasks than many ActiveX controls. Many Java applets, especially the most popular ones, offer aesthetic features, such as scrolling text, or bouncing text, or color cycling text, and so on. Other Java applets are very complex programs that contain their own pull-down menus, and so forth. This doesn't mean that ActiveX controls can't perform the same complex tasks; they can. And, conversely, this doesn't mean that Java applets can't be created that provide enhanced buttons and form elements; they can.

Using Java applets on our Web page is quite easy with the FrontPage Editor. The process is similar, but simpler than, using ActiveX controls. We'll look at how to acquire Java applets, insert an example or two into our Web page, and then call it a day.

Where the Applets Come in Bushels

Java is not as "automated" as ActiveX. To insert a Java applet into our Web page, we first need to obtain the applet file, and place it somewhere sensible, such as within our FrontPage Web. An Applet file is a filename which ends in the extension *.class*. Thus, a Java applet which animates text might have the filename *animtext.class*.

An applet may require more than one .class file, however. While many Java applets consist only of one .class file, some require two or more. In such cases, we'd need all necessary .class files for the applet to function in our Web page.

The natural question, then, is where do we get these Java applets, and their .class files? Read on.

The Easy Way to Acquire Applets

There are a number of Web sites that provide "applet orchards," where we can browse a variety of applets. The most popular such site is Gamelan, at http://www.gamelan.com.

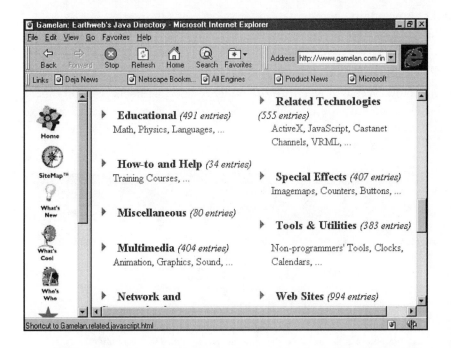

Gamelan, the mother of Java applet orchards. Pick and choose from the selections listed.

At Gamelan, we can browse the available applets by category. Once we decide on an applet to view and click its link, we'll see a page showing off the applet in question. On many pages, there will be some instructions on how to download this applet for our own use. Usually this will involve clicking a link to a .class file, or a .zip file containing several necessary .class files, which we then download to our computer. This is the "easy way" of acquiring applets; we download the .class files, and save them on our hard drive. Later, we can import the .class files into our current FrontPage Web if we decide to use them.

Preserving Applets

For the sake of organization, it's probably best to keep all our applets in one folder on our hard drive. This way, when we later need to pick an appropriate applet for our Web page, we have the whole bushel to choose from in one place. For instance, I've created a folder on my hard drive called c:\docs\html\java, wherein all downloaded .class files are saved. I also have an additional subfolder, in c:\docs\html\java\docs where the documentation files for each applet are stored.

Many of these pages also contain documentation for the applet's properties. Just as ActiveX controls had configurable properties, so do Java applets. However, our only way of knowing the Java applet's properties is by the documentation, so if the page includes documentation, save it for future reference.

Consider the picture below. We've moved into the category **Special Effects: Text** on the Gamelan site, and clicked the entry of an applet named **Scrolling Text,** by Matt Howitt (mhowitt@husc.harvard.edu). It represents a Web page containing an applet, which we're invited to download for our own use.

Picking a Java applet for our own recipe. Download the .class file(s) and save the property documentation. Screen shot from http:// www.hcs.harvard.edu/ ~mhowitt/fun/ scrollingtext/index.html.

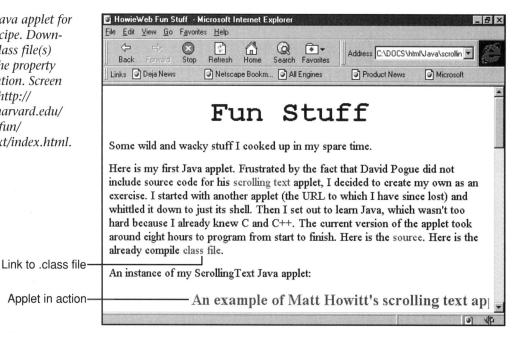

In the previous figure, we would first want to save the .class file. If we only require one .class file, there's probably a link to it, which will launch our browser's Save dialog box, and we can select a suitable place to save the applet. Applets that require multiple .class files are most likely downloaded as an archived .zip file, which we can unzip at some later point. In this example, after clicking the link to the .class file, our browser asks where to save it. We enter our path for Java applet .class files—**c:\docs\html\java**—and it's saved to that location.

In addition, we should save the documentation for this applet's properties. We'll need to refer back to it when configuring the applet in our Web page later in this chapter. The simplest way to save this documentation is to save the whole Web page, by selecting our browser's **File, Save As** (or the equivalent) menu, and saving the .html file in some suitable spot. When we need it again, we can reload it into our browser for reference. In this case, we save this Web page as **c:\docs\html\java\ScrollingText.html**.

The Hard Way—Bobbing for Applets

Unlike ActiveX, Java applets do not install and register themselves in a clean way. FrontPage 97 has no way of knowing which Java applets we have on our computer, nor does it have any way of knowing an applet's properties. This poses a problem if we encounter an applet we like, on a page which contains no downloadable .class files, or property documentation.

In these cases, we must become a sleuth. If we are viewing the applet in action, the necessary class files *must* have been downloaded to our computer. However, because of the way in which Web browsers work, they've probably been saved in a temporary directory. To save these .class files for our own use, we need to copy them from that temporary directory to some other place. Unfortunately, it's impossible to provide step-by-step instructions on how to do this; each browser, and each computer, may save temporary files in different places. Thus, I recommend the following general guidelines for saving Java applets from pages that provide no alternative method:

> **Check This Out...**
>
> **Words to the Weary** In this section, we're examining sleuthful methods for capturing applets from Web pages. Don't worry if the material seems confusing; this is advanced stuff, and not necessary in many cases, since most applets are available from the well organized applet orchards described earlier. However, the more adventurous reader can glean some tips in this section on grabbing applets from pages which offer no easier alternative.

1. Assuming the page containing the applet in action is loaded into our browser, we should view the source code. Most browsers have such a feature, such as **View, Source** (Microsoft Internet Explorer).

2. In the source HTML file, we need to find the applet tag, which looks like <applet code=appletname>. This tag will list one or several names, these being the .class files that have been downloaded to our computer. Thus, if we saw the tag <applet

code=animtext>, we can conclude that animtext.class is the file we need. We can then search our hard drive (or just the temporary browser cache, if we know its path) for that file, and copy it to a more permanent place.

3. Still, we need to know the applet's properties. Here, our only reference is this same source code; the tags following the <applet> tag, which looks like <param name=something value=somevalue> show us at least some of the applet's properties. This is far from ideal—only the properties this author chose to configure are shown—but it's a starting point. Again, this info is for more advanced users, who can make heads or tails of these guidelines.

An Applet in Your Web

We've created a very simple sample Web page for our applet, which merely contains the banner text, Wow, what a beautiful Java applet! Needless to say, the procedure we'll now trace for inserting a Java applet into this page applies equally to any of the other Web pages created throughout this book.

Picking the Applet

First things first, we need to locate the applet's .class file(s) where our Web page will be able to reach them once published to the server. For instance, we might create a "java" subdirectory within our Web site, or we might simply locate the .class file(s) along with the other files in our Web site. In this case, for the sake of organization, we'll create a java subdirectory in our Web site. Below is the current state of our Web site, as displayed in the Folder View of the FrontPage Explorer:

Our current, simple, Web site, prior to creating a java subdirectory, where our applets will bunch together.

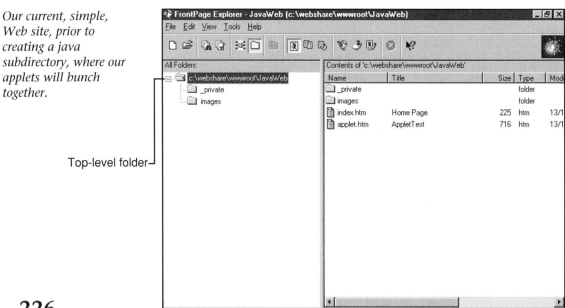

Top-level folder

We click the top-level folder in the All Folders window (as indicated in the previous illustration), and then select the menu item **File, New, Folder**. The folder appears in the right-hand contents window, and we'll set its name to **java**. Now, we must import the necessary applet .class files into the newborn java subdirectory on our Web site. First, we select the menu item **File, Import** from the FrontPage Explorer. Next, we click the **Add File** button of the import window, and locate the ScrollingText.class file, which we earlier saved into c:\docs\html\java.

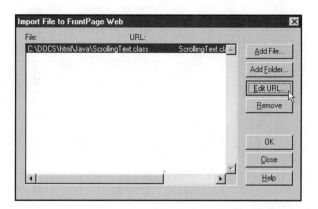

Importing the applet .class file into our Web site. We'll need to click Edit URL to send it into our java subdirectory.

Next, we click the **Edit URL** button, and we're asked for its location within our Web. The filename itself is fine, but we want to preface it with the java subdirectory, so that the .class file lands there. Thus, we change this URL from ScrollingText.class to java/ScrollingText.class. After clicking **OK**, the .class file or files will now be copied into the java subdirectory of our current Web site.

Finally, then, we're ready to roll. Applet file(s) are in place within our Web, and we can insert it (them) into our Web page. Thus, we turn our attention to the FrontPage Editor.

Placing the Applet

As usual, we begin by positioning the FrontPage Editor cursor where we want the Java applet to appear. You can insert the Java applet in one of two ways:

➤ Select the menu item **Insert, Other Components, Java Applet**

 ➤ Select the Insert Java Applet icon from the Advanced Toolbar

Configuring the Java applet; all applet behavior is set from this window.

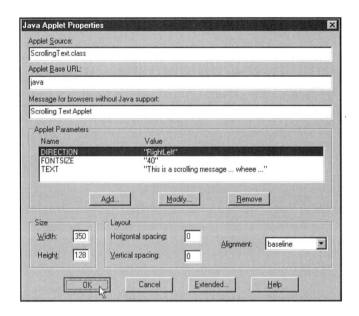

The Java Applet Properties window appears, as pictured in the previous figure, with a set of properties for us to configure.

First, we must fill in the Applet Source property. This is the filename of the applet's .class file. In our example, it is **ScrollingText.class**. Note that with regards to Java applets, the .class filenames are case-sensitive. Thus, we must preserve the proper capitalization of the filename; in this case, the "S" in "Scrolling" and "T" in "Text" are capitalized. A common cause of errors when inserting Java applets into a Web page with the FrontPage Editor is mis-typing the capitalization of the .class filename.

Next, we're asked for the esoteric-sounding property, Applet Base URL. Actually, this refers to the subdirectory our .class files reside in. In this case, it's in the *java* subdirectory of our Web, thus we enter **java**. If, for instance, our .class files resided at some other Web location entirely, we might enter an Applet Base URL such as "http://some.othersite.com/~me/applets". In any case, the browser will look for the Applet Source .class file in the Applet Base URL location.

In thinking kindly of readers whose browsers do not support Java, we may enter a message for browsers without Java support. Something descriptive, such as **Scrolling Text Applet** would do nicely.

Now we face some of the most important properties of the Java applet, its Applet Parameters. These are properties specific to each applet, which customize its behavior. We learn these properties, and what values they may contain, from the applet documentation, which is why we saved it earlier. When saving this ScrollingText applet, we saved its Web page as scrollingtext.html. Now we re-load that Web page, and focus on its documented properties.

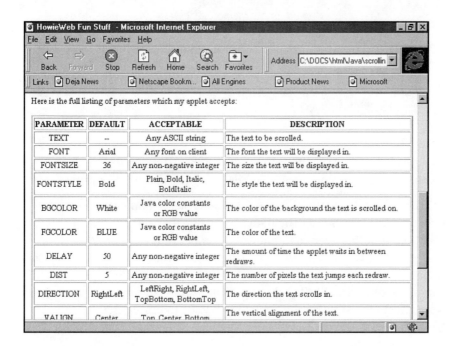

Documentation of this Java applet's properties. Matt Howitt, the author of this applet, has provided a nice property table for easy reference. Thanks, Matt!

Each applet parameter has a name and a value. In the documentation above, written by Matt Howitt for his ScrollingText applet, these properties are well explained in an easy-to-read table. Other applets may format the documentation in different ways, but however they are described, they will provide the parameter names and possible values.

Looking at Matt's table, we see that the ScrollingText applet has a number of parameters, the first of which has the name TEXT. As it's described, this parameter's value defines the actual text to be scrolled, and may be any valid text (known as ASCII in computer-speak). Looking at the table, we see other sensible parameters, such as FONT, FONTSIZE, FONTSTYLE, and so forth. The parameter DIRECTION controls which way the text should scroll, and its value may be any of LeftRight, RightLeft, TopBottom, or BottomTop. Each of the parameters has a default value, as Matt specifies, which takes effect if we decide not to define the parameter in our Java Applet Properties.

Applet Behavior

Now, then, we're ready to define these parameters for our use of the applet. Turning back to the FrontPage Editor, in the Applet Parameters section of the Java Applet Properties window, we click the **Add** button to define a parameter. A new window, named Set Attribute Value, pops up.

229

Adding and configuring parameters for the current Java applet.

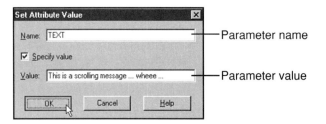

Parameter name

Parameter value

We'll enter **TEXT** for this parameter's name, and, with the check box **Specify Value** enabled, we enter **This is a scrolling message ... wheee ...** as the parameter's value.

After clicking **OK**, this name and value now appear in the Applet Parameters window. Repeating this same procedure, we can set the name and value for each parameter this applet supports. We needn't define every parameter; remember that there are default values which take effect in the case of an unnamed parameter. In this instance, we'll also add the **FONTSIZE** parameter name, and set its value to **40**, and the **DIRECTION** parameter name, setting its value to **RIGHTLEFT**. Later, we'll likely want to return to these parameters and tweak them to customize the applet's behavior to our desires.

Final Touches

At the bottom of the Java Applet Properties window we can define some typical image properties for this applet, including its Width and Height, as well as Horizontal Spacing, Vertical Spacing, and Alignment. These properties all apply as with any image on our page. Keep in mind, however, that they apply to the entire Java applet window; not the contents within the applet window. In other words, the Alignment property aligns the entire applet window with respect to an adjacent element on the Web page. It does not control alignment of the applet contents *within* the applet window; that's why the applet has its own alignment parameter, as configured in Applet Parameters.

We can now click **OK** on the Java Applet Properties window, and return to our Web page in the FrontPage Editor, where a large J represents the applet. Because the FrontPage Editor cannot display the actual applet, it shows a placeholder. If we left-click the applet placeholder, a sizing box appears around the applet. We can use placeholders to visually size the applet's width and height. These changes will be reflected in those properties when viewing the Java Applet Properties window, which we can return to by right-clicking the applet placeholder.

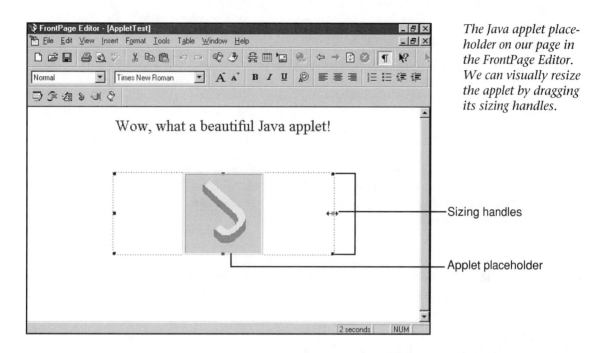

The Java applet place-holder on our page in the FrontPage Editor. We can visually resize the applet by dragging its sizing handles.

Sizing handles

Applet placeholder

To test the applet in action, we must preview this page in our Web browser, such as by selecting **File, Preview in Browser** from the FrontPage Editor menu. As we can see in the picture below, the scrolling message appears on our Web page when viewed in the browser.

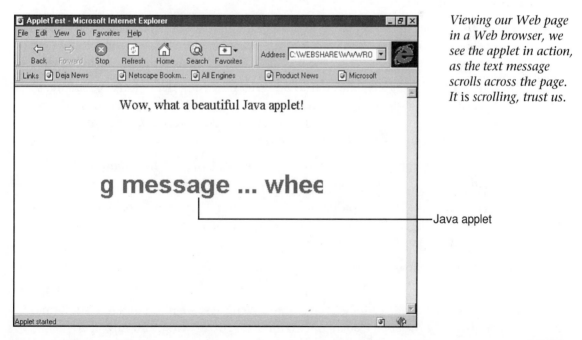

Viewing our Web page in a Web browser, we see the applet in action, as the text message scrolls across the page. It is scrolling, trust us.

Java applet

231

Obscured by Applet

When inserting applets, you may notice that they always contain an opaque background. When we have a Web page with a background color, this can be hidden by setting the applet's background color parameter to the same color as the page's background.

However, consider a Web page which uses a graphical background texture. In this case, regardless of what background color we choose for the applet, it will obscure the background texture. The obvious question, then, is "how can I make the applet's background transparent?" Unfortunately, as of this writing, the answer is "You can't." Hopefully, a future version of Java will allow transparent backgrounds, but for now, it is not to be.

Because each applet has a different set of parameters, learning the documentation for each parameter is the bulk of the effort when inserting Java applets into our Web pages. As far as the FrontPage Editor goes, the actual insertion process is quite simple, as we've seen in this chapter.

The Least You Need to Know

Java applets provide the chance to extend the possibilities of our Web page by including pre-made programs created by others. This is similar to ActiveX, although more Web browsers support Java.

➤ Before inserting an Java applet into our Web page, we need two goodies: the .class file or files which make up the applet, and the documentation which defines its properties. These can usually be had from the Web page of the author who created the applet.

➤ Import the applet's .class file(s) into our Web site, using the FrontPage Explorer's **File, Import** feature. We may want to first create a subdirectory within which to save Java .class files in our Web site, by selecting **File, New, Folder** from the FrontPage Explorer while in Folder View.

➤ We insert the applet using the FrontPage Editor's **Insert, Other Components, Java Applet** menu. This brings up the Java Applet Properties window.

➤ Configuring the applet's properties requires entering its .class filename into Applet Source, and the location (if any other than our main Web) of this .class file (such as java, if we've created a java subdirectory).

➤ With reference to the applet's documentation, which we acquired earlier, we use the **Add** button to enter parameter names and values, which control the behavior of the applet.

➤ With respect to adjacent elements on the Web page, we may configure additional properties of the applet, such as its Width, Height, Spacing, and Alignment.

Chapter 18

Pump Up Your Page: Plug-Ins and WebBots

In This Chapter

➤ Plug it in, Plug it in

➤ WebBots: Automation of the future?

Continuing along the merry theme of this section, we take a slice of time to consider a couple of additional options for extending the capabilities of our Web pages. Both technologies discussed in this chapter—third-party plug-ins and FrontPage WebBots—are less complex and less likely to be widely used in the future, in comparison to ActiveX and Java. Nonetheless, FrontPage 97 supports them, and well, heck, this *is* a book about FrontPage 97, *n'est pas*? (French for "nespa" which is the Latin neuter plural for "Nescafe").

Where to Stick It: The Plug-In

Throughout this section of the book, we've looked at Web page extensibility via prefabricated modules. Both ActiveX and Java relied on computer programs which we plopped into our Web page, and then customized through properties and parameters. Enter the technology known as the "plug-in," which (surprise) is designed to serve much the same purpose.

In fact, along the line of technological chronology (say that four times after a few Long Island Iced Teas), plug-ins predate both Java and ActiveX. Introduced with Netscape

Navigator, plug-ins are computer programs that can be inserted within a Web page. By and large, plug-ins have been created by software companies to allow browser users to view files created for that particular software—for instance, the popular Macromedia Shockwave plug-in allows Web browsers to display Macromedia Director files within a Web page. Macromedia Director, in turn, is a commercial software package with which people create multimedia presentations.

Without any claims for Nostradamus's status, it's not much of a stretch to predict that plug-ins will soon fall into disuse, since ActiveX controls and Java applets can easily take their place. Furthermore, while ActiveX and Java both automatically install their components, the user must manually download and install plug-ins. None of this bodes well for their future.

In fact, Macromedia has already released a Shockwave ActiveX control, thus rendering the plug-in version obsolete for users with ActiveX-capable Web browsers. Nonetheless, plug-ins are still used here and there, and it's not our place to dictate such matters. Readers who want to use a plug-in with their Web page—perhaps there is no alternative yet for a particular application—can do so with the FrontPage Editor.

Socket to Me! How the Juice Flows

Before inserting a sample plug-in onto our Web page, let's take a moment to understand how plug-ins operate; it's a bit different than ActiveX or Java. Although most plug-ins operate on the same principle, we'll refer to the Shockwave plug-in to help explain the concepts involved.

Imagine, then, that we have created a Web page, on which we'd like to include a multimedia effect we've created with Macromedia Director (overlooking, for the moment, that said application is very expensive, and if we could afford that, we could probably hire someone who knows how to use plug-ins). For the Web user to see our page, with its multimedia effects, he needs the capability to view the files produced by Director. The Shockwave plug-in does just that. Our Web surfing fellow, desirous to see our Web page, downloads the Shockwave plug-in and installs it on his computer. In doing so, there are two important consequences:

➤ The plug-in now resides somewhere on his hard drive.

➤ His Web browser is configured to launch the plug-in whenever it encounters the appropriate type of file within a Web page.

Thus, he visits our page, and his browser thinks to itself, "Ah, this page contains a Macromedia Director file! According to my settings, I'm supposed to launch the Shockwave plug-in to process that file. Boy, I'm thirsty." As a result, the correct plug-in is launched, and everyone is all smiles.

Therefore, the key principle here, other than the fact that Web browsers do indeed grow thirsty, is that we do not actually insert the plug-in *itself* into our Web page, but rather the *type of file* which triggers the plug-in. Keeping this principle foremost in mind, let's now insert a plug-in onto a sample Web page.

Power On

Both Netscape Navigator and Microsoft Internet Explorer include plug-ins for playing audio files. When we create a Web page that uses these plug-ins, a graphical interface appears on the Web page that allows the reader to control the playing of the audio—for example stop, pause, play, volume. Consider the following two images, which depict each browser displaying a simple page using an audio plug-in.

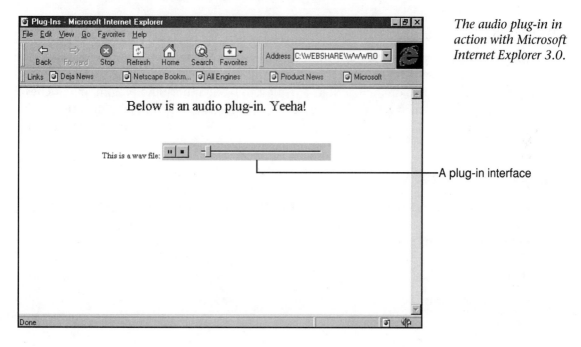

The audio plug-in in action with Microsoft Internet Explorer 3.0.

A plug-in interface

The audio plug-in looks equally charming in Netscape Navigator 3.0.

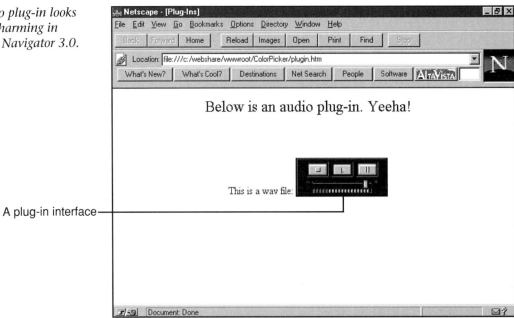

A plug-in interface

The actual plug-in that is launched will depend on how the browser is configured—we, the Web page designer, cannot specifically control that factor. For instance, when Microsoft Internet Explorer encounters a request to launch the audio plug-in, it launches the audio plug-in which Microsoft distributed with the Internet Explorer. Similarly, Netscape Navigator launches its own plug-in. As the Web designer, we can merely tell the browser, "launch whichever plug-in you've been told to for this type of file."

Plug-In Placement

Beginning our example, then, we've loaded a Web page into the FrontPage Editor. Our modest goal is to insert an audio plug-in onto this page. Thus, we begin with the traditional placing of the cursor, to locate where we'd like the plug-in interface to appear. Following that, we select the FrontPage Editor menu item **Insert, Other Components, Plug-In**.

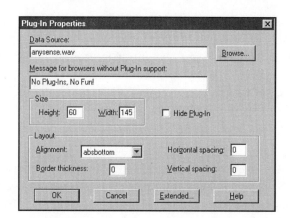

Triggering a plug-in on our Web page. A mere handful of properties.

The Plug-In Properties window appears, as pictured above. It's first, and most important, property is Data Source. Here, we must select which file to include in the Web page. Remember that this file will trigger whichever plug-in to which the browser is configured. Thus, if we insert an audio file (such as a *.wav* file) as the Data Source, the browser will trigger its audio plug-in. If we insert a Macromedia Director file, the browser will trigger its Shockwave plug-in. Should the browser not know what plug-in to use for a file, it will prompt the user to either download the plug-in or give up. There's nothing that we, the Web designer, can do to help that situation—the outcome rests entirely in the hands of the individual visiting our page (one of the disadvantages of using plug-ins).

Popular Plug-Ins

Although Plug-Ins are probably on the "out" as far as browser technology goes, several popular ones are still in wide use (a full list of available plug-ins can be found at Netscape's Web site *http://www.netscape.com*):

Macromedia Shockwave: Plays Macromedia Director files, which often end with the filename extension *.dir*

Apple QuickTime: Plays QuickTime format videos, whose files end with the extension *.mov*

RealAudio: Plays RealAudio format "streaming" audio files, which can be heard as-they-download; commonly found as files with the extension *.rpm*

Live3D or any other VRML plug-in: Allows for viewing and navigation of three-dimensional "worlds"; filenames end in *.wrl*

LiveAudio, Crescendo, other MIDI plug-ins: Play MIDI-format music files, which end in the filename extension *.mid*

In this case, we want to trigger an audio plug-in, so we include a .wav file as the Data Source. We've included a snippet of a song which we downloaded from a music site some time ago, but since books can't (yet) play music (although, curiously, greeting cards can), you'll simply have to take our word for it. In the next property, we can configure a Message for Browsers without Plug-In support. A simple note, such as an "Audio plug-in of 'Any Sense of Time' by the Inbreds" should suffice in letting the reader know what they're missing.

Next, we can set the Height and Width for the graphical aspect of the plug-in. These properties may take some experimentation. We want these dimensions to match the size of the plug-in, and so we may need to preview this page in our browser several times, tweaking these properties.

Peek-A-Boo Plug-Ins

Note that some plug-ins, such as the Internet Explorer audio plug-in, ignore the Height and Width properties, and display their full interface regardless. The Netscape audio plug-in, however, conforms to these properties, and if we make the dimensions too small, the plug-in interface will not fully display (for the record, the Netscape audio plug-in has dimensions of approximately 60 pixels high and 145 pixels wide). Then again, if we enable the Hide Plug-In property, then the plug-in interface will not appear at all. For some plug-ins, such as Internet Explorer's audio plug-in, hiding the interface will not play the file. Netscape's audio plug-in does play the file with the interface hidden, although the default volume is too low to hear it very well!

Lastly, in configuring the Plug-In Properties, we can set the typical layout controls that are available for any image. The Alignment, Border Thickness, and Horizontal and Vertical Spacing properties all behave as usual, determining the plug-in's arrangement with respect to adjacent page elements.

For many plug-ins, that's all. Test the page as usual by loading it into a Web browser. Some plug-ins contain extra customizations that are documented by their creators; for instance, they allow us to select which portions of the interface to display by specifying special parameter names and values. Any special customization must be added via the Extended button at the bottom of the Plug-In Properties window. There, we can add additional parameter names and values, similar to when we customized Java applets in Chapter 17, "Java (I Simply Refuse to Make a Coffee Joke)."

WebBots: Use, Care, and Feeding

Finally, we close out Part 4 of this book with a look at WebBots. These little cretins—er, creatures—are spawns of Microsoft, and are specific to FrontPage 97. This fact has two ramifications: only Web designers using FrontPage 97 can include them in Web pages, and only Web servers which have the FrontPage extensions installed can deliver Web pages with functioning WebBots.

The best way to describe a WebBot is as a little "doohickey" that we can include in our page. They are not grand in ambition, as are ActiveX, Java and Plug-Ins. Rather, WebBots are modest little gadgets which perform certain tasks on our page. The FrontPage Editor includes only a couple handfuls of WebBots to choose from. Presumably, if they're a hit, more will be released in the future. The more useful WebBots can perform the following tasks:

➤ An **Include**, which allows a specified page to be inserted into the current page; if using this, we can include one page into several other Web pages, and by editing only the one included page, the others are automatically up-to-date.

➤ A **Substitution**, allowing us to insert a variable into the page, whose value can be changed from within the FrontPage Explorer, without directly editing the page itself.

➤ A **Search form**, allowing reader's to search for any text within our Web site; hyperlinks to each match are provided in the results.

➤ A **Timestamp**, which automatically reflects the date and time of the last page edit or update.

Let's create a simple Web page that uses each of the WebBots; it's quite simple. However, do keep in mind that these WebBots will *only* work if our page resides on a server with the FrontPage extensions. Using one of the Personal Web Servers provided by Microsoft (to be discussed in Part 5, "Broadcasting from Bed: The FrontPage Web Server") will work, but if our page is hosted by a service provider, we'd better ask them if they support the FrontPage extensions.

The Include WebBot

We begin with a blank page, created in the FrontPage Editor. At the top, in bold centered letters, we type the headline:

Welcome to Harry's Fishmarket Quote of the Day:

Our first WebBot, then, will be an Include. We'll design a specified Web page containing our current quote of the day. Each day, then, we need only edit the quote of the day page, and our Harry's Fishmarket home page will reflect the new quote. Clicking the line just below Quote of the Day, we select the FrontPage Editor menu item **Insert, WebBot Component**. A selection window appears, from which we choose the WebBot to place.

Choosing a WebBot doohickey for our page.

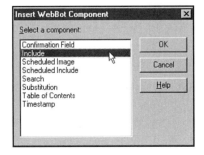

After selecting the **Include** WebBot, we're asked for the page to include. Here, we enter *qotd.htm*, which is the page containing the quotation (created some time previously). When creating the page to be included, keep in mind that it will be displayed just like any Web page. Any formatting or design we want applied to the quote of the day should be done on the qotd.htm page. In this case, we previously created a page called qotd.htm which contains the one line, centered, italicized, red quote, "He who lives by the sword-fish, dies by the swordfish."

Previewing our Web page in our Web browser, we see the following result:

Harry's Fishmarket page, with an Include WebBot representing the quote of the day. The robot pointer icon represents the location of the WebBot component.

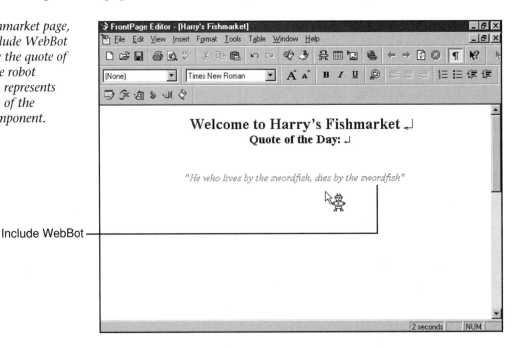

Include WebBot

On future days, then, to change the quote of the day, we need only edit the qotd.htm page—the Fishmarket page will automatically include the new quote.

The Substitution WebBot

Very similar to the Include WebBot is the Substitution WebBot. In the same manner as the Include WebBot, the Substitution WebBot acts as a placeholder for data. Rather than including another Web page, the Substitution WebBot represents the value of a variable which we can define in the FrontPage Explorer. Let's use this WebBot to create a price table, which can change frequently in this business. On our current Fishmarket page, we create a three-row, two-column table. In the left-hand cells, we enter our products; in the right-hand cells, we will insert the Substitution WebBots:

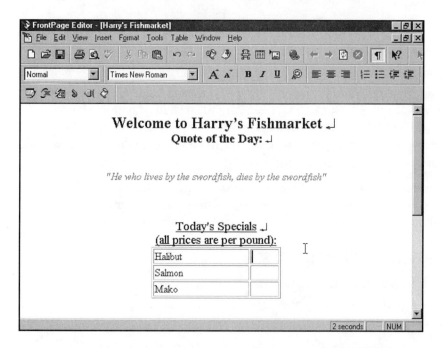

Creating a price table, in which we'll use the Substitution WebBot to reflect changing prices at the Fishmarket.

Now, we're almost ready to insert the Substitution WebBots. First, we must define the variables we want to substitute. We do this in the FrontPage Explorer, by selecting the menu item **Tools, Web Settings**, and clicking on the **Parameters** tab.

Defining variables for use on our Web page with the Substitution WebBot.

Add new variable——

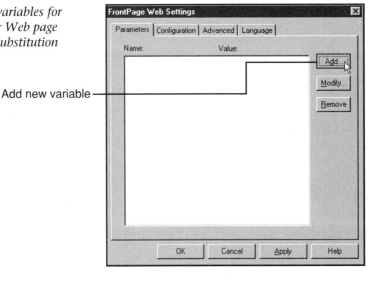

We click the **Add** button, and when prompted, enter a name and value for our variable (or "parameter" as Microsoft calls it). Our first variable/parameter shall be named **Halibut**, and will contain a value of **8.50**—its current market price per pound. Following that, we create two additional parameters: **Salmon**, with a value of **6.99**, and **Mako**, with a value of **3.99**. We now return our attention to the FrontPage Editor, and our price table.

Clicking in the right-hand column on the top row, we place the cursor within the cell beside **Halibut**. Next we select the menu item **Insert**, **WebBot Component**, and select the **Substitution** WebBot from the list provided. We're then asked what to substitute for it.

Configuring the Subsitution WebBot; selecting which parameter's value to display here.

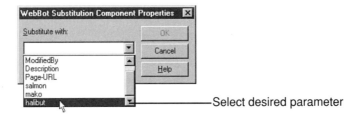

————Select desired parameter

We notice that **halibut** appears in the drop-down menu, and after choosing it and clicking **OK**, the current value of halibut (8.50) appears in the table cell. Thus, we need only click the remaining two cells, and insert a Substitution WebBot in each, choosing the appropriate parameter (**salmon** for the salmon price and **mako** for the mako price).

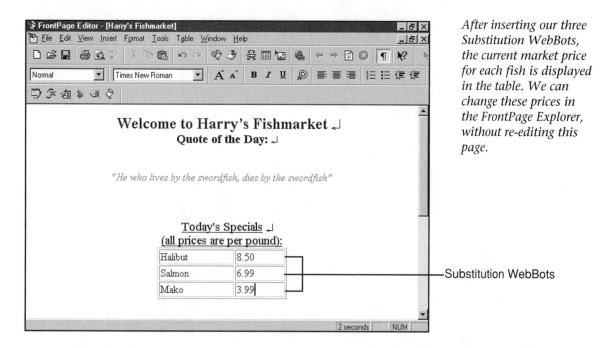

After inserting our three Substitution WebBots, the current market price for each fish is displayed in the table. We can change these prices in the FrontPage Explorer, without re-editing this page.

Substitution WebBots

In the future, then, when fish prices change, we needn't re-edit this page. Rather, we can simply return to the Parameters tab in the **Tools, Web Settings** window in the FrontPage Explorer (with this Web site opened in the FrontPage Explorer), and modify the values of each parameter. Those changes will automatically be reflected in the price table on the Fishmarket page.

Take that, AltaVista!: The Search WebBot

Now, let's imagine that our Fishmarket site also contains a number of other pages—information and recipes, for instance, on preparing various fish products. We could (and should) create hyperlinks to these pages in the normal way, but can also use the Search WebBot to provide a simple search engine for visitors to use. The result is that a reader of our page can enter any keyword into the search form, and they'll receive a list of hyperlinks leading to each page within our Web site which contains that keyword. The Search WebBot makes this very simple, and is perhaps the most useful WebBot of all.

First, we locate a position on our page where we want the search form to appear. Then, we simply select the menu **Insert, WebBot Component**, and select the Search WebBot from the list offered. We're then asked to configure the Search WebBot properties.

Customizing the Search WebBot, which will allow readers to find any pages in our site with ease.

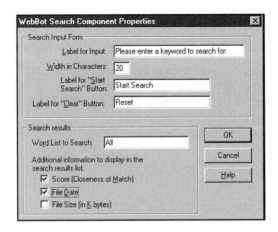

First, we may customize the prompt which appears beside the text box form field, known as the Label for Input. Search for: is the default, although we might replace that with a more descriptive phrase, such as, **Please enter a keyword to search for:**. Then we may set the Width in Characters of the keyword search field; the default of **20** is reasonable. Following that, we can configure the labels to appear on the Start Search Button and the Clear Button.

The property Word List to Search should be set to **All**, and we can then enable any of the additional information which we'd like to appear with the search results; the **score** of the match, the **date** of the file containing the match, and the **size** of the file containing the match.

We click **OK** when satisfied, and the search form appears on our Web page, ready-to-use.

The search form, automatically generated by the Search WebBot.

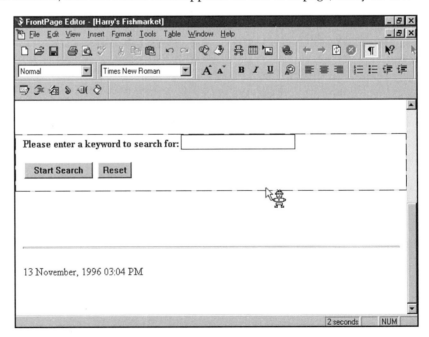

When a reader visits our page, and enters a keyword in the search form, he'll receive a list of hyperlinks to each match (if any) in a table display, such as those shown in the next figure.

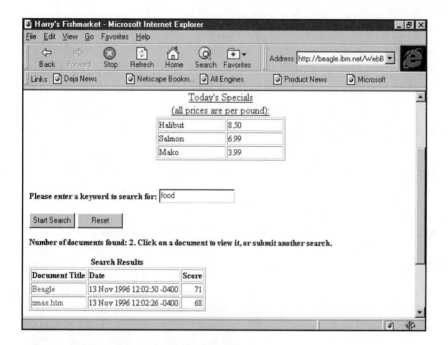

The results of a search performed by the Search WebBot.

The TimeStamp WebBot

We might end our Fishmarket page with the Timestamp WebBot, which will display the date and, optionally, the time of the last edit or update to this page. After positioning the cursor where we want this notation to appear, we select **Insert**, **WebBot Component** and select the **Timestamp WebBot** from the list.

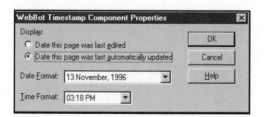

Configuring the Timestamp WebBot, which lets the reader know just how fresh this page is. Hot outta the oven!

If we select to display the **Date this page was last edited**, the date will reflect the last time we tinkered with it in the FrontPage Editor (actually, merely loading the page into the FrontPage Editor will update the timestamp). On the other hand, if we go with the **Date this page was last automatically updated**, we'll see a date that reflects the last time some of the included or substituted data was changed. In this case, we want the reader to know how fresh the price table is, so we opt for the latter.

245

Lastly, we can select a cosmetic format for the date, and, optionally, the time, as it will appear on the page. Anything is fine—it's a matter of personal taste. Which, as they say, there is no accounting for.

At last, our page is complete; full of light and fluffy WebBots. These doohickeys can be great enhancements to a page, performing tasks which would otherwise require more complex scripting or form handlers. But, remember, they *only* function properly when these pages are delivered by Web servers with the FrontPage extensions.

The Least You Need to Know

In a final look at ways to extend the functionality of our Web pages, we considered two less-popular technologies: the plug-in and the WebBot. The former is old and probably on its way out of usage, while the latter is very new, but its proliferation remains to be seen.

➤ A plug-in is a premade computer program that is designed to view/play/show a certain type of file; usually one produced by a certain company's application. One example is the Shockwave plug-in, which plays multimedia files created with Macromedia Director.

➤ In a Web page, we create a reference to the type of file which triggers a plug-in. Which plug-in is actually triggered is defined by the configuration of the user's Web browser, and therefore it is not something which the Web designer has control over.

➤ Using the FrontPage Editor, we can insert a plug-in trigger with the **Insert, Other Components, Plug-In** menu. We can select which file to trigger with (for instance, a sound file will probably trigger an audio player plug-in), and the graphical dimensions for the plug-in interface.

➤ WebBots are small doohickeys which automate functions that we'd otherwise need to script into our Web page using more complex means. WebBots can only be inserted using the FrontPage Editor (**Insert, WebBot Component**), and can only function properly if our Web page is handled by a server which has the FrontPage extensions.

Part 5
Broadcasting from Bed: The FrontPage Web Server

For the experienced or adventurous readers, running your own Web server puts information delivery squarely into your own hands. It takes some knowledge of matters that are necessarily technical. We work through those issues, and, at the least, get your Web server running. For the especially advanced readers, security issues and other access restrictions are covered. At the conclusion, we run our server through a battery of tests to ensure its health and well-being.

Chapter 19

Bringing the Server to Life

In This Chapter

➤ Server semantics

➤ To serve or not to serve

➤ Perplexion: Which server for me?

➤ Wrangling with ports

➤ The glow of success

A long, lone time ago, in a chapter far, far away (Chapter 1, "Why We Web (and How)," in fact), we considered the kindly, pastoral Web server. Designed to deliver Web pages to visitors near and far, the server occupies a simple concept. We likened the Web server to a waiter in a restaurant, and at the time, the analogy "served" us well. In actuality, though, the Web server can be a complicated, snarling beast. And that's when he's in a good mood. Okay, we don't mean to seem *too* intimidating here, but the truth remains that the server can be slightly confusing. Over the next three chapters, we'll attempt to disentangle the concepts involved, and help readers install, setup, and manage a small Web server from their own machine. By and large, this part of the book may appeal most to two groups: readers who want to test their Web site locally before uploading it to a service provider's server, and readers who run small, possibly home-based organizations, businesses, or those that are on an intranet. Larger organizations or businesses will use more robust and expensive servers than we'll discuss in these chapters; furthermore, they'll also have hired specialists to run them.

The Server's Role

At its core, the Web server plays waiter in the great restaurant of the Internet (or any other network on which it's used). Readers open connection to the server and request Web pages—the server delivers. However, due to budget cuts and staffing shortfalls, the server must take on other responsibilities as well. It acts as maître d', processing incoming requests and determining the order in which they will be served. It acts as security guard, preventing anyone not on the guest list from dining at that Web site, and only allowing authorized cooks (Web authors) into the kitchen. Grandest of all, the Web server also acts as chef, processing orders—sometimes simple and sometimes complex—and cooks them up.

From the technological point of view, the Web server is a software application. As such, there are a variety of Web servers available on the market, just as there are a variety of restaurants in the city. All of them aim towards the same basic goal — delivering Web pages — but their quality varies. Some servers are adept at every role; some have no capability to play some of the roles (such as security guard). Most servers fall somewhere in between, and are generally priced accordingly. Of course, as the server's quality increases, so does its complexity. These chapters focus on two particular Web server products, both of which are (surprise!) included with FrontPage 97.

Fast Food or Sit Down

Two groups of people should be reading these chapters:

➤ Readers who want test their Web sites on their own machine before publishing them to a service provider's Web server

➤ Readers who run small (perhaps home-based) businesses or organizations, and, just as in the case of an additional phone line or FAX machine, they are interested in serving their Web pages either within the organization (intranet), or to the Internet

Not that we don't enjoy a crowd as much as the next loner, but readers can save some reading, and possible confusion, by skipping these chapters altogether if one of these descriptions applies:

➤ You create very simple Web pages and have no need or desire to test them in a server environment before publishing, or you want only to test them on the service provider's server

To briefly elaborate on the above point, Web pages that do not contain any "special" features usually don't need to be tested on a server; that is, loading them into a Web browser directly from a file on the hard drive is fine. Web pages that use special server features, such as pages containing ActiveX controls, Java applets, WebBots, forms and form fields, and server-side imagemaps, *do* need to be tested on a server; simply loading these types of pages from the hard drive into the Web browser will not suffice. Even in this case, however, one need not test them on one's *own* server. We could publish the site to our service provider's server first, and then test them. However, this can be a time-consuming process, and for that reason, some people prefer to set up a server on their computer for testing purposes, before publishing.

➤ Readers who create Web sites for large organizations or businesses, who use advanced, expensive server software, and have hired specialists to run them. In these cases, don't worry about the server issues at all—someone else is being paid to do that.

Now, after some consideration, we've decided whether we are interested in serving Web pages or not. Readers who don't care to become entangled in the server side of things may advance to find out what happened to Jane and her monkey after they fell into the cave...Everyone else, read on!

A Tale of Two Servers

By their nature, Web servers are confusing organisms. Interesting, then, that Microsoft devised a plan to make their Web servers even more so. We begin our discussion of using Web servers with FrontPage 97 by disentangling a few points of confusion, which can save a heap of trouble down the road.

The FrontPage 97 product actually ships with two suites of software:

➤ FrontPage 97, which contains the FrontPage Explorer, the FrontPage Editor, and the FrontPage Personal Web Server.

➤ The Bonus Pack, which contains the Image Composer, the Web Publishing Wizard, and the Microsoft Personal Web Server.

Thus, everyone who has purchased the FrontPage 97 product owns both sets of software listed above (whether or not it has all been installed is the matter of the Appendix "Semper Paratus: FrontPage 97 Installation Tips"). Notice, then, that we listed two Web server products. This brings us to:

Critical Point #1: The FrontPage Personal Web Server and the Microsoft Personal Web Server are two completely separate, distinct products. Although their names are distressingly similar, they have no connection to one another. Both are Web server applications, that is true, but we only want and need to use one of them. Which one?

The short answer: The Microsoft Personal Web Server.

The long answer: The FrontPage Personal Web Server is a Web server with few capabilities. It can play the role of waiter, but that's about it. It is a weak security guard, and a limited chef (more of a short-order cook). Its primary purpose is to allow for the testing of basic Web pages. In contrast, the Microsoft Personal Web Server is a fairly competent Web server that can adequately play most of the roles for small-time users. As we discussed earlier in this chapter, there is no real need to test basic Web pages on a local server—obviating the purpose of the FrontPage Personal Web Server. If we *do* want to perform any testing on our own server, we may as well use the more capable Microsoft Personal Web Server. The only exception to the following applies to users of Windows NT; the Microsoft Personal Web Server only runs under Windows 95. Most users of Windows NT are in a specialized office environment, and thus probably don't need to run their own server. In case you do want to run a server on Windows NT, ask the office information manager for further information.

It is the recommendation of this book, therefore, that we do not use the FrontPage Personal Web Server at all. We want to use the Microsoft Personal Web Server. Have we repeated that enough? Is it annoying yet? Good. It's critical that we begin on the right foot (not that there's anything wrong with a nice left foot).

Unfortunately, when we install FrontPage 97, we're offered the opportunity to install the FrontPage Personal Web Server, and may not have known Critical Point #1. Ideally, we'd suggest not to install the FrontPage Personal Web Server, as noted in the Appendix. However, we realize that many readers may have gone ahead and installed the entire FrontPage 97 suite before reading the Appendix. Not to fear, there is help.

Ultimately, our aim in this chapter is to install and start-up the Microsoft Personal Web Server. Readers who have *not* already installed the FrontPage Personal Web Server can skip ahead to the section titled "Finally — the Microsoft Personal Web Server." Those who did install the FrontPage Personal Web Server or aren't sure, continue reading.

Overcoming the FrontPage Personal Web Server

We've been given the superior Microsoft Personal Web Server with the FrontPage 97 package, so we may as well use it. Unfortunately, if we've already installed the FrontPage Personal Web Server, we must jump through a few hoops before we can successfully install and use the Microsoft Personal Web Server instead. The crux of the problem is a conflict of "ports."

Ports? Remember that each computer on a network has a unique address, not unlike a building in a city. Computer addresses, which we're probably familiar with by now, exist as numbers, such as 128.253.160.5, and often have English-friendly names mapped to the numbers (such as bobshouse.companyco.com). Think of the computer as an apartment building, though. While the whole building has a number, there are suites within the building, which have their own assigned addresses. For instance, I might reside at 2500 Mina Bird Lane, Apt. 42. Similarly, each computer has a number of "ports" which are analogous to apartments within an apartment building. Thus, we could speak of bobshouse.companyco.com:80, which means "port 80 on the computer named bobshouse.companyco.com."

Typically, servers live in these ports. Each type of server (FTPd, HTTPd, POP mail, and so on) has a traditional port in which it lives. For instance, POP mail servers live in port 110. Web servers (also known as HTTPd) live in port 80. Because this is assumed, we usually don't specify the port when making a request of the machine. When our Web browser attempts to connect to bobshouse.companyco.com, it assumes that it should knock on port 80. We could locate our Web server in a different port, but then we'd have to specify that in the URL; e.g., http://bobshouse.companyco.com:8080 would attempt to contact the Web server at port 8080.

Evicting the Old Server

When the FrontPage Personal Web Server is installed, it's "bound" to port 80, meaning that it lives there. Problem is, if we simply try to install the Microsoft Personal Web Server, it, too, will try to move into port 80, causing a conflict—pushing, shoving, possibly some spitting. Therefore, what we first need to do is evict the FrontPage Personal Web Server from port 80.

We begin by launching the FrontPage Server Administrator, which can be found in the main Microsoft FrontPage directory, located wherever we installed FrontPage (default: C:\Program Files\Microsoft FrontPage). After double-clicking the FrontPage Server Administrator, we're greeted with the administration window:

In the upper-left-hand region of the Administrator window, we see a list of port numbers currently being lived in; at least, there should be one entry labelled 80, as pictured in the next figure. We click **80**, and information about the server living at that address appears to the right. As illustrated above, we see that the FrontPage Personal Web Server is the current resident of this port, as it reads beside Server Type:. Following that, we're also given the location of the Server configuration file, the Content directory, and additional properties which won't concern us until next chapter. The important point here is that we've verified that the FrontPage Personal Web Server is living in port 80. Thus, with **80** selected, we click the button marked **Uninstall**. A confirmation box appears reassuring us that the Web pages themselves will not be deleted, only this server's relationship with the port. After selecting **OK**, the hard drive will whir for a bit. Eventually, the Administrator will display the new current settings:

Our first meeting with the FrontPage Server Administrator. Order of business: evict FrontPage Personal Web Server from port 80.

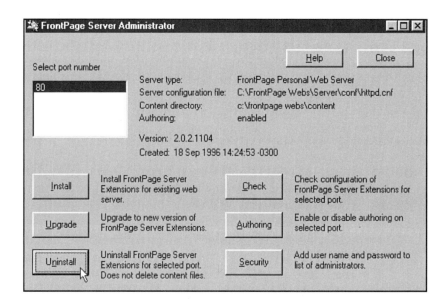

After evicting (uninstalling) the FrontPage Personal Web Server from port 80, we now have no servers residing on any port.

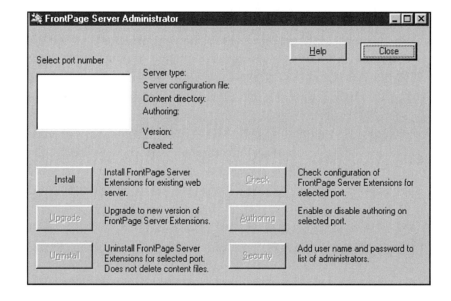

For the record, the FrontPage Personal Web server itself has not been deleted from our computer. It's merely been severed from port 80. We could re-install it into a different port if we wanted both Web servers to co-exist (by editing its configuration file), but there's no strong reason to do so. Rather, we can simply leave it unattached to any port, where it will homelessly do no harm. Now we can close the Administrator.

Finally, the Microsoft Personal Web Server

Welcome back to those readers who skipped ahead. To the readers who followed the paragraphs to oust the FrontPage Personal Web Server, Congratulations! Now, every one of us, tall and short alike, should be ready to install and prepare the Microsoft Personal Web Server.

The first step, of course, is to install the Microsoft Personal Web Server from the Bonus Pack included with FrontPage 97. This is the easy part; simply launch the Bonus Pack's set-up program, and choose to install the Microsoft Personal Web Server. If it asks any questions prior to installation, the default answers are all correct for our needs. After this process is complete, Windows may request that we restart the computer, to which we'll agree, and grab a cup of coffee in the meantime.

Later that Day (or however long it takes for Windows 95 to boot up again)...

Before we re-launch the FrontPage Server Administrator, we need to verify that the Microsoft Personal Web Server is currently running. Take a look at the Windows 95 taskbar—it should display a series of icons, one of which represents the Microsoft Personal Web Server (the other icons that appear may vary from system to system):

Microsoft Personal Web Server is running

If the above icon does not appear, then the Web server needs to be manually kick-started; simply go into the Windows 95 Control Panel and double-click the Microsoft Personal Web Server. When its Properties window appears, click the **Startup** tab, followed by the button marked **Start**, as pictured below.

*Starting the
Microsoft Personal
Web server. Vrooom.*

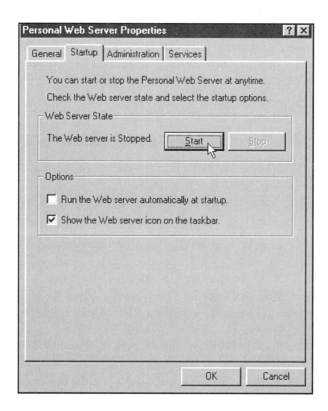

Moving in Day

Now that the Microsoft Personal Web Server is running, we can close its Properties window, and re-launch the FrontPage Server Administrator.

Back in the **FrontPage Server Administrator** window, we now click the button marked **Install**. A drop-down menu appears, from which we are asked to Configure Server Type. Simply select the **Microsoft Personal Web Server** from the selection list.

After clicking **OK**, the drive will whir for a bit. Upon realizing that port 80 is now vacant, and because it is the preferred Web server port, the Administrator will attempt to attach the Microsoft Personal Web Server to port 80. Before any final changes are made, we're shown a summary of what the Administrator intends to do.

As pictured, we see that the Microsoft Personal Web Server will be moved to port 80, and that the home directory for Web pages delivered by this server will be the path c:\WebShare\wwwroot. Assuming that's all agreeable (which it is), we click **OK**.

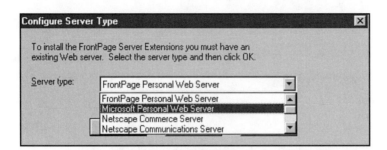

Selecting the server to move in to port. Choose the Microsoft Personal Web Server; it will drift into port 80 by default.

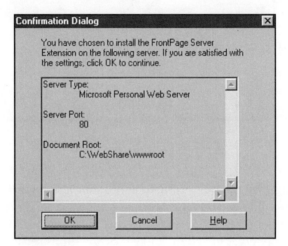

The Administrator displays its intentions, before we approve any changes made to our server setup.

Handing Out the Keys

Next, the Administrator asks us to create an account name to use when authoring Web pages or making other changes on this server. By default, it prompts us with the account name (if any) assigned to the current Windows 95 login session. Whether using that name or another, we should select an account name with its purpose in mind: Whoever uses this account name will be able to have full access to our Web pages and this Web server; if you are unsure about the security features configured on this machine's Windows 95, select a administrative name different from the default (if you'll be the only one ever operating this machine, these security mechanisms are less important, and you can select basically any administrative name). The ins and outs of Web server security are the focus of Chapter 20, "Tinker Tinker Little Server," so for now, select an administrative name, and in the next chapter, we'll examine the role it plays.

Once we've decided on an administrative name, we click **OK** again. Lastly, the very amiable Administrator informs us that it needs to restart the server for the changes to take effect. We agree, and a few seconds later, our new server configuration is displayed.

Ah...at last. The Microsoft Personal Web Server is installed in port 80. We're finally ready to rock. And roll.

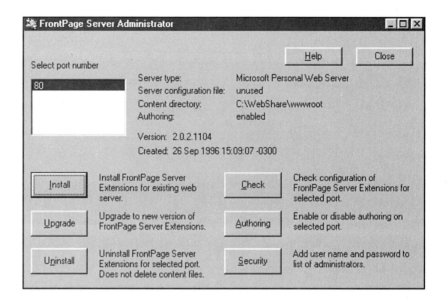

The Good Life

Yahoo! We've completed the most difficult part of our journey with Web servers. At this point, all readers should have the Microsoft Personal Web Server installed on their machine and residing in port 80. The server is ready for prime-time. In the next chapter, we'll demonstrate the server in action, and get cozy with its security-guard personality. The hard part is over; take it easy for a bit. Have a Zima.

The Least You Need to Know

The most challenging aspect of using a Web server with FrontPage 97 is actually installing it. The products and procedures involved can be confusing at first glance, and so we dedicated this chapter to disentangling the issues, and prepping the correct server for prime time.

➤ Installing and running a Web server is a matter of choice. Readers who either create simple Web sites, or create Web sites for larger business who hire server administrators needn't concern themselves with running their own server.

➤ Readers who want to test their Web sites before publishing them to a service provider's server, or readers who want to serve pages directly from home, such as in a home-based business environment or possibly an intranet, should install a Web server on their own computer.

258

➤ The FrontPage 97 package includes two entirely separate Web server products: the FrontPage Personal Web Server and the Microsoft Personal Web Server. In all cases, we want to use the Microsoft Personal Web Server; the FrontPage Personal Web Server is too weak to recommend.

➤ Readers who already installed the FrontPage Personal Web Server before reading this chapter will need to uninstall it from port 80, by using the FrontPage Server Administrator (located in the main Microsoft FrontPage directory).

➤ Once there are no servers occupying port 80 (verified by running the FrontPage Server Administrator), we can install the Microsoft Personal Web Server from the FrontPage Bonus Pack. Following that installation, we use the FrontPage Server Administrator to install this Web server to port 80.

➤ Sound confusing? Then be sure you read through this chapter!

Chapter 20

Tinker Tinker
Little Server

In This Chapter

➤ Behave, you server!

➤ Configurations and more configurations, and a few more

➤ Guarding the gates: Access permissions

➤ Restricting Web sites

➤ Paranoia—it's not all bad

The Web server is a multi-faceted sort, with a wide array of configurable properties that guide its behavior. In a real sense, this is a good thing, as it means that we have a fair amount of latitude in customizing how our Web server behaves. On the other hand, it also means that there are that many more parts to play with (and concepts to understand), some of which can seem confusing at first. In this chapter, as we near the final few unrumpled pages of this book, we'll zoom in on the Microsoft Personal Web server, and how to configure its behavior. Special attention is paid to security issues, where we dictate who can do what. And who can't.

Checking Your Roots, and Tilling the Fields

There are some rational, and some less rational, reasons why the Web server configurations are spread out over four different applications. "What??" you say, "Four?" Yes, in fact, it turns out that to fully access the different tweaks and knobs to customize our Web server, we need to conscript (at least) four applications, menus, and utilities that Microsoft has provided. Having said that, we'll look at each in turn, to minimize confusion.

Familiar territory being what it is (well, familiar), let's take another look at the FrontPage Server Administrator. We used this application in Chapter 19, "Bringing the Server to Life." It's an application that we launched from the Microsoft FrontPage directory on our hard drive, when examining or changing which Web servers were installed into port 80 on our computer. Recall that its friendly face smiled as in the following figure.

The friendly face of the FrontPage Server Administrator. Here we can allow or disallow authoring of Web sites, and define new administrators.

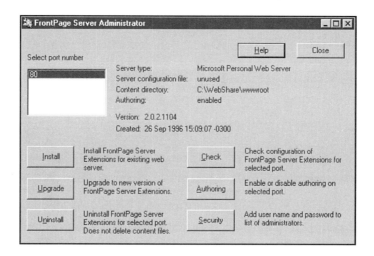

Be sure that the Microsoft Personal Web Server is currently running; check for its icon on the taskbar, or kick-start the server as explained toward the end of Chapter 19.

The FrontPage Server Administrator offers two additional options (other than those we've already looked at) to customize our server:

Authoring: Clicking this button allows us to enable or disable authoring. Put simply, *authoring* is the ability to edit a FrontPage Web on the server. If authoring is disabled, any Webs on this server's port are "write-protected" and cannot be modified. If it is enabled, we can modify the Webs on this server. Checking the option marked **Require SSL for authoring** will only allow Webs on this server to be modified if the author has chosen to **Connect using SSL** when opening the Web with the FrontPage Explorer. This guarantees that only secure (encrypted) transactions will occur in modifying the Web site, keeping out spies. Of course, this does require that the Web server in question support SSL transactions. If the server reports an error when this option is enabled, it may not be configured to support SSL.

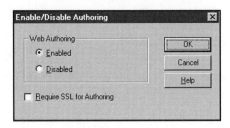

Scribble, scribble... allowing or disallowing the authoring of Web pages on this server.

Security: An administrator is a user who has full access to Webs on this server. He can view, edit, add to, or delete from the Web, and he may administer the Web, such as by determining who else has privileges. When we initially installed the Microsoft Personal Web Server, we already created an administrator name for the <Root Web> (the main Web, which we'll explain shortly). If we like, we can add additional administrator names, and specify which Webs on this server they have power over. Specifying <Root Web> gives the administrator power over all Webs on this server. For users who work in a solo environment (for example, designing Web sites on one's own personal computer), a single administrator name is fine. Those designing Web sites with groups of people might want to create additional administrators.

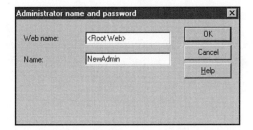

Aye, aye, captains. Adding additional administrators to this server.

That completes our brief tour of the FrontPage Server Administrator. Its functions are few, but necessary.

Web Server Properties

Now, to continue customizing how our Personal Web Server behaves, we turn our attention to the Microsoft Personal Web Server Properties. There are two ways to access these Properties: Either open up the Windows 95 Control Panel and double-click the Personal Web Server icon, or right-click the Personal Web Server icon in the Windows 95 taskbar and select **Properties** from the pop-up menu. Via either route, the following window appears.

*The General Proper-
ties tab of the
Microsoft Personal
Web Server. Tweaks
and tunings.*

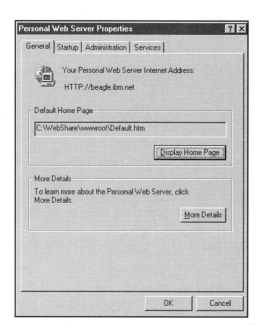

General Properties

We first see the General Properties tab for the Microsoft Personal Web Server. At the top
of the window, beside the little compu-globe icon, it tells us the "Internet Address" for
our server. Do, however, swallow this with a few grains of salt. At the least, this is the
address we can use when testing Web pages on our server from the same machine (local
testing). It may not, though, be the address we can use to access our server from elsewhere on the Internet (see Chapter 21, "Leave No Server Untested," for a full explanation
of this).

Moving on down, we see the property Default Home Page. This represents the page that a
reader will see if he opens a URL to our server without any further path specifications.
Saying that again in the English language, if the reader points his Web browser to http://
our.server/, he will see the page specified in this property. Clicking **Display Home Page**
will merely open this default home page into our browser. For the record, when we
choose to open the <Root Web> on this server in the FrontPage Explorer, it is this page,
and any pages related to it, that we are opening. Should it suit us, we can change the path
for the Default Home Page, but not in this properties sheet. That comes later.

Clicking the button **More Details** will open the Microsoft Personal Web Server help pages
in our browser—not a bad idea, to supplement our discussion in this chapter.

Startup Properties

The **Startup** tab brings us to a new sheet of properties, which is represented in the next figure.

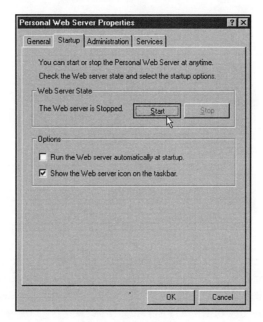

Giving the Microsoft Personal Web Server a real start.

Whether the server is currently running is reflected in the Web Server State property. Clicking **Stop** will halt a running server, and clicking **Start** will run a halted server. Tough concept, that. Below, we can enable **Run Web Server automatically at startup**, which will, as advertised, start the Web server whenever Windows 95 boots up. If you use the Web server frequently, it's probably best that it start up automatically. Otherwise, you can manually start it when needed. Finally, and it is generally recommended, we can **Show the Web server icon on the taskbar.** Whether to automatically start the server, or manually use the **Start/Stop** buttons, is a matter of choice. The only important point, albeit a somewhat obvious one, is that the server needs to be running when performing administrative tasks, or viewing and editing Web pages that reside on it.

Services Properties

Briefly skipping over the Administration tab for the moment, let's click the **Services** tab. Here we can configure the server's delivery of certain types of data.

Service, service, service. Delivering data is the server's primary function in life. We can enable or disable Web (HTTP) or FTP services.

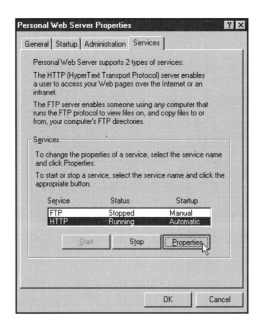

The Microsoft Personal Web Server supports two types of data delivery services: HTTP is the service used for typical Web page delivery. FTP is a service strictly meant for delivering files. By default, HTTP service is active and FTP service is not. This should suit most readers. The availability of the FTP service, however, is a convenience to those who would like to offer FTP access. Only readers who understand FTP should consider enabling it, otherwise there may be a security risk to one's personal files. Leaving FTP service stopped will not negatively impact those who intend to deliver most typical Web pages.

Selecting either service allows us to click the **Start** or **Stop** buttons, to immediately start or stop each service. Clicking the **Properties** button with a service selected, we can further configure some characteristics of the service. For instance, we'll select the HTTP service, and click **Properties**.

The top-most, and slightly confusing, property is labelled Startup Options. If we choose **automatic**, then we may use the **Run Web server automatically at startup** option in the Startup Properties sheet. Choosing **manual** means that we must start and stop the service by hand. This is not much different from the similar option on the Startup Properties sheet.

Next, we see the Web Server Home Root Settings. This refers to the local storage path for all Web pages and related files that reside on this server. The Microsoft Personal Web Server's default path is c:\WebShare\wwwroot, and unless there is some reason to choose a different path on a particular computer (perhaps you want Web pages stored on a different drive than C:), this path is fine. For the record, this path is where <Root Web> will reside, as explained in Chapter 12, "If I Only Had a Crane—Hauling Your Web to a Server." Lastly, we can change the path for the Default Home Page, as first encountered on the General Properties sheet. Usually, there's no reason to change this either, although if we've changed the Web Server Home Root path, we probably need to change the Default Home Page accordingly. For instance, if we only have a 300 megabyte hard drive on C:, and a 1 gigabyte drive on D:, we might prefer our Web pages to be stored on the larger drive. In that case, we could change the Web Server Home Root to D:\WebShare\ wwwroot and the Default Home Page to D:\WebShare\wwwroot\Default.htm.

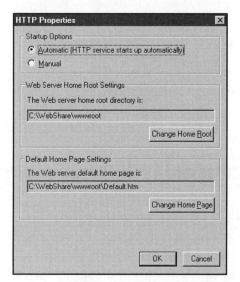

Delivering Web pages via the HTTP service, we can further configure this service's behavior.

Third Application—The Administration Tab

One tab remains in the Personal Web Server Properties, and that is labelled Administration. At the outset of this chapter, we warned that server configurations spanned four different applications. Thus far, we've covered two of them: The FrontPage Server Administrator and the Personal Web Server Properties. The Administration tab only contains one button, marked **Administration**, and clicking it launches the third configuration application.

Launched from the Personal Web Server Properties, and operated through our browser, the Internet Services Administrator allows us to configure security fundamentals for our server.

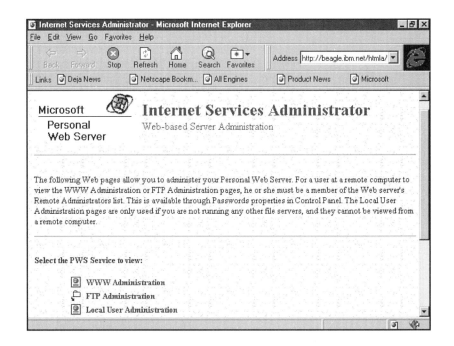

The Microsoft Personal Web Bureaucracy—Administrating the Server

As pictured above, the Administration button has launched our Web browser, and opened a page titled Internet Services Administrator. Yes, all these names do become confusing, and that's unfortunate design. Bear with it; fortunately, most of these configurations and properties are only used from time to time, if ever. This Internet Services Administrator allows us to further configure the Web and FTP services, as well as maintain a list of authorized users and passwords. But that's simply an overview; let's begin, in earnest detail, by clicking the link named **WWW Administration**.

We begin on the Service property sheet, as illustrated in the previous candid photo. If a connection established to our server doesn't respond within Connection timeout seconds (600, by default), the server will close the connection to that visitor. In addition, the server is willing to accept the Maximum Connections number of simultaneous connections from visitors (300, by default). To reduce potential overload of our server computer, especially if it has other work to do besides serving Web pages, we might want to reduce both of these values, especially Maximum Connections. For instance, if we try to serve pages over a 28.8 kbps connection (which is not advisable, but is possible), we should reduce the maximum number of connections to one. The number of connections should be proportional to the speed of your Internet connection.

268

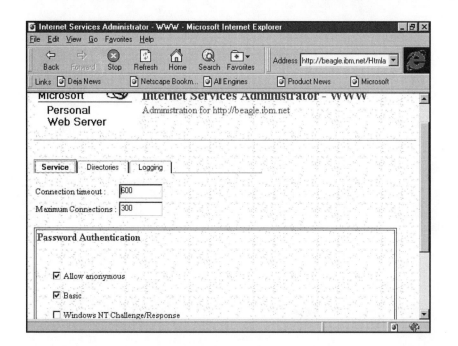

Administering WWW services through the Internet Services Administrator. Sure would've been nice to have one application that handled all configurations.

In beginning our look at restricting access to our server, and at least some of its Web pages, we consider the Password Authentication properties. If we enable **Allow Anonymous**, then anyone may visit our unrestricted Web pages (we'll look at how to restrict certain Web pages later in this chapter). Except for intensely private intranet environments, we usually want to enable anonymous access (hence, it is enabled by default).

For those Web pages that we later choose to restrict, we may select what sort of password authentication to use: **Basic** is the standard choice, although it exposes a risk to snoopers, who could intercept passwords as they are transmitted across the network. **Windows NT Challenge/Response** prevents snoop attacks on passwords, but can only be used within intranets that have at least one Windows NT machine. For most servers, then, we leave **Basic** enabled.

Lastly, we may click the link leading to **Local User Administration**.

Advanced Administration: FTP Returning to the initial page of the Internet Services Administrator, the next link leads to FTP Administration. As mentioned earlier in this chapter, we're not directly explaining FTP server support in this book, because it is not essential to serving Web pages, per se. Readers who are familiar with FTP services can feel free to configure them—clicking this link leads to a predictable set of properties, including the number of connections, server messages, directory permissions, and logging options. Readers unfamiliar with FTP can ignore this administration tool.

Creating a list of users and groups who may be given permission to edit or view the Web pages on this server. It's good to be king.

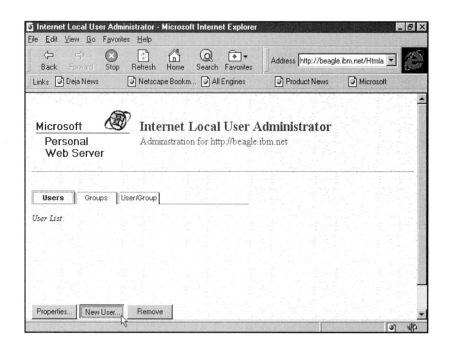

Axis and Allies: Creating User Name and Groups

In the final section of this chapter, we're going to examine Web site restrictions—limiting who can view, edit, or administer a Web site on our server. In doing so, we'll need to reference a list of "users," names we've created, to whom we will grant the various levels of privilege. It is here, on the Local User Administration page, where we create these user names.

As pictured above, no names are listed; we've not created any yet. Let's create three names, each one to be used again later in this chapter. In addition, we're going to create one group. A group is a set of user names who share a privilege level.

1. First, though, we create each user name. We begin by clicking the button marked **New User**, and a new screen appears.

2. Next, we'll assign our first user the name **KingLear**, and decide upon a password for KingLear. We enter the password in both the User Password and Confirm Password entry forms, to prevent against a typo.

3. Then, we click **Add**, which returns to the user list page, which now has a population of one.

Adding a new user to our user list. "I hereby knight thee…"

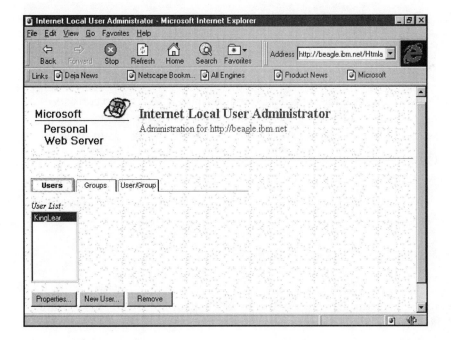

Our newest user appears in the user list.

4. Repeating the above, careful not to induce carpal tunnel syndrome, we create two additional user names: **Shakespeare** and **Peeper**. Afterwords, our user list appears like the next figure.

Three user names, all in a row. Now, to create a group.

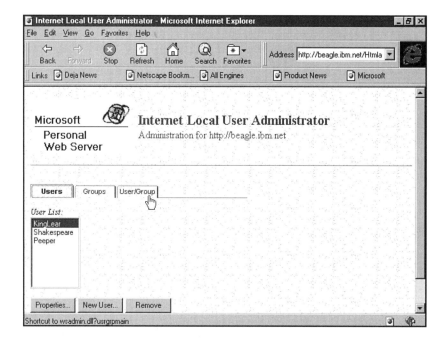

5. Now we'd like to create a group, which can be a more efficient way of assigning the same permissions to multiple individuals (as we'll see later). This group consists of two users: KingLear and Shakespeare. Thus, click on the **Groups** folder tab, and a group list appears, empty. We click **New Group**, and assign to this group the name **Scribes**.

6. To add users to the group, we click the folder tab marked **User/Group**.

7. Finally, with the group name **Scribes** selected, we select the user name **KingLear** from the user list, and click **Add User to Group**. Repeat this step for the user **Shakespeare**. To verify which users are in a group, simply click the **Groups** tab, select the group to view, and click the **Properties** button.

Thus, we have created four new potential privilege-holders: the users KingLear, Shakespeare, and Peeper, and the group Scribes, consisting of KingLear and Shakespeare. Having completed our lessons with the Internet Services Administrator, we now look at how to assign privileges to the above users and groups. We can close the Web browser now, as the Internet Services Administrator is no longer needed.

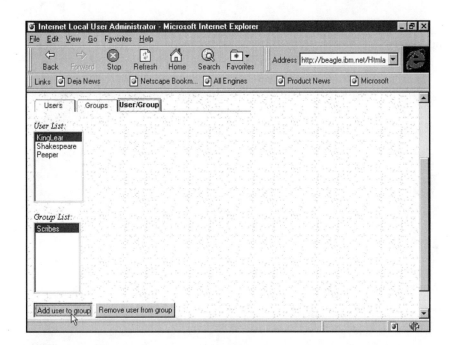

Choose a user name from the first list, a group from the second, and voila!

Who Goes There? Access Restrictions

The vast majority of Web authors and designers want their sites to be accessible by the general public. After all, it is called the *World Wide Web* for a reason. Therefore, restricting access to view Web pages is not extremely common. On the other hand, it's not unheard of either. Some sites contain pages with information that only certain people are allowed to see; perhaps beta testers of a software application. Or employees of the FBI, although one assumes they have alternative methods of distributing their secrets (ouch!).

When it comes to restricting access to our Web sites, there are three levels of privilege that may be granted to individuals or groups:

➤ **Administer, Author, and Browse**   Users or groups with this, the most prestigious level of privilege, may view the Web pages in this site; they may modify, add to, or delete them; and they may grant privileges to other users or groups.

➤ **Author and Browse**   This privilege allows for viewing, modifying, adding to, or deleting from the Web pages in this site. It does not allow for granting of privileges to anyone.

➤ **Browse**   Only allows viewing of these Web pages, without authority to alter them, or to grant privileges to anyone.

Privileges are hierarchical in nature; that is, they apply to any Web that resides within the Web that the privileges were applied to. Huh? Let's consider the structure of Web sites on our server. The main, top-level Web site is known as the <Root Web>. We can open the <Root Web> in the FrontPage Explorer by choosing to open a FrontPage Web. Assuming that we have entered the correct name for the machine running our Web server (e.g., mycomputer.domain.com), we click **List Webs**, and at the least, <Root Web> should appear in the list of FrontPage Webs, and we can open it.

Any other Web sites that we've created on our server are sub-Webs of the <Root Web>. As a consequence, any privilege permissions that we apply to the <Root Web> automatically apply to every sub-Web. We can also override these permissions for a particular Web site on our server, if necessary.

Granting Permissions

But let's begin at the beginning: Applying permissions to the <Root Web>. Be sure that it is currently opened in the FrontPage Explorer.

*Our <Root Web> open in the FrontPage Explorer. By selecting the menu item **Tools, Permissions** we can set permission privileges that apply to all our Web sites on this server.*

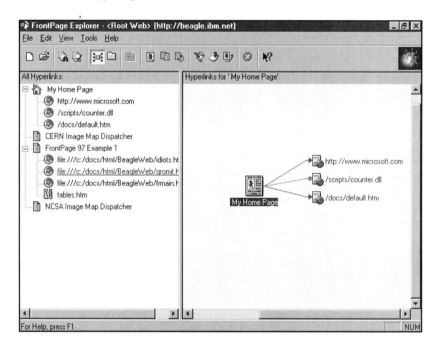

Configuring permission privileges is done through the menu item **Tools, Permissions**, which yields the panel pictured in the next figure.

274

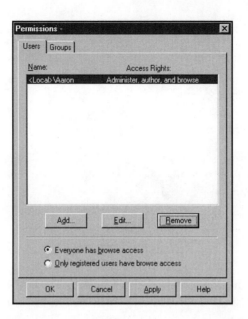

Determining permission privileges for this Web site, and any Web sites within it. In this case, permissions applied to the <Root Web> apply to all Web sites on this server, unless specifically overridden.

By default, the **Users** tab is selected, and we see which users have permissions granted. In this case, only one user, coincidentally named Aaron, has permissions; and he has all of them. Recall that we didn't create this user when adding users to the user list with the Internet Services Administrator. Where did he come from, then? He was created as an administrator when installing the Microsoft Personal Web Server into port 80, with the FrontPage Server Administrator. Any other administrators created there would appear here, as well.

Note that at the bottom of the permissions window, **Everyone has browse access** is selected. This allows any visitor to view Web pages on this server. Later, if necessary, we can restrict access to particular pages, but now we're working with the <Root Web>.Thus, we've created a default situation in which anyone can visit our pages, unless otherwise specified by us in future permissions. We'd want to apply **Only registered users have browse access** to the <Root Web> only if this were a private intranet, and we wanted all of its pages to always be restricted.

Imagine, though, that we'd like to apply permission privileges for two other users: KingLear, who is also allowed full privileges, and Shakespeare, who is allowed only authoring and browsing privileges. To do so, we'd click the **Add** button, and see the next window for managing our additions:

Selecting a level of permissions, and the users to whom they are granted.

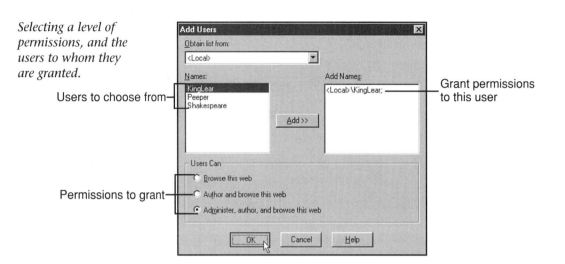

Users to choose from┐

Grant permissions to this user

Permissions to grant┐

At the bottom of the window, we select the level of permissions to grant. In this case, we'll start by choosing all permissions: **Administer, author, and browse this web**. The only user to whom we wish to grant these is **KingLear**, and so we select his name from the Names list on the left, and click the **Add>>** button. His name then appears in the Add Names window on the right. Since we are done, we click **OK** to add this permission. We're returned to the Permissions properties, where we click **Add** again, to set the permissions for Shakespeare. This time, we select the permissions **Author and browse this web**, followed by **Shakespeare** in the Names list, and then click **Add>>**. Our permissions properties now reflect the permissions for each assignment we've made.

The permissions assigned to each user—both Aaron and KingLear have full authorities, while Shakespeare can only author and browse pages on this server.

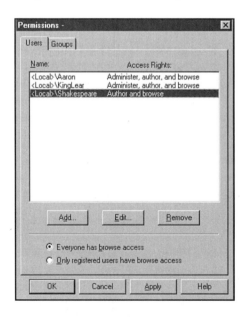

Permission Inheritance

To repeat an important theme, the permissions we've just applied to the <Root Web> automatically apply to any other Web site residing on our server (that is, those Webs that appear when we select our server and click **List Webs** when opening a site in the FrontPage Explorer).

Nit-picking: Page-Specific Restrictions

In many cases, the above is sufficient, and we needn't worry about more specific permissions. However, consider an alternative scenario: We have several Web sites on our server, and while most are available for public browsing, one of the sites is restricted to pre-approved users only. Perhaps it contains sensitive information, or information that we charge for, and thus only allow access to those who've paid us. Imagine, then, that this Web site is called PrivateWeb, and we want to restrict access to it, while allowing public access to our other sites.

Fortunately, the matter is not so difficult. We've already applied suitable permissions to our <Root Web>, allowing the public to browse any of our sites by default. Now, then, we must open our PrivateWeb into the FrontPage Explorer. Once that is open, we again select the menu item **Tools**, **Permissions**. Note, though, that a different window appears than in the previous example.

Override <Root Web> permissions

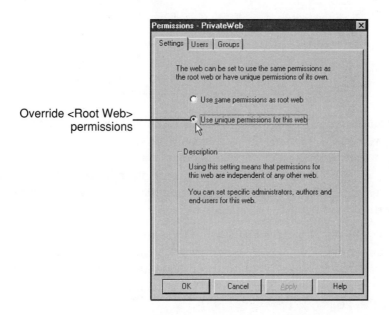

When configuring the permissions for a Web within our server's <Root Web>, we can either inherit the permissions "from above," or override them.

Upon opening, the option "Use same permissions as root web" is selected. This would, as it explains in the window, inherit the permissions we applied to <Root Web>. In this case, we do not approve of that, because the <Root Web> allows for public browsing, and we want to restrict viewing of this site. Thus, we select **Use unique permissions for this web**, which allows us to override the <Root Web> for this particular site. Next, we click **Apply**, which will allow us to then click the **Users** tab.

We're now faced with the permission settings as before, except that whatever we create here will only apply to PrivateWeb. In this case, we want to select **Only registered users have browser access**. When that is done, only users whom we add to this list may browse PrivateWeb. First, we'll add two folks from within our organization, KingLear and Shakespeare. Remember that we defined a group, known as Scribes, containing them both. So, we click on the **Groups** tab, followed by **Add**. We're then asked to add groups, just like we added user names in the previous example.

Adding the group Scribes (KingLear and Shakespeare) to our access list, complete with permission to browse and author.

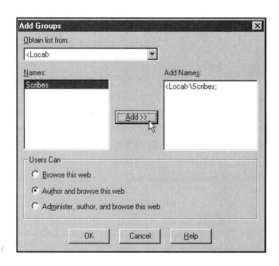

These two folks are members of our organization, and so we choose to grant them **Author and browse this web** access. Then we click again on the **User** tab. Imagine that we have one paying customer so far, named Peeper. Consequently, we want to grant Peeper permission to browse PrivateWeb. Being sure that **only registered users have browse access** is still selected, we click **Add**. Facing the now-familiar screen, we add **Peeper**, giving him (or her!) **Browse this web** permissions.

Be sure to click **OK** in Permissions properties window, so that these changes are relayed to the server. To take a refreshing look back, we've applied certain administrative and authoring permissions to our <Root Web>, and consequently, all other Webs on our server—except for PrivateWeb, which has its own set of permissions, allowing only one member of the public, Peeper, to browse it.

A Few Words about Paranoia

Paranoia is not necessarily a bad thing, although the word has negative, spiders-crawling-on-my-arm-aliens-are-after-me connotations. In the world of computer security, paranoia is a measure of safety. In the last half of this chapter, we've considered server properties that address issues of paranoia: who is allowed to administrate, author, and view our Web pages. The degree to which these settings matter is wholly proportional to the degree in which security matters to one's site, and organization.

One of the first steps in typical security consultation is to evaluate the security needs of an individual or an organization. Obviously, the CIA has a different set of security requirements than Frank's Fishmarket. Additionally, a Web server that runs on a computer shared by many people may require more security than a Web server that runs on a home computer with one primary user and a cat sleeping on the monitor.

When re-reading this chapter, which is probably a must, given the convoluted and sprawling nature of accessing Web server configurations, consider how much security is appropriate for the particular situation. Adding security, as can be gleaned from reading this chapter, adds additional complexity to the maintenance of the Web server. Some situations require this increased complexity, some do not.

The Least You Need to Know

The truth is, there really isn't a *least* you need to know for this chapter. There's quite a bit to know, if one is going to delve into server configurations, which no short summary can cover adequately. If you are running the Microsoft Personal Web Server, then it needs to be configured, and you need to read this chapter. Besides, it has some good jokes!

Leave No Server Untested

Some of the cooking programs on television are fascinating. While some stick to the basics, there's a segment of the culinary world that finds great joy, perhaps a sadistic kind, in combining disparate ingredients into an exotic concoction. In fact, it seems that the trendy thing to do is to highlight its eccentricity by naming it descriptively: while the old school has the modest "Chicken Cacciatore", the new school proffers the more explicit, "Cubed Breasts of Poultry with Mangos, Beets, and Kiwi Sauce." But food isn't math, and the viewer of these recipes cannot simply add up the ingredients to calculate the score. "Hmm, I like chicken, and mangos, and kiwis, so I'm sure I'll love them all cooked together" simply doesn't add up. The only reliable way to evaluate this recipe is to try it. Long-winded introduction excused, the same is true for our Web server. Staring at its configurations all day only gets us part-way there —to test the server, we've got to try it.

From the Inside Looking In

When we say "test" a server, we basically mean, "request Web pages from it." Ultimately, the test of whether the server works or not lies in whether the Web pages work as designed. That's the obvious part.

The first issue we encounter, though, is how should we send requests to our Web server? To answer this, consider the two perspectives on our computing environment:

➤ The computer on which our Microsoft Personal Web Server resides is part of our internal network; sometimes called a Local Area Network, sometimes called an intranet. The size of this internal network can vary—it may consist of only one computer. We do everything on that computer, from designing the Web pages, to serving them. Or, our internal network might consist of several computers, one of which runs the server. However we slice it, there *is* an internal network.

➤ Depending on which computers can contact our internal network, there may also be an external network. Most commonly, this external network is the Internet. If we have no connection to the Internet, we may *only* have an internal network.

Most readers of this book will fit into both perspectives above: They have an internal network of at least one computer (by necessity), and an external network via their connection to the Internet. In this case, we'll want to test our Web server from each perspective, asking it to deliver Web pages within the internal network and asking it to deliver Web pages across the Internet.

The few readers who only possess, and desire, an internal network need only test it from within. In this half of the chapter, we'll look at testing the server from within the internal network. In the second half of the chapter, we'll test the server across the Internet. After that, we party.

Browser, Meet Web Site

Ultimately, to test our Web sites, we are going to visit them with our Web browser. Any special functions should be reviewed, such as submitting forms, viewing Java applets, and so forth. If we have an internal network of one computer, then obviously we must run the Web browser on the same computer as the Web server. If we have an internal network of two or more computers, then it's a good idea to run the Web browser on a computer other than the one which is running the server. This provides the best test of the internal network and the server.

After the Web browser is running, let's consider how we'll access Web sites on our server. Recall that when we open a URL in a browser, we're essentially sending a request to the server on the specified machine. Consider, for instance, the URL:

http://somemachine/Catalog

The URL requests the Web site named *Catalog* from the server running on *somemachine*. Because we didn't specify an exact Web page to open (a .htm or .html file), the default home page will be opened within the Catalog directory (*default.htm* as is the standard configuration in the Microsoft Personal Web Server). We could point a URL to an exact page, as in:

> http://somemachine/Catalog/items.html

Or to the <Root Web> of a server, which will open its default home page:

> http://somemachine

In all the above cases, we're sending our requests to the server on *somemachine*. Therefore, to send requests to our own server, we must determine by what name to refer to it. The answer, in fact, is that we can use any of several names to refer to the computer running our server. However, some names are safer bets than others. Because we're still testing our server from within our internal network, we should use the following two guidelines to determine the address of our server:

For readers whose internal network consists of only a single computer:

We'll be testing our server by running the Web browser on the same computer. In this case, we need to determine the address of our computer. In fact, our computer probably has several addresses, each of which are synonymous. To illustrate this, launch the FrontPage Explorer. Then, select the menu item **Help, About Microsoft FrontPage Explorer**. This yields a pop-up window with the registration information for our copy of FrontPage, as well as a button labelled Network Test:

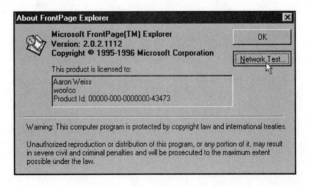

The About window in FrontPage Explorer hides a special utility for testing our network.

Click the **Network Test** button, and a new window appears, named **FrontPage TCP/IP Test**. Click the **Start Test** button in this window, and some information will appear as follows:

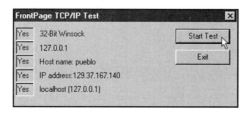

After running the network test, the information revealed helps us determine the network name and address of our computer.

We're basically interested in the bottom three bits of information:

Host name: This is the "name" of our computer; *pueblo* in the image above. This name was configured when Windows 95 was originally installed.

IP address: This is the Internet network address of our computer. It may read 127.0.0.1 if we're not currently connected to the Internet, or it may have some other IP address, such as *129.37.167.140* as in the picture above.

localhost: Localhost is a network term which means "this computer." Assuming our network is setup properly, this should read *localhost (127.0.01)*

So, what do we learn from the above? To address the server on this computer, we can use any of its hostname, IP address, or localhost in the Web page URL. In other words, we can launch our browser and attempt to open a URL to:

http://pueblo

http://*129.37.167.140*

http://localhost

All of these addresses are synonymous, and will open the <Root Web> on this machine's Web server. If we wanted to open a subweb of the <Root Web>, such as *CandyCatalog*, we could open a URL to *http://localhost/CandyCatalog*, for instance. While there is no "preferred" address of the three above, for the sake of consistency, we'll use the *http://localhost* syntax, as it is the most traditional when referring to a server on the same machine as the client.

For readers whose internal network consists of two or more computers:

In this situation, the above names are inapplicable, because they refer to whichever computer the Web browser is running on. Remember that we want to run the Web browser on a computer *other than* the one running the Web server. Within a local network, though, each computer has an address. This address may be a number, as in the form xxx.xxx.xxx.xxx, or it may be a word, such as *Mambo*. The best bet is to find out the address of the computer running the Web server from someone who knows. You might also try running the Network Test in FrontPage Explorer on the machine running the Web server. You can then find out which address or name to use when opening a URL to a page on the server.

Because the configuration of local networks vary in many ways, we cannot provide sure-fire step-by-step instructions on how to determine the name of the machine running the Web server. If one does not know, and asking whomever is in charge of the local network is out of the question, one idea is to sit at the computer running the Web server and open the Network Properties from the Windows 95 Control Panel. Once the Control Panel is displayed, click the **Identification** tab, and it will report a Computer Name. This is the name you can use in the URL to address this machine from another Windows machine within the local network; for example, http://computername/CandyCatalog.

There's Somebody Out There

For those who intend for their Web sites to be accessible across the Internet, testing our server from outside the local network—from the Internet, in fact—is the best way. The basic concept for doing so is the same as in the first half of this chapter: Launch a Web browser and open a URL which points to our server. What differs in this scenario is the address of our machine running the server, and on which machine we run the Web browser.

Determining the address of our server machine is the first, and most critical, step to testing it over the Internet. As we're probably quite familiar with by now, each computer on the Internet has a unique numerical address (known as an IP address), in the form xxx.xxx.xxx.xxx. In many, but not all cases, a human-friendly equivalent is assigned to the IP address; for instance, bob.machine.com may be assigned to 130.150.43.5. In such a case, either the human-friendly or IP address may be used.

Due to the way we may connect to the Internet, readers will fall into one of two categories of addresses:

➤ *Static IP addresses*: A static IP address is an IP address which always remains the same. For instance, let's say that our service provider provides our computer with a static IP address of 130.150.43.5. Therefore, everytime we connect to the Internet, assuming that we don't own a dedicated connection (24 hours a day/7 days a week), our computer has the same IP address: 130.150.43.5 (in this example). This is very convenient, and oftentimes, a human-friendly name will be assigned to us as well.

➤ *Dynamic IP addresses*: Unfortunately, many of us home users fall into this category. Our service provider doesn't provide us with a single IP address that is always ours. Rather, we are assigned an IP address each time we connect to the Internet. Therefore, our IP address may be different every time we connect. A human-friendly name is not assigned to us, because it has no single address to be equivalent to. Dynamic IP addresses are inconvenient, because we cannot rely on a single address for our computer, and we must look up its current address each time we need to refer to it. Most problematically, a dynamic IP address prevents us from establishing a permanent location on the Internet. In such a situation, we really can't use our computer a reliable Web server for others to visit. This would require obtaining a static IP address, for which most service providers charge extra.

Whether or not one has a static or dynamic IP address, we can find out the current IP address of our computer in a simple manner: Assuming that we're currently connected to the Internet, we select **Start**, **Run** from the Windows 95 taskbar, and run the program named **winipcfg**.

Determining our current IP address, by which we'll address our server.

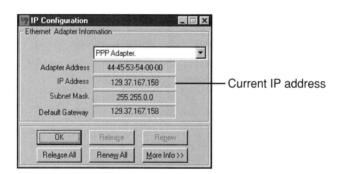

— Current IP address

Of course, we should run this program on the computer that is running the server. If one has a static IP address, we need only determine it once. Those with dynamic IP addresses will need to run winipcfg everytime they reconnect to the Internet, to find out their current IP address. Those with static IP addresses, but don't know it, will find out soon enough if they keep running winipcfg after making their net connection, and consistently find it reporting the same IP address. For the record, we can also find out our current IP address by running the Network Test from the FrontPage Explorer's Help menu, as explained earlier in this chapter. It works equally as well as **winipcfg**.

An Alternative Test

In either case, we now know at least the current IP address of the computer running our server. The ideal test, then, is to contact this server from a machine elsewhere on the Internet; that is, a machine with a different address than our server. This may not be so easy; after all, we'd need to have access to a computer with its own connection to the Internet. Not many home users have two computers, each connected individually to the Internet. Users in an office environment may have better luck finding another machine connected to the Internet.

Nonetheless, the ideal test is a machine unconnected to our own server. If feeling scrappy, one could always find a friend or neighbor with an Internet-connected computer, or rent time at a hip "CyberCafe," or Kinko's, or any of those other shops who charge outrageous fees for an hour of Internet usage. Aside from these options, an additional option remains.

Run the browser on the same computer as the server, but open the URL using the IP address, rather than localhost. For instance, while we could open a URL to http://localhost/CandyCatalog, we could also open it to http://130.150.43.5/CandyCatalog. The latter would be a better test of how our server operates across the Internet.

The advantage of the above is that we can view our Web site with full graphics, and test any functions such as form handling and Java applets. On the downside, checking our access restrictions may not work, because the server may assume that we're the Web administrator (because we are), and therefore automatically allow us full browsing privileges.

Testing 101

By and large, once we've connected to our server and viewed the Web page, *testing* it, per se, is fairly obvious.

Does it look as designed?

Does it behave as designed?

Do Java applets appear and ActiveX controls function?

Do form fields work properly, and does submitting a form yield the correct results?

The key is to be thorough. While non-interactive page elements merely need to appear aesthetically correct, interactive functions should be tested extensively. Try to imagine yourself as the visitor, and engage in any and all of the actions a visitor might take.

Perhaps even more importantly, attempt to make any mistakes a visitor might make. Submit incomplete forms, attempt to choose multiple options when only one should be selected at a time, and so forth. Anticipating visitor errors is one of the smartest approaches to designing a foolproof page. In doing so, we also run the server through its paces.

A situation may arise where a page function is not working (such as a certain form not yielding the correct results) and we're not sure if the page contains a design flaw or if the server is misbehaving. In these cases, we may need to try publishing the page to another server on someone else's computer, and attempt to test it from there. If possible, try testing the page on a server product which is different from one's own; for instance, if we're trying to deliver the page with the Microsoft Personal Web Server, try publishing it to a computer which is running Netscape's Web server, or NCSA's Web server. Certainly, these are all ideal cases. When possible, they'll provide the most thorough test. When they are not, we do what we can.

The Least You Need to Know

In closing out our time together in this book (except for the Appendix "Semper Paratus: FrontPage 97 Installation Tips," Glossary "Speak Like a Geek: The Complete Archive," and the always-exciting Index), we've considered ways in which to test our Web server.

➤ All readers can test their server from within the local network, whether it consists of only one computer, or more.

➤ On local networks with only one computer, the Web browser must be run on the same machine as the Web server. To reference this server when opening a URL in the browser, use **localhost** as the address for this machine; for example, http://localhost/CandyCatalog.

➤ On local networks with multiple computers, run the Web browser on a different machine than that which runs the Web server. Reference the server machine by using its Windows name in the URL; for example, http://mambo/CandyCatalog. The Windows name of the server can be determined via the Identification tab of Networking Properties in the Windows control panel.

➤ Readers who intend to make their Web sites accessible over the Internet should test the server from an Internet site other than their own, if at all possible. One must refer to one's server by its machine's IP address. The IP address is determined by running the program **winipcfg** from the Windows 95 **Start, Run** taskbar; for example, http://130.150.43.5/CandyCatalog. This URL should work from any machine anywhere which has an Internet connection.

Semper Paratus: FrontPage 97 Installation Tips

Let's look at the well-known model of post-software-purchase-response, or PSPR. After all, there are two sorts of people: those who bring home their shrinkwrapped software, snip the end open with a scissors, and after peeling the plastic film off in one whole sheet, gently place the CD-ROM or diskettes near the computer, and settle into an easy chair with a hot cup of tea and the software manual.

Then there are the *normal folks*, who nearly break the front door down after returning with the software, shred the plastic wrap with horrific, violent strokes, rip the carton in half with a burst of energy typically reserved for lifting an automobile off a trapped child, and, after pausing briefly to consider whether to burn the manual in effigy or merely toss it into another room, they insert the CD-ROM and launch the installation program. Total time from arrival home to loud shout of "D-oh!": one minute, 24 seconds, on average.

We all *know* that we should read the manuals first, but few of us can stand to. I am Guilty as charged. That said, we recognize that some readers of this appendix have already installed FrontPage 97, perhaps because they purchased it long before this book, or perhaps because they just purchased it, but they have the patience of a ferret. Not to worry: in this appendix, we'll look at some tips for installing FrontPage 97, which are of use to either psychological orientation.

What's in the Box, and Why We Don't Really Know

There's at least one good reason to read the manual—at least the "Quick Start" portion of it—which comes with FrontPage 97: It was written with inside knowledge. While we can describe some basic concepts, and specific caveats, with regards to the FrontPage 97 suite, we cannot provide an exact inventory of what comes in the box, or even the filenames on the installation CD-ROM. The answer, or excuse, is a matter of delay. After all, this book has been written long before FrontPage 97 hit the shelves, so we cannot know exactly how the final version will be packaged.

What we do know, among other things, is this: The FrontPage 97 package consists of approximately seven pieces of software. Microsoft has chosen to categorize these applications into two groups:

Microsoft FrontPage 97 (requires approximately 30 megabytes of hard drive space for a full install), which includes:

> FrontPage Explorer
>
> FrontPage Editor
>
> FrontPage Personal Web Server

Microsoft Bonus Pack, (required hard drive space for a full install, in megabytes, listed beside each component) which includes:

> Microsoft Image Composer (17)
>
> Web Publishing Wizard (1)
>
> Microsoft Personal Web Server (1)
>
> Microsoft Internet Explorer (13)

Note to Current Users of FrontPage 1.1

Microsoft has probably included special instructions, either in printed form, or in a Readme file on the CD-ROM (likely in the main directory), for users who want to upgrade from FrontPage 1.1 to FrontPage 97. At the time this book was written, it was recommended that FrontPage 97 users either install to a different location than FrontPage 1.1, or uninstall FrontPage 1.1 first. However, as these instructions may have changed for the final FrontPage 97 release, please check the included documentation carefully.

In this book, we've touched upon every application listed here except for the Microsoft Image Composer. In short, it is an image processing program similar to Adobe Photoshop or Paintshop Pro, and while it is useful for designing graphics for the Web (or any other purpose), it's a fairly complex program with its own detailed documentation.

Presumably, one will be able to launch separate install programs: one which installs the Microsoft FrontPage 97 applications, and the other which installs the Bonus Pack. Both of these should be readily apparent upon opening the contents of the CD-ROM in Windows 95. It's also possible that Microsoft will include an "all-in-one" installer, which combines the above two, allowing us to install any of the listed applications from one installation program. If so, that should be apparent as well. Fortunately, none of this is very difficult or unusual to any reader who's installed a software package before.

Microsoft has designed a "Setup Wizard" which walks us through the install process for every application. That's good for everyone: Easier for the user, less for us to write in this Appendix!

Of course, installing FrontPage 97 is the main focus of this package, so let's walk through a typical install procedure, and point out any caveats along the way.

Muscle Power

Every software application advertises its hardware specifications (the computer equipment you'll need to run the software). More often than not, though, these specifications are minimum requirements, and while they may suffice, they may not suffice very well.

Potential users of FrontPage 97 should have at least a 486 processor. Of course, enough hard drive is necessary to store the program files (approximately 50-70 megabytes to install every application included in the package). It is recommended that you have at least a 256 color video display for designing Web pages, although 16- or even 24-bit displays are preferable: in short, the more colors the better, considering the graphic nature of many Web pages. Because FrontPage 97 is a suite of applications, several of which are usually running simultaneously (the FrontPage Editor, the FrontPage Explorer, and possibly the Microsoft Personal Web Server, at the least), plenty of RAM is the most important hardware benefit. While 16 megabytes of RAM can run the suite acceptably, 24 megabytes or more will improve performance considerably. FrontPage 97 will function with only 8 megabytes of RAM on a Windows 95 system, but quite slowly.

Ready, Set, Install

After launching the FrontPage 97 install program from the CD-ROM, and, if necessary, choosing to install FrontPage 97, the hard drive will whirr for a bit, and we'll eventually be greeted with a screen which resembles the following illustration:

Remember, because our screen shots are taken from an early version of the software, the final results may appear slightly different on your own screen. On the opening screen, we're given a number of instructions, such as to close any other application which we have running right now. This is a good idea that will prevent any conflicts during installation. Once this message is read, we click **Next >** to move into heartier territory.

First, we must select where on our system to install FrontPage 97. This is an important decision, since it's a rather large program, and it requires sufficient storage space. By default, the Wizard prompts us to install it to c:\Program Files\Microsoft FrontPage. For many users, this path may be adequate. A full installation of FrontPage 97 itself (not counting the other applications included in the package, although they can be installed to other drives) requires approximately 30 megabytes of hard drive space. If we'd prefer to install FrontPage to a different path than the default, clicking the **Browse** button will allow us to select a new directory or hard drive for it.

A prototype of the FrontPage 97 Setup Wizard's opening screen.

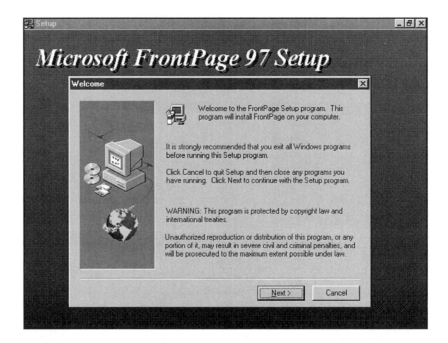

Selecting a Destination Path for FrontPage 97.

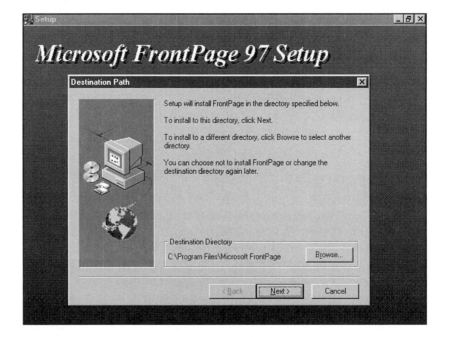

Once that is decided, we click **Next >** to move ever onward in the Setup Wizard. We're now asked whether to perform a Typical or a Custom installation. Choosing **Typical** will automatically install FrontPage 97, the FrontPage Personal Web Server, and the Server Extensions (thus binding the server to port 80; see Chapter 19, "Bringing the Server to Life," for details on why that's an undesirable thing). A Custom install allows us to have some say over this process, which is exactly what we want. Thus we click **Custom** followed by **Next >**.

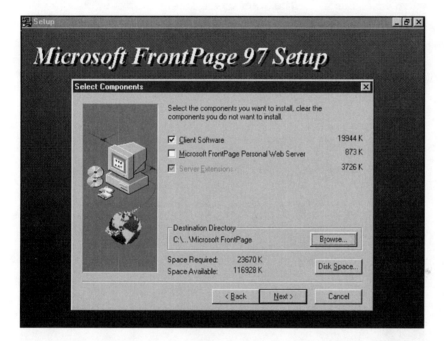

Selecting which components to install. We choose to omit the server components, which will ease matters when we read Chapter 19.

In the screen above, we may place a check mark next to each component we want to install. Note that we have only checked one: **Client Software**, which consists of the FrontPage Explorer, the FrontPage Editor, and associated files. We have *not* checked Microsoft FrontPage Personal Web Server, and that decision prevents us from checking the Server Extensions.

We can see at the bottom of the image above that the Setup Wizard has calculated the storage space requirements for our installation. We'll need approximately 24 megabytes of space for FrontPage 97 without the server or extensions, and we currently have about 117 megabytes of free space on the drive we've chosen to install to. We decide that this is acceptable, and click **Next >**. Had we decided that this was not acceptable, we could click **Browse** to select a different destination path for the installation.

293

Stop that Server Installation!

There is a very good reason for this. In fact, the first half of Chapter 19 is devoted to this reason. In the interests of a quick preview: we do not want to use the FrontPage Personal Web Server, because the Microsoft Personal Web Server, which is included in the Bonus Pack, is a superior Web server. Installing the FrontPage Personal Web Server now will cause potential headaches later, when we decide to use the other server. Sound confusing? Read Chapter 19!

If you're reading this chapter thinking, "D-oh! I've already installed FrontPage 97 with the FrontPage Personal Web Server, and was only reading this Appendix because the book fell open to it while I was eating my Rice Krispies," do not fear: Chapter 19 also explains how to undo installation wrongs.

The Setup Wizard summarizes its intentions for final approval. It's a go!

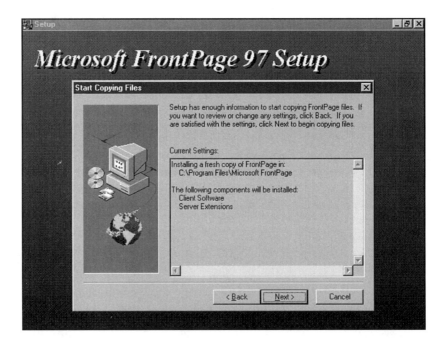

The Setup Wizard now displays a summary of its intentions. As pictured in the previous figure, it intends to install a "fresh copy" of FrontPage into the path indicated (C:\Program Files\Microsoft FrontPage, in this case). It intends to install only the Client Software component, as we customized earlier. Since that is all settled, we click **Next >** and the install process begins.

Reading from source

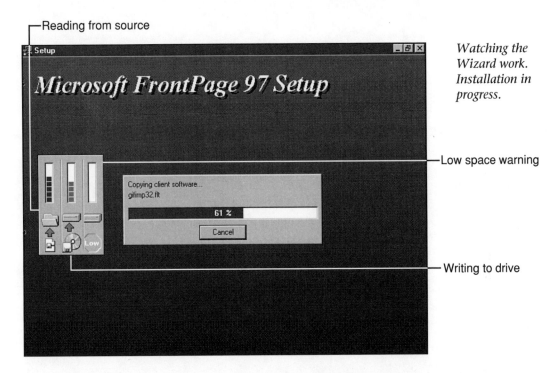

Watching the Wizard work. Installation in progress.

Low space warning

Writing to drive

The progress window in the center of the screen displays the installation progress as a percentage, as well as which file it is currently installing. On the left of the screen are three usage meters, which represent, from left to right: writing files to the destination drive, reading files from the source drive, warning of low space remaining on destination drive.

Once done, the Setup Wizard will probably ask to reboot the computer. We happily agree, and can rush headlong into Chapter 1 "Why We Web (and How!)."

When installing the remaining applications, follow the same procedure as above. The only minor exception is the Microsoft Personal Web Server, whose installation and setup we detail in the second half of Chapter 19.

WHAT..?

Speak Like a Geek: The Complete Archive

action   In the context of scripting, we select an *action* to occur, as triggered by a preceding *event* (see *event*).

action pane   The upper-right portion of the Script Wizard window, containing a list of possible actions for each object on the page (see *object*).

ActiveX   A Microsoft technology which allows you to add prefabricated program modules to a Web page. These modules, known as *controls*, can be preprogrammed to perform a wide range of possible functions, from aesthetic improvements to complex information management. ActiveX controls can interact with the user via scripting. (See also *control* and *scripting*.)

applet   A prefabricated Java module, which you insert into a Web page. Analogous to, but not technologically compatible with, an ActiveX control. Applet behavior can be customized by setting their parameters in the FrontPage Editor (see *parameter*).

association   Typically, the relationship between a particular software application and a type of file, based on its file extension. For instance, a GIF image file whose filename ends in .gif may be associated with the Microsoft Image Composer application. The FrontPage Editor contains configurable associations—these associations apply only to FrontPage 97, and do not override file associations configured in the Windows operating system itself (see *file extension*).

AVI   A type of file that contains video (and possibly audio), also known as "Video for Windows." AVI files can be inserted into Web pages using the FrontPage Editor, but only Microsoft Internet Explorer supports browsing such Web pages.

background   An image or plain color which appears behind the text and other elements of a Web page. If a background image is smaller than the browser window, it is repetitively "tiled" to fill in the entire browser window. Backgrounds can also be individually applied to tables and table cells (Netscape Navigator 3.0 only supports viewing table and cell background colors, not images).

bookmark   An invisibly marked location on a Web page, to which a user can be sent directly via a URL or hyperlink. In a URL, bookmark names are represented by a pound sign, such as **http://www.server.com/mypage.html#bookmark1**. Also known as an *anchor* by some people, but not in FrontPage 97 parlance.

broken link   A hyperlink which points to an invalid, nonexisting, or nonresponding destination. Broken links appear graphically in the Hyperlinks View of the FrontPage Explorer.

browser   The Web "client," which is the software application used to view and interact with Web pages; examples include Microsoft Internet Explorer and Netscape Navigator (see *client*).

button   On a Web page, a button is typically a rectangular graphic element, which the user can click to commence a defined action. Buttons are commonly form fields, but may also be ActiveX controls or Java applets.

cell   A single unit of space within a table. Cells may contain text, images, forms, Java applets, or any other valid page element.

CGI   "Common Gateway Interface," the most widely used method for passing form data to form processors. (See also *form* and *form processor*.)

check box   A form field, or ActiveX control, which the user can either check on (enable) or check off (disable). The state of the check box can be accessed by a script, or sent to a form processor when the user submits the form.

child Web   A Web site (a.k.a subfolder) which resides within the main Web on a server (known as the <Root Web>). (See also *subfolder* and *<Root Web>*.)

.class file   The heart and lungs of a Java applet. To use a Java applet in your own pages, you must save that applet's .class file, or .class files if it requires more than one. For example, a Java applet called *AnimText* requires the single .class file *AnimText.class*.

click   The act of pressing a mouse button. If the left or right button is not specified, "click" refers to the left-mouse button. Conversely, "right-click" refers to pressing the right mouse button.

client   A software application that sends requests to a server, usually across a network such as the Internet. The client receives the data delivered by the server, and processes it in some way; for instance, displaying it as a Web page. (See also *browser* and *server*.)

command pane   In the Script Wizard, the bottom portion of the Wizard window, which displays the currently selected event, and which action it triggers.

control   An ActiveX prefabricated program module, which can be inserted into a Web page to add new features to the page. Controls can also interact with the user via scripting (see *scripting*).

default   In a general sense, the value of some option if not otherwise specified by a user. For instance, if you choose not to assign a value to a certain property, the property may have a *default* value which is assumed (see *property*).

default.htm   When requesting a Web page from the Microsoft Personal Web server, if no particular .htm or .html file is specified, the file named *default.htm* will be delivered.

domain   A general organization identity for a computer in a network. For instance, the domain *ibm.com* identifies generally any computer within the IBM organization which is on the Internet. As more information is added to a domain, it increases in specificity: gromit.ibm.com refers to any computer within the *gromit* network within IBM, unless *gromit* is a single computer, in which case the example identifies that exact machine named *gromit*.

download   When one computer requests data from another, the data is said to *download* from the destination of the request to the origin of the request. (See also *local*, *remote*, *host*, and *upload*.)

drag   The act of holding down the left mouse button while sliding the mouse in any direction. This technique is most often used to move an on-screen object from one place to another.

drop-down menu   Within the context of a Web page, a drop-down menu is a form field which contains a list of items, from which the user can choose one or possibly several.

dynamic IP address   An IP address which is newly assigned everytime a connection is made to the service provider. Prevents the possibility of establishing a permanent, reliable location on the Internet (see *IP address*).

event   In scripting parlance, an event is "something that occurs" on the Web page, such as the user clicking a button, or typing in text, or moving the mouse pointer over an element. (See also *action* and *scripting*.)

event pane   The upper-left portion of the Script Wizard, which contains a list of possible events, any of which can trigger any number of possible *actions*.

file extension   In Windows, the common three-letter suffixes that appear to the right of the dot in a file name; for example *dogimage.gif, house.jpg, music.mid, readme.txt*.

folder   A section of files on a hard drive, folders are stored in hierarchies of subfolders. For instance, the C: drive may contain a folder named *docs*, which contains a number of files, as well as a subfolder named *html*, which also contains files, plus a subfolder named *java*, in which there are yet more files. (See also *subfolder*.)

font   A typestyle design which is applied to a portion of text, such as Times New Roman or Courier.

form   In a Web page, a form consists of one or more data input regions, known as form fields. All of the data in form fields within a single form is sent to a form processor when the form is submitted. In the FrontPage Editor, a form is bounded by dashed lines, visually illustrating which fields reside within a form. (See also *form field*, *form processor*, and *submit*.)

299

form field   A single data input region within a form, form fields can take the shape of text boxes (where a user types in data), check boxes, radio buttons, or drop-down menus.

form processor   A computer program that receives and in some way interprets the data entered into a form upon its submission. The form is sent to a form processor as determined in the **Form Properties** settings available by right-clicking a form region in the FrontPage Editor.

frame   A window-within-a-Web-page. A Web page can consist of two or more windows, known as frames, each of which can contain its own content. Frames can be navigated (scrolled) independent of one another, although an event in one frame can change the content that appears in another (see *frameset*).

frameset   For a single Web page, the frameset defines the geometry (dimensions, position) for all frames which make up the page. When a user visits a page containing frames, he actually visits the page containing the frameset, which automatically places the designed content into each frame.

FrontPage Editor   The FrontPage 97 application that is used to create and edit the content of a particular Web page.

FrontPage Explorer   The FrontPage 97 application that is used to create, manage, and publish entire Web sites.

FrontPage Extensions   A set of computer programs added to a Web server, which allow it to deliver pages with special FrontPage-specific features, such as WebBots and simple Web publishing.

FrontPage Server Administrator   The FrontPage 97 application that is used to install and configure a Web server.

FTP   Short for "File Transfer Protocol", a client/server system that is commonly used to transfer files between computers over a network such as the Internet.

GIF   A common file format for storing graphic image files; it is an acronym for "Graphics Interchange Format"

group   In the context of Web server administration, a group is a specified set of users who may be assigned specific permissions to access or edit Web pages (see *permissions*).

host   Any computer on a network that delivers data to another computer. Generally speaking, a server resides on a host computer (see *server*).

hotspot   A defined region within an image which acts as a hyperlink; that is, when a user clicks on that region of the image, she is taken to a new page. (See also *imagemap*.)

HTML   An abbreviation for "HyperText Markup Language", HTML is the code language in which Web pages are written. FrontPage eliminates the need for the Web designer to know the

HTML language, as FrontPage 97 generates the HTML code for a page behind the scenes. (See also *WYSIWYG*.)

HTTP   The client/server protocol used to deliver Web pages and related data between a Web server and a Web browser; stands for "HyperText Transport Protocol".

hyperlink   The heart and soul of Web pages, a hyperlink is a region of text, an image, or a region within an image that, if clicked or "followed", takes the user to a new page, or a specific location in the current page. (See *bookmark*.)

image   A graphic which appears on a Web page, either as a background or an element on the page. Images can be passive or interactive, behaving as *hyperlinks* or *imagemaps*. Usually stored as GIF or JPEG format files.

imagemap   An image that contains defined subregions, known as *hotspots*, each of which is a hyperlink. Not all browsers support imagemaps, although Internet Explorer and Netscape Navigator do.

import   In the context of the *FrontPage Explorer*, the act of copying images or HTML files from a location on the hard drive into the currently opened Web.

index.htm   Analogous to *default.htm*, some Web servers will deliver the page with the filename *index.htm* when no other page is specified in the requested URL. This varies among brands of Web servers—some deliver *default.htm* and some deliver *index.htm* when no specific page is specified.

Internet   The vast, dynamic network of computers around the globe which can intercommunicate by using compatible protocols over wide-ranging transmission lines (such as telephone lines).

Internet Explorer   Microsoft Corporation's Web browser, included with the FrontPage 97 Bonus Pack.

intranet   A new market-friendly term for a local area network; a system of interconnected computers within a particular organization, such as a business or academic environment.

IP address   The unique address that identifies a particular computer on the Internet. Represented as a series of four sets of numbers, each set a value of 255 or less, such as 200.134.9.80. May also have a human-friendly name mapped to the numerical address, such as *mail.mom.provider.net*. (See also *dyanmic IP address* and *static IP address*.)

Java   A technology for inserting prefabricated program modules into Web pages, developed by Sun Microsystems. Analogous to, but not technologically compatible with, ActiveX by Microsoft. Currently, more browsers support Java than ActiveX.

JavaScript   Not directly related to Java, JavaScript is a computer programming language, developed by Netscape, used to write scripts that control the interaction of elements in a Web page (see *scripting*).

JPEG   Another common file format for storing graphic images. Can achieve high compression rates, allowing complex images to be stored in small files, albeit with some loss of quality. The filenames of images stored in JPEG format usually end in the extension .jpg.

link   Synonym for *hyperlink*.

Live3D   Plug-In included with Netscape Navigator 3.0 which allows for viewing three-dimensional hyperlinked "worlds", known as VRML. Files containing such worlds usually end in the extension .wrl.

local   The computer that is in front of you right now. In the context of a network, the local computer is the one that you are currently operating. Every other computer is known as *remote*.

Microsoft Personal Web Server   A Web server software product included with the FrontPage 97 Bonus Pack. Superior to the other Web server included with FrontPage 97, known as the FrontPage Personal Web Server.

MIDI   A file format for storing music. MIDI files are often very small, and therefore quick to download, because they only contain a musical score—the actual instrument sounds must pre-exist on the local computer. An acronym for "Musical Instrument Digital Interface," these files usually end in the extension .mid.

multi-select   The act of selecting multiple choices, such as in a menu or file dialog box. Multiple selections are made, when allowable, by holding down the Ctrl key on the keyboard while left-clicking each desired choice.

Netscape   The company that makes the Web browser named Navigator, and in which you should have bought stock three years ago.

network   Any collection of computers that can communicate with each other. (See also *Internet, intranet.*)

object   In the context of scripting, an object is any element on the Web page at which events can occur, or actions triggered. Objects include form fields, ActiveX controls, and the browser window.

page   Content that is viewed within the Web browser window. A single "page" consists of all content displayed in the browser window at one time (including scrolling). A page can consist of text, graphics, hyperlinks, sound, form fields, ActiveX controls, Java applets, and any other elements.

parameter   With respect to Java applets, a parameter customizes a certain aspect of the applet's behavior. For instance, an applet that animates text on the page may have parameters that control font style, font size, direction of animation, and so on.

path   Generally speaking, the location of a file. Usually, this includes specifications of storage device, subfolder(s), and filename, such as *C:\DOCS\HTML\WELCOME.HTM.*

permissions   Privileges granted to specified users or groups; in the context of a Web server, permissions can be granted which allow browsing pages, editing pages, or granting permissions to others.

pixel   A single "picture element" on the computer screen—a tiny dot. The computer screen consists of tens or hundreds of thousands of pixels. In placing elements on Web pages, such as tables or images, some measurements (such as extra spacing) can be specified in terms of pixels.

Plug-in   A self-contained computer program that can be tied to the content of a Web page; for instance, a Web page containing a three-dimensional VRML file can launch the Live3D plug-in, which allows the user to browse VRML files. The plug-in usually achieves integration into the browser by placing its navigational controls within the Web page.

pointer   Sometimes known as a "cursor," the pointer is the icon which represents the location of the mouse.

property   Similar to a *parameter*, a property customizes the behavior of a page element, or FrontPage itself. Form fields, images, and even the FrontPage Explorer, to name a few, all possess properties which can be modified to customize their behavior (see *parameter*).

protocol   A set of communications rules that computers use to exchange data between one another. To intercommunicate compatibly, both computers must use the same protocol. Examples of common protocols include HTTP (Web pages), FTP (any computer files), and POP (e-mail messages).

provider   The organization that provides your Internet connection or Web server space, such as a commercial business, employer, or academic institution; also known as "service provider," "Internet service provider," or simply "ISP".

publish   To make Web pages available to anyone on the network (intranet or Internet), the act of copying Web page files to the Web server.

QuickTime   A file-format and plug-in produced by Apple, which allows viewing of QuickTime images or videos. QuickTime files usually end in the file extension .mov.

radio button   A multiple-choice form field, which allows the user to choose only one selection from several choices.

RealAudio   A file-format and plug-in produced by Progressive Networks, which allows for realtime streaming of audio files, allowing them to play in transit. RealAudio files often end in the extension .ra, .ram, or .rpt.

remote   In the context of a network, any computer other than the one currently being used (see *local*).

right-click   Simply, the act of pressing down the right mouse button.

<Root Web>   The main Web on a Web server. The <Root Web> is delivered by default if a URL is opened to the server with no further path specifications. All other Web sites on the server are subwebs, or child Webs, of the <Root Web>.

scripting   Similar to a directory with a screenplay, scripting is used to guide the interactions between a user and the Web page, and the relationships between page elements. The Script Wizard in the FrontPage Editor is used to construct scripts without needing knowledge of the JavaScript or VBScript programming languages. (See also *JavaScript.*)

server   In the context of a network, the server accepts requests from clients, contains the data to deliver, and delivers the requested data to the client (see *client*).

Shockwave   A plug-in created by Macromedia that plays multimedia Director files within the Web page, which are created with other Macromedia products.

site   Literally, any server on the Internet. In practice, a Web page on a server is often referred to as a "Web site".

SSL   "Secure Sockets Layer", a protocol used to transmit secure, encrypted data between a Web server and browser.

static IP address   An IP address that remains constant everytime a connection to the Internet is established; allows for the presence of a permanent Web site. See also *IP address* and *dynamic IP address.*

subfolder   Any folder that resides within another folder. In fact, every folder on the hard drive, other than the main C: folder, is a subfolder. (See *folder.*)

submit   An on-screen button that the user presses to send any data input for a form to the form processor. (See also *form processor* and *form.*)

subweb   Synonymous with child Web, any Web that resides within the <Root Web> on a server. (See *child Web.*)

table   A page element that defines a specific structure of rows and columns, in which reside a set of cells. A table can be used to structure text content, or contain images and other page elements (see *cell*).

text box   A form field in which the user can manually enter information. Text boxes can either consist of one-line only, or multiple-lines with a scrollbar.

texture   Synonymous with background, a texture is a graphic image that is seen behind the main content of a Web page, or table, or cell (see *background*).

toolbar   In FrontPage, a set of icons that allow quick access to certain functions. For instance, the form toolbar allows the user to quickly create form fields.

transparent   On a Web page, a graphic image with "invisible" areas, through which the background color or texture can be seen. Only GIF images can be configured to contain transparent areas.

upload   Opposite of *download*, sending data from the local computer to a remote computer. (See also *local* and *remote*.)

URL   "Uniform Resource Locator"—The syntactical format for sending a Web page request to a Web server, such as **http://server.com/mysite/mypage.htm**. In a Web browser, you "Open URL" to connect to a server and view a web page.

video   A digital "movie"—as opposed to a single graphic image, a video is a series of images, which sometimes include sound. (See *AVI*.)

watermark   A background image which does not scroll with the rest of the page. If a background image is configured as a watermark, it always remains in the same spot on the page, even if the user scrolls the page content up or down.

WAV   A file format for audio clips whose file names usually end in the extension .wav.

Web   A set of content pages that are interconnected via hyperlinks. On the Internet, the set of all potentially interconnected pages is known as the World Wide Web.

Web Publishing Wizard   A component of the FrontPage 97 Bonus Pack, which allows FrontPage Web sites to be published to remote Web servers that don't support the FrontPage Extensions.

WebBot   A small preprogrammed module, included with FrontPage, which can be inserted onto a Web page. WebBots can be used to perform small useful tasks, but only function properly on pages that are delivered by servers with FrontPage Extensions. (See *FrontPage Extensions*.)

wizard   A utility that walks you through a configuration process step-by-step, such as the Import Wizard or Frames Wizard of FrontPage 97.

WYSIWYG   Acronym for "What You See is What You Get"—The design philosophy employed (mostly) by the FrontPage Editor, wherein you design the page on-screen as it will appear to the end user. Eliminates the need to know HTML code. (See *HTML*.)

Index